Leaving Breezy Street

Leaving Breezy Street

A Memoir

Brenda Myers-Powell

with **April Reynolds**

Henry Holt and Company Ⓗ New York

Henry Holt and Company
Publishers since 1866
120 Broadway
New York, New York 10271
www.henryholt.com

Henry Holt® and Ⓗ® are registered trademarks of Macmillan Publishing
Group, LLC.

Library of Congress Cataloging-in-Publication Data

Names: Myers-Powell, Brenda, author. | Reynolds, April, author.
Title: Leaving Breezy Street : a memoir / Brenda Myers-Powell with April
    Reynolds.
Description: First edition. | New York : Henry Holt and Company, 2021.
Identifiers: LCCN 2020034256 (print) | LCCN 2020034257 (ebook) |
    ISBN 9780374151690 (hardcover) | ISBN 9780374719401 (ebook)
Subjects: LCSH: Myers-Powell, Brenda. | Ex-Prostitutes—United States—
    Biography. | Prostitutes—Rehabilitation—United States—Biography. |
    Drug addicts—Rehabilitation—United States—Biography. | African
    American women—Biography.
Classification: LCC HQ144 .M94 2021 (print) | LCC HQ144 (ebook) |
    DDC 305.48/896073—dc23
LC record available at https://lccn.loc.gov/2020034256
LC ebook record available at https://lccn.loc.gov/2020034257

Our books may be purchased in bulk for promotional, educational,
or business use. Please contact your local bookseller or the Macmillan
Corporate and Premium Sales Department at (800) 221-7945, extension
5442, or by e-mail at MacmillanSpecialMarkets@macmillan.com.

First Edition 2021

All photos public domain or courtesy of the author

Designed by Meryl Sussman Levavi

Printed in the United States of America

10 9 8 7 6 5 4 3 2 1

I'd like to dedicate this book to every young girl
and boy out there who is sexually abused and
trafficked who couldn't find their voice: I believe you—
and I believe IN you.

I also dedicate this to my frontline Family that
supported me through my Journey,

Edwina Gateley my mentor/mother,

and my best friend, Stephanie Daniels-Wilson,
who convinced me I had a book.

Contents

Part iii: Fake love can never own you

Part iV: Running

Leaving Breezy Street

Author's Note

Respect. That's how I lived my life: needing respect, demanding respect. And actually that's how I got into a lot of trouble I found myself in. In the hood, it was all about the words—we used words that played the dozens, we used words that lifted us. Lately, I've been reading the words I've written in this book. Are they going to lift you? Are they going to cut you down? I hope they do both. I know nowadays we are more careful with our words. We respect words to convey respect. But back then we didn't. We let it fly. So you should know, I'm not trying to tell you a story about my past using the careful words of right now. I call myself a prostitute and a ho in this book because those words are my truth. If you want to really know my story and how it went down, you should know what I was hearing and what I was telling myself. Because it's the truth. It may turn your stomach or make you mad, but that might be a good thing. Look around, we need a little truth-telling. God help; God bless and good reading.

Every Road Has to End Somewhere

I woke up to a beautiful day. I was in Gary, Indiana, staying with my brother Todd. A few weeks back, he had saved me from myself and California. I left my family twelve years before as a drop-dead beauty and came back a messed-up crackhead. But they still loved me; I was still their sister. Todd was always trying to rescue and help me. He had just bought me a new outfit. Really nice jeans with the zipper that circled my hips and a white fitted top. White gym shoes. He got my hair done. My brother wanted me to look good; he didn't want my daughter Prune seeing me look any kind of way. I hadn't seen her yet, but I knew she was twenty-something years old, accomplished, and somebody I wanted to look up to. My brother had told me I could sleep as long as I wanted; I could stay with him as long as I needed. I took him up on it. The crack cocaine had me worn out. For a couple of weeks, all I was good for was sleeping and eating a little bit. But that day, April

Fool's Day, was the first time I woke up and wanted to stay woke. I wanted to wake up and appreciate my brother's basement.

When my brother bought the house, it was a mess. He had moved away from Chicago when he had been robbed. They had carjacked him. So he decided to move to Gary. He found a one-story house and worked all day and at night and on the weekends until he had his house just the way he wanted. He'd made a laundry room and a very nice bathroom; in the basement, he'd made two rooms. Green leather sofa, big-screen TV in one, and in the other, a pullout couch, but a really nice one. Wood paneling all around. Big rug. I was sleeping on the nice pullout couch. My brother Todd was so good to me. Gave me the whole basement. Get your thoughts together, he told me. "You really looking wretched, girl."

When I woke up that morning, I noticed the spring weather right outside. Sunshine coming in through the basement windows. I could smell the brand-new leaves growing on the bushes in my brother's backyard. And I was hungry.

I went upstairs to the kitchen. Todd had made me breakfast. A bowl of grits and eggs were set on the table. So was a nice pile of money. I stole glances at the cash and scooped the warm buttered grits into my mouth. I dug in.

"Brenda!" my brother called out from the other room.

"Yeah?"

"Don't take all my money, now!"

I yelled back, "I'm not!" But I took a little. Not enough to hurt him, you know. I counted it. Four hundred dollars. I peeled off a hundred and twenty and stuck it in my titty. That was just enough to do what I needed to do. See, with all that sleep and good food in me, I could finally hear it: the crack cocaine calling. I finished up breakfast and took off toward Broadway. I can't remember if I told my brother I would be back.

+ + +

I knew I couldn't get drugs from the crack dealers down the block. I didn't want them telling my brother, "Your sister was out here buying crack cocaine from us." Plus, he had already asked them very nicely to move their business down the street. He was trying to have a nice house. Todd ran his mechanic shop out of his garage, and he had a lot of women and older guys as his clients. Folks wouldn't come out to him if they had to push through dealers and crackheads just to get their brakes fixed.

I had a plan, though. I was gone go to Chicago, get my high on, and then come back like I ain't done a thing. That was the plan. As soon as I made it to Madison Street, I didn't care how amazing the day was. I just wanted to get high. It was a shame how I spent that day hustling to try to get high. A day that was so beautiful. The flowers were smelling good. I was looking good. Todd was taking care of me. I had on new clothes and my hair was done, but I couldn't wait to get back to that greasy, nasty-ass city and get high. I think about it now, I think that day was supposed to happen cause I needed to get to the end of that life. It was a hell of a day. I hopped on the South Shore Line train and headed to Chicago.

+ + +

When I got to the city, I found out there was a drought. Wasn't no drugs on the street. It happens every now and then. Sometimes drug dealers get a big shipment, and the police snatch it up. There wasn't nothing nowhere. I promise you. I hooked up with my homeboy Petey. He was one of those dudes who wore work clothes even when he wasn't working. Work boots, jumpsuit. The whole thing. He worked in construction, doing a little work in the neighborhood for ten dollars. Together, we searched everywhere. People who did have some drugs was holding on to it or selling it for outrageous prices. Folks were getting *pissed off*. It was a whole bunch of mess.

Me and Petey stopped on Pulaski Street. That was the spot where I used to go to get high, but they didn't have anything. We walked to a couple more spots on the West Side, but didn't nobody have nothing. And I was ready to shake loose from Petey. The more we looked for drugs together, the more complicated it got. Petey started having ideas about my money. He started pulling at me, saying, "Let's go get something to drink."

"Nah, man."

"Let's go spend some of this money."

No way, I told him. He was trying to block my action. Plus, every time I turn my head, here go Petey rubbing on my ass. So I separated. I didn't give away my honeypot. I been a ho too long for that kind of nonsense.

+ + +

I went up on Madison to the ho stroll, near Kilbourn, because I knew you can always get drugs up there. JR's Hotel—it was a two-hour hotel that the girls could use with no questions asked—was nearby. See, even if you couldn't find it no place else, you could bet your damn dollar they was gone have crack up there. And I wanted my fix right now. I could feel it in my stomach. I went up to Madison, and I went to this furniture store that this old guy owned. Back when I used to roam K-Town, he used to let me come in there and use the bathroom, you know, do my thing. And he had this young girl he was keeping. She was a friend of mine, Diane. Young girl, seventeen years old. Chocolate and pretty all over. And he must have been sixty-eight, sixty-nine years old. Old, bald-head church guy with this young girl. He controlled her terribly. He could control her because she had a habit. I went and asked her if she knew where to go and get some, and she did. Diane asked if she could go in half with me, so she went in to him to get some money, and I could hear them going back and forth, "I don't want you doing that stuff. Wait till later." But I guess he had some weak ways, too, because he gave her money and she went out and got some.

That ten-dollar rock was so small. Just pebble size. And I'm thinking, *This is bullshit, friend.* But once I had taken that hit of cocaine and I couldn't see that beautiful day anymore, all I could see was making sure more of that monster got inside of me. I couldn't see nothing else. Just that one hit took all that away from me. I changed just like that. I was shaking all over. I could feel my skin crawling. When I got to that point, the first thing I'd want to do is get a drink. And my drink of choice is cheap wine. I left the furniture shop and Diane. I saw some wine heads on the corner, and I saw one of my wine-head friends. I told him, "Give me some of that."

"You better get me another one," he told me.

"Alright, I'm gonna get you another one. Calm down." But I would have told him anything, cause I was strung. The crack had me strung, and you'll say anything to keep that feeling going. That's why so many girls will do anything under the influence—cause they strung. I'll do anything you want me to do, as long as I get some more. I'll suck your junk; I'll suck her snatch. Listen. I done seen some girls do some pretty awful things. You take chances and do things you wouldn't have done if you hadn't had been high.

It took a couple of swigs of wine to bring me down. I didn't have a straight head, but I knew one thing: I needed to go get me some money. I needed to get some money, so I can go get me some smoke. It was so simple in my mind. I went out to some of the guys selling on the stroll. And they were like, "Wait a minute and I'll get it for you," but a couple of them were honest and just told the truth: "Look, girl, we ain't got it." Nobody knew where the smoke was, everybody was speculating. I'm walking up and down Madison. I'm standing in front of the Tavern, where in the past me and the other ladies sat in cars in the parking lot and got high. That's also where working-class guys and truck drivers hung out to get access to whatever they wanted: poontang, drugs, gambling.

I remember standing there and seeing him. He stood out because he was a white guy in a crisp business shirt. Very clean-cut. Maybe he was thirty-five, forty years old. Good-looking. Brown hair. Black suit. Medium build. Not the type of trick that normally comes down there. He was driving a black Mercedes. And when I saw him, I thought,

Okay, that's my trick right there. I looked around and thought I didn't have no competition. There was one girl working the stroll who looked better than I did, looked fresher than I did. But in my mind, I claimed him. I claimed him to be my trick.

I stood on the corner, and he motioned to me, and we made eye contact. He drove around the corner, and I walked to the middle of the block, cause sometimes guys didn't want to stop on the corner. Don't this sound like it's all happening in the middle of the night? But no, this was all happening in the middle of the day. They didn't have any respect for our community; they picked up our Black women in the middle of the day. They used us like toilets and then hopped on the interstate and went back to their half-million-dollar homes and kissed the kids and took the wife flowers. And when they get caught with us, the police don't dare take them to jail, they take *us* to jail. Cause *we're* the problem. Black women are the issue. Not this white guy from Skokie or Wilmette, or the western suburbs and Naperville. He lives forty minutes away from us, but he's over here getting Black pussy.

So, what happened was, he started playing a game with me. He pulled down the block and pulled over by the street, but as soon as I got up close to him, he drove off. This went on four, five times. He was getting off masturbating and watching me. Getting off watching me run toward his car. When we get to the fifth, sixth time, I'm pissed off. I'm thinking, alright, you playing with me. Now I could have walked off and been like, you just playing, but I didn't because I had a vendetta by then. I'm cronked and I'm thinking, *I'm getting in this car and I'm taking his money.* I would like to tell you that that day I was a victim, but point of fact, I had turned into a predator. I wanted to get him. I wanted to show him you can't play these games with me. How wrong I was.

So when he came around again, I had already seen his play and how he did his move. In other words, I knew he was going to come over and pull down the block and when I got close to the car, we'd have a couple words and then he'd speed off. See what I'm saying?

So this seventh time, after the six times he done played me like a fool like this, I'm thinking I know what to do. When I got to the car this time, I snatched open the door real fast and jumped in. And I looked at him and said, "Hi."

"No, no, no, no, no," he said, talking real fast. Punk ass.

"Drive." I'm really forcing him because he had kept playing with me, and I thought he owed me something for messing with me and my community, on my time, on my turf, and I was going through a mental thing cause I'm sprung and I don't have no drugs. Here I am messed up, and you gone pay for it. So I said, "Turn right here, pull over." He looked at me real nervous, and I looked him dead in his eyes, because I'm turned his way, and I said, "What you want to do?" He gave me forty bucks. I took the forty bucks, and I put the money in my pants and when I turned back around, he hit me.

I could see stars. I've been hit a lot. But he was hitting me with everything he had, and I knew if I kept letting him hit me, he was gonna knock my ass out. He knocked me over my ears and the top of head. He hit me in both eyes. I raised my hands in front of my face, and my back is to the passenger door, and now I'm kicking him so he can stop hitting me. And I got the door open with my hand, but I was still trying to protect my face and he's still hammering me. It feels like this is happening simultaneously: as the door opens, he started up the car.

I started falling backwards, and the car was moving. I was caught off-balance. I done jumped out of cars before. I done jumped out of cars on the expressways without a scratch. But I had been able to do that without getting dragged. This time I wasn't. My clothes caught on the car and he dragged me. It seemed like he was tearing me from my meat. I could feel it. Especially on my face and on my side. I had pants on, so all of my leg didn't get messed up, but the concrete ripped my pants. After I got up, my face was filthy from the ground, and there was gravel and little pieces of glass in my face.

The first face I looked at was a little girl's; she had all these colored beads in her braids and she was wearing this lime-green short set. She was on her bike. Looking at me, she shook her head, then took off and came right back with some toilet paper. When I was in the hospital, I thought about that little girl, about what I made her see. I worried I had taken the light from this little girl. Made her see too much, too soon. We all did. We were out here like animals. Niggers. Walking the street in our panties. Sucking some white man's penis in the broad daylight. Every time I think about that little girl, I pray to God to help me make it right with the universe.

It's amazing how blind you become to the children who are out there on the street; kids you prostituting in front of, that you're buying drugs in front of, that you are dressed inappropriately in front of. It's amazing how desensitized you become to these little angels and how it will affect them. Because the drugs put blinders on you. And the drugs tell you, your vision has only one thing to look at: see how you can get high.

I looked that little girl in her face and said, "Did you see what happened?"

She said, "Yeah, I saw everything."

I said, "Am I messed up?"

"Yeah."

She rolled away on her bike, and I started walking toward where she was headed. I could feel people looking at me from their porches. Whispering. Nobody came to help me, but I could feel their conversation. I still had the bloody money on me. I had it in my hand. I went and passed where three drug dealers were on the street, and one of them—a most disrespectful son of a bitch—said, "Tell that ho keep on walking and get on off the tip, she gone make it hot. She bleeding; she gone make it hot over here." I kept walking.

I got down back to where it first all happened, and a car pulled up next to me and I looked in there and I recognized the guy. Randy Johnson. He was with two of his homeboys. And he said, "Breezy, what happened to you?"

I started crying, and I told him, "This trick dragged me and did all this to me!"

And Randy, in the car, said, "Get in, girl. Let's find this punk."

So now I'm in a car with three guys who have pistols and we looking for a trick to kill. Thank God somebody in the car had a bright idea, cause I didn't. The driver said, "Man, that dude's gone; let's take this girl to the hospital."

And Randy said, "You want to go to the hospital, Breezy?" And I said, yeah, I do, cause I was hurting. I didn't know how messed up I was, I really didn't. I had no idea the damage he had done; I just felt bad. I felt like my body and face were burnt. I went to the county hospital. As I got out the car, Randy said, "Call when you get out and you can stay at the safe house." Crazy as it sounds, that made me kind of happy. Staying at the safe house had a lot of perks. You sat around, helped out, and got as high as you wanted to. So when he said that, I said, "I'll call you when I'm done." That was my goal. That was the plan.

Fortunately, that wasn't God's plan. He had a whole other schedule for me. I had no idea that that was going to be the last day that I turned another trick, sucked another penis, saw Madison Street under those conditions. You couldn't have told me that this was going to be the end for me, cause I had always had success in prostitution. I mean, I was the baddest ho out there. I was. In my own mind. I always wore the latest outfits; my body was tight. On my best night I could pull in fifteen hundred dollars, and if I robbed somebody, I could come back home with five thousand dollars. Is that what made me a bad ho? Is that what made me the coldest? Or made me an excellent prostitute? I don't know, but for whatever reason I thought I was. My pimps brought me up that way. To get me out there and get more money, they brainwashed me to feel I was the coldest bitch out there, with the best thieving hands. I knew how to catch a trick and take everything and bring it back to them. So yeah, I was one of the baddest, stupidest hos out there because this lifestyle was made for me and to change meant I had to give up my title. Why would I come this far without being the best? And trust me, I was always going to be in the game. You wouldn't believe the shade and slick-ass things I could say about being a prostitute, about being able to get that kind of money from tricks. If it ever came to the point that I couldn't turn a trick, if I ever got too old, I always thought I could sell other people's poontang. I'll retire, I thought, and I'll sell me some hos. Cause I'm a cold bitch, right? That's what they used to say about me. *You a cold bitch.* How can you hear anything but a compliment? *You one of the baddest bitches I know. Bitch* was always in the equation, and I ate that up. That was the medal on my chest. "You don't know me? I'm one of the baddest bitches out here." That's the bullshit I had told myself to stay out there. *I'm the coldest; I'm the baddest; I'm the best bitch out there.* I was the bomb.

But when I hit that hospital that day, I went in there as a victim. Nobody wanted to help me. And I needed help. The people dealing with me didn't think I was a bad bitch; they called me a crackhead whore. I heard the police tell the nurse, "She's a prostitute, and she probably did something to some poor guy and got what she deserved." The hospital curtain was pulled, but I heard every word. And she was giggling with him cause she and the police, they're friends. This smug-faced white nurse just giggling her ass off. And I knew the cop, too. Old fat dusty bald dumbass. I had run into him before. Stupid-ass beard. Fat ass. He had busted me before. I always wondered if that laughing nurse knew that the minute her back was turned, he probably talked shit about her, too. *He was talking about you, too.* I laid there in pain and in panic, and I wanted to stop my face from burning and my side from burning. I needed help so bad. I didn't know what to do, and I couldn't really talk, cause my face hurt when I moved it. I couldn't really see out of my eye cause my eyelid was torn. I was in so much pain. My breathing was crazy cause I have asthma. Everything was just messed up. I became afraid. *Am I going to die? Are they going to let me die?*

When they came back, that nurse went and pushed me out into the hallway, as if I didn't exist. Like I was invisible. I looked at her. "I see you," I told her.

She saw the tears roll out my eyes and she half-assed looked at me. Then she said, "Somebody'll see you soon." She walked away. I remember turning my head, and I whispered, "God, these people don't care about me. Could You please help me?"

After a while, I had to go pee, and somehow, I made it to the bathroom. I got to the stall, then washed my hands. The mirror was right there. I was scary to myself. The first thing that went through my mind was, *I guess I won't be going to the safe house. I ain't going to be going nowhere. Where can I go? My face is gone.*

I didn't have no face.

There were people passing me by, looking at me like I was a monster. I wanted to cover my head up, but I couldn't breathe good under the covers. I laid there and I cried till I went to sleep. When I woke up there was a doctor over me. She was a petite little lady and talked with a Russian accent. She had brown hair, and she was white. She was nice. She admitted me into the hospital, and she nursed me. Real cool lady. She didn't say nothing jazzy to me about being a prostitute or ask me a bunch of questions—how did this happen? What you do? She just said, "It's going to take a lot to get you back together, young lady. I hope you don't leave, so we can help you." Just real encouraging, you know? And like after a day or two or three, I woke up and I saw her sitting in the chair. She was doing her charts. She looked up and said, "Oh, look who rose from the dead! I been waiting for you to wake up. How everything is going with you? How you feel?" I looked at her and my whole heart broke. I couldn't think. I couldn't talk cause my heart was broken. And I felt like the biggest piece of shit that ever walked the earth. I didn't want to live; I wanted to leave here, forever. I had always told my people, if you find me dead, know I didn't commit suicide, somebody done killed me, but that day I wanted to go. It was too much; I didn't want to be here. I was so tired.

The doctor lady kept talking. It was positive stuff. It wasn't about me, really; it was just about life in general. And I started thinking about, how did I get here? How did I get to that monster in the bathroom mirror? Being tore up from the floor up? How did I get to having all these scars on my body? How did my life get here? How did that white businessman know that he had come to get me off the streets, because that's what he did. I don't know what his motive was; I don't know what kind of freak he was; I still haven't figured out what was on his mind while he was hitting me, but I know one thing for sure: this wasn't the first time he had done it. And I figured that's why he didn't want me to get in the car. He probably sized me up. Neither one of us knew how much he could mess me up.

Still. How did I end up like this? That doctor with her pretty accent was telling me to keep my head up, but I couldn't think of anything happy. That's when I started thinking back over things. Not just this day, the day I became the lady without a face, but all the days that led to it. Because truth was, if I slipped into a big sleep and died, everybody would be okay with that.

I was thirty-nine years old.

You know, County Hospital in Chicago is one of the biggest hospitals in the country, and it has saved a lot of people's lives, and I guess it saved mine. If anybody had seen me laying in that bed, I don't think they would have thought somebody like me could rise up and start from scratch. Or that I could leave the life of prostitution that spanned most of my childhood and all of my adulthood. I never thought that after years of trying to make a home for my daughters, Peaches and Prune, they would come back to me, forgive me, let me hold my grandchildren. I had years of birthdays and Christmases and anniversaries waiting on me, but I didn't know it. I had no idea that I would find my best friend and business partner, Stephanie Daniels-Wilson, and together we would build the Dreamcatcher Foundation, an organization that helps young women who are on the verge of walking my road and women who are living the chaos I have lived. Lying in that hospital bed, I had no idea that I would someday lead a life where I worked so hard and yet felt so blessed. Little did I know that somewhere out there was the love of my life and that I would find him. Or that God would let me raise a son and be the mother I couldn't be to my daughters. None of that was on my mind as I lay on that hospital bed. I was steeped in the past, wading through everything that had gotten me there.

I think maybe all that had happened for a reason.

Part I

It starts in the family

Chapter 1

Life with Ma'Dea

Every day I wonder how God works things out. How He do that? How He allow so much to happen? How He make my first memory, my first memory? And why?

I was three years old. I woke up and it was Christmas. I don't know if I woke up or if Christmas woke me up, but all these people—my grandmother; my cousins Charles, Dennis, and Renee; my uncle Cleveland; Uncle Lee and Uncle Joe; my aunt Josie; my uncle LC; Ike, the man who was a grandfather to me—were in the house. I could smell Christmas. We were living in one of the biggest apartments we ever had. It was a six-floor building. We had the first-floor apartment on the right-hand side. Our apartment was huge. The front door opened into the living room; down the hallway was the bathroom, and then the bedroom and then another bathroom and the dining room, and then there was a back door and a back porch. I remember being little, crawling out the bed with my grandmother and feeling my way to the fridge. Dark everywhere. But I felt safe. And when I turned on the lights . . . there was a little girl stand-ing in front of me. There was a silver Christmas tree in the corner of the living room. Doilies covered everything. My grandmother's name was Ruth, but all us grandkids called her Ma'Dea. She loved a knickknack. I don't know where she got them all, but she had little crystals all over the place. We had these plants on top of the TV and in the windows. And there was this beautiful girl.

I walked up to her, and I said, "Hi." She didn't say anything. So I said, "Hi!" But she still didn't say anything. Everybody around me started laughing, but I was trying to figure out why this little girl in front of me didn't say nothing, so I pushed her and she fell down.

It was a damn doll. An "I walk, I talk" doll. Everybody was laugh-ing and shouting, "Pick the doll up." Back then everybody called me Fat Mommy. "Pick her up, Fat Mommy!" they yelled. Ma'Dea couldn't stop laughing. She had a beautiful laugh. I think. It scared you a lit-tle, but it made you want to laugh, too. My grandmother was a good-looking woman with a nice shape. Thick. One of those Black women who was built like a brick house. Nice curves and strong muscles. Everybody knew if Ma'Dea hit you, you were going to get knocked out. So didn't nobody mess with her. Her hair was always red, Miss Clairol #33R Flame. And she was stylish. Jazzy. Beautiful. She was the kind of woman who looked good in a housecoat, which is what she was wearing that Christmas morning when she was laughing at me and that doll.

"Ma'Dea, you laughing at me!"

"I'm laughing *with* you, Fat Mommy!" She threw back her head and laughed some more. "You gone love that doll." And that was my first recollection as a child.

I remember dragging that doll around the house by her hair, cause she was the same size as me. She was three feet tall. And she was Black. I ain't never seen no Black baby doll like that. Chocolate skin with blue eyes. I dragged her around, danced with her and stuff. She had so much style. A little pleated skirt and a white blouse, with ankle socks and bow-tied shoes. I think my aunt Josie and my uncle LC bought that doll for me.

But what I remember most was a lot of spankings and a lot of whoopings. Sometimes I think God made my first memory a Christmas memory filled with happiness because He knew I would always remember the first time somebody tried to mess with me.

+ + +

He was one of my uncle's friends. His name was Woody. He was very tall. Six feet four, six feet five, and he had very long legs. I liked it when he came over with his long legs and wanted to give me the bouncy knee ride. I started bouncing on his knee, and then I bounced all the way down to the end again and he'd pull me back. The bouncy knee ride was so much fun. I was bouncing on Woody's knee, and I could smell the food Ma'Dea was cooking. Candied sweet potatoes and fried chicken. Collard greens that smelled so good, your head turned. The windows were sweating from the heat coming out of the kitchen.

You know, when you are a little kid and you're the only child in the house and the only time you have any playmates is when your cousins come and that's the only time you can go outside—all that makes up for a lonely childhood. But my grandmother was working all the time, at Learner's Cleaners, so there was nothing to do about it. I was a child in an adult world. And in our house, it was mostly adults popping off. Getting drunk and bossing me around. I grew up during a time when being a good girl meant being a mannered child. Stay out of grown folks' way. All my grown kin said, "I don't want to catch you on somebody else's knee. Can't be sitting in everybody's lap." But I wanted attention, I wanted love. I wanted to play. That "I walk, I talk" doll only said so much. "Quit sitting in everybody's damn lap, you little fast-ass girl!" Ma'Dea said, and I thought, *I ain't fast. They like me. I'm four.* I wasn't even going to school yet.

So I got in his lap, and he was giving me a knee ride, and I was laughing. You know how when you a little kid, you got next to nothing on? You got your little panties on, you got your little slip on? Cause it's warm in the house and everything. I think I had one of my slips on and a pair of panties. He was bouncing me on his knee and it was fun. And all of a sudden, I felt his fingers slip inside my panties. His fingers went inside my little coot. I got stiff as a board. "Shh, shh. Hush up, hush up. Don't say nothing." His breath was hot against my cheek. I kept thinking, he didn't even smell like a man anymore. He smelled like an animal. Musty. Sour. He starts fumbling my privates. He was doing his fingers in and out. I couldn't talk. My grandmother walked in the room and he released his grip on me. She looked at me and said, "Girl! What's wrong with you! Brenda Jean, what wrong with you?"

"Nothing." She had scared me. He scared me. She scared me cause she had always said don't let me catch you in nobody's lap no more and here I was breaking that rule. And he scared me cause he had done something wrong to me and I was scared to tell her. So I'm afraid of her and I'm afraid of him and I'm four years old and I don't know what to do. You know I had a little irritation in my pie after that. I remember her putting a little cap of that Campho-Phenique on my stuff. And it started to itch, cause he'd had no business in there. And my grandma was like, "How long you had these panties on for, with your nasty self? What wrong with your body?" I didn't know how to explain to her what had happened. She washed out my pie with that red Lysol. Lord, You know, old people put anything on you back in the day. It's a good thing we still alive after all that. Swear to God—those old folks were trying to kill us. They put bleach in the goddamn bath water. Ma'Dea was like that. Good-natured, but she thought if Lysol was good enough to clean a floor, it was good enough to clean a child. But I made it through.

I remember after that not feeling good at all. There was nothing my life-sized doll could say to help me. Woody and his nasty ass still came around, and he was still looking at me, and I would go to another room. But when I saw him, I didn't know what to make of it. I didn't even know how I felt about it. Wasn't this my fault? How many times had I been told to stay out of folks' laps? I tried my best to stay out of his way and I hoped he stayed out of mine. It took a minute, but I learned how to be satisfied with my doll's conversation, because anything else could get me in a kind of trouble I couldn't explain.

I chalked the whole thing up to my little girl pains, and like all hurt, it faded, replaced with better memories. Not everything was bad. I remember listening to Mary Wells and Curtis Mayfield and Rufus Thomas, "Walk the dog, baby." In the living room, out on the sidewalk, we did the Dog. We couldn't do it too nasty or our mommas pulled us off the floor. "You fast." Teenagers were listening to brothers singing on the corner, they were doo-wopping. My grandmother watched our carrying on and made dinner while singing Tommy Tucker's "Hi-Heel Sneakers." My grandmother wore this knit dress buttoned down in the front that she looked great in. I always think about my grandmother in that red dress and how that red dress got her in trouble. That red dress brought out the fire in her. And Ike, my play granddaddy, would look at her and say, "Where you going dressed like that?" He knew he better ask, cause Ma'Dea looked damned good. And she best have the right answer or they were going to fight before she left the house. The dress was fly, the makeup was set, and her wig was cool. My grandmother had a wig or two. One was red and long and had a flip-up. The other had bangs. It was also red. Wigs were optional back then. The wig man came by with the big case, the stand, the whole shebang. My grandmother didn't wear a lot of wigs because when she was drunk, they went crooked on her head. Her wigs were crooked a lot.

But drunk or sober, wig or no, we had music in our lives. We used to play a lot of the Temptations' "Ain't Too Proud to Beg." I got a lotta quarters if I sang that song. I would throw in a little drama. Those Motown songs spoke for us and to us. Renee, my cousin, who was around the same age I was, and I used to sing the Supremes. We crooned the Marvelettes' "Don't Mess with Bill" or the Staple Singers' "Respect Yourself."

While we were all singing the Spinners, Ma' Dea was always cooking something in the kitchen. She was a special cook. She cooked for us all—me, Uncle Lee, Uncle Joe, my aunts, my cousins, the strangers who floated in and out of my life. I loved, adored my uncles, especially Joe. He was a pretty boy, and his reputation was that he was the coolest brother on the planet. No need to panic. He was the type of guy who could slide into the set, and everybody wouldn't even know he'd been there. My grandmother used to call him sneaky, but that's not true. He had swag; he just had some real cool-ass swag. My uncle was cool, but he was a dangerous guy. He was a bully. He knocked a brother out just for the sake of knocking a brother out. He would be like, "I don't like that nigga. I'm gonna knock that nigga out."

My grandmother was the only person who could control him. You know, people came to her, "Please, Miz Myers, your son down there beating my brother up and he won't let him go." And my grandmother slipped on her house shoes and put her duster on. She put something in her pocket because she going down there to knock him out. She know he down there hurting somebody, right? She said, "I'm gone down there and kick his ass." You could see where Uncle Joe got his fight from when you looked at my grandmother; she was just as hard-core as he was. She went down there, and he saw her coming and then he started laughing. "Hey, old girl."

"Come here, sonny," my grandmother said.

"I'll meet you at the house, old girl." Joe was holding the man up with one hand.

"Let that man go."

"Ain't nothing wrong with him." Joe turned to the man he was holding. "Tell her ain't nothing wrong with you."

That man was shaking in his boots. "Naw, ma'am. Ain't nothing wrong with me."

+ + +

My uncle Joe was something else. This was the sixties, and these were our communities. Back then, everybody watched out for everybody. Didn't nobody want to mess with Joe. They didn't want to be up under his wrong side, and they figured out the way to get out from under him was to call my grandmomma to come and get him.

I remember my grandmother saying, "Alright, sonny, fuck with him again, why don't you?" When they both got home, my grandmother turned to him with her fists up and said, "That's right, I got you now."

My uncle started laughing and trying to hold her. He told her, "Ah, come here and give me a hug."

She started laughing. "Gone now. Get somewhere." My uncle Joe knew if he didn't make her laugh, she was gonna whoop his ass. She loved her boys more than any momma I ever knew. Sure, she whooped them over the head, but she kissed the hurt right after. I think that was because she knew the police wanted to kill my uncle Joe.

One time they told her, "No, ma'am, we don't want to take your son to jail, we wanna kill your son." That was the Fillmore Police Station, Chicago. They had a lotta nasty cops there. Lotta old stories came out that precinct. Up there on Pulaski and Fillmore. I guess it was the right kind of policing for the community, cause there was some tough brothers. My uncle was one of them. I mean, one time he knocked a cop out. After that, they really wanted to do him in. Every time he went to the penitentiary, they made him box. And my uncle was the star boxer. He brought trophies home. The institution crazy, ain't it? Fighting brothers against each other. My uncle was good with his hands; he was real, real good with his fists. He could have been another Sonny Liston or another Cassius Clay, but he was such a little stinker. He was a criminal. I missed him when he was in jail, but I had the rest of my family to love.

There was five of them: my aunt Josie; my mother, Ernestine; my uncle Joe; my aunt Suzie; and my uncle Lee. Lee was the baby. My grandmother said he sucked a bottle till he was five years old. He would go to the refrigerator and fix his own bottle. Can you imagine this big-ass kid going to the fridge and pouring his own bottle? We all laughed about that.

All my uncles and aunts were young—my mother was only fifteen when she had me—but they weren't like brothers and sisters to me; they were my uncles and aunts. I was the only kid in the house. My five half brothers—Jethro, Jerome, Wiley, Terry, and Todd—all lived with my daddy and his wife.

Ma'Dea didn't care for my daddy, so I rarely saw him. My grandmother kept me close. My uncles and aunts kept me closer. I was their dead sister's kid.

Every time we went over to one of our relatives' on the weekends, we did a fish fry and everybody got together and played spades. I danced and danced to a whole lot of Sam Cooke, and everybody told me stories about my mother, who died before I could walk, before I even had crawling down good. "Your momma was built like a Coke bottle, Fat Mommy. She was Ma'Dea's favorite child. Did you know that?" I did. I did know. Ma'Dea told me stories about my mother almost every day. In those stories my mother was beautiful, and she had men down the block wanting to court her. "Who you waiting on today, Ernestine?" And my mother would shrug her beautiful brown shoulders. Once, some man had given her the biggest engagement ring anyone had ever seen, but my mother just looked at it and said she'd think about it. Those were the stories my grandmother and uncles and aunts told me. And when we went to their houses, we would be having so much fun, there'd be so much laughing and Sam Cooke and dancing, but when I heard the voices start to elevate, I always knew my grandmother was in it. My grandmother and her liquor didn't go together. Every time she drank, she wanted to fight somebody about something that happened before anybody was born, or just *because*. I pretended I was asleep so she would leave me behind, but she never did. She'd come and wake me up. I could hear people saying, "Don't wake her up! Let her stay here!"

She'd turn on them and say, "This motherfucker here is going with me. She's my responsibility, not yours!" As if I were her property. "Get your motherfucking ass up and let's go!" I was nervous. Shaking all over. When I talk to my family about some of this now, they say, "I don't remember that." And I'm thinking, *Naw, you don't want to remember it, but it happened.* I don't want to remember Woody, but I do. I remember it all. The drinking and beatings. You think I'm gone to sit up here and make this up? Y'all act like you don't remember, but do you remember when you came and got me? You came and got me cause I got so many extension cord marks on my back. Do you remember that?

I remember Aunt Josie taking me into the bathroom and lifting up my blouse and saying, "Oh my God," and her face looked like she was about to cry, and she didn't let me go back to Ma'Dea's house that night. "You just stay here, Fat Mommy." Oh, but now she don't remember none of that? My grandmother is gone now, and know I loved my grandmother more than anybody, but I knew who she was. And I'm talking about me now. I'm talking about how intimidated I was. There's this wonderful picture of her I have. She was drunk in the photo. Could anybody else tell? Let me tell you: when she wasn't drunk, she was the smoothest, coolest lady on the planet. She cooked fried pies; cooked anything you could ask for. In the mornings, she'd sit up and read me the funny papers. She was so together. Sometimes in the early evening, especially if it was nice outside, she would look at me and say, "Come on, get the dog. Let's take a walk." And we would go for a walk. We lived maybe three, four blocks before our community cut off into the white folks' neighborhood, called K-Town. And we would walk down to the white folks' neighborhood—maybe they were Italian or Polish, but I was so young I didn't know; white was white at that time—and look at the yards and how pretty they were because ours didn't look like that. Around Christmastime, we would stop and look at the lights. We went on our evening walks, and Ma'Dea would stop and get "a taste"—that's what she called it.

You know what I really hated? When those assholes came through during the week with their brown bags and got her drunk. Cause not only did she stay up all night with the drinking; *I* stayed up all night with the drinking. When she got drunk, she would call me up out of my bed. "Come here and sang for Ma'Dea."

Their nasty asses used to sit back and say, "Nah, you ain't got to make her do that."

And my grandma said, "She gone do what I tell her to do. Wake up!"

They knew I was intimidated. They used that. Especially when they brought the little drinks around. They knew what kind of state they were going to get her in. They wanted that, so Ma'Dea would be so drunk she wouldn't notice them messing with me. She drank vodka, Smirnoff. And my grandma, my Ma'Dea, who was a good-looking woman even when she wore a housecoat, changed and turned ugly. Fight. Fight, fight, fight. Every weekend I tried to hide in the closet. Every weekend she was nursing a black eye. She was a pro at nursing black eyes. She did her share, too. She didn't get whooped all the time. They might have got a lick in, but she was the winner. When you did my grandmother wrong, she was not nice. Once, when my granddaddy Ike came home from work at the carwash, she scalded him with a pot of beans. She wasn't kidding. If you came to her house, you knew that. This was how she talked to me: "Motherfucker come in here with some bullshit? You better watch me. I'll get up and light me a cigarette, and you think that's all I'm doing, but I'm gone light that cigarette off the stove and I'm heating my water up."

She kept what could be weapons in the house. White women came to the front door, and she had a hammer and hatchet under the couch cushion if they acted up. She kept things around that she could get to if you messed with her. And she loved to start it. "Oh, don't worry, I'll start it." That's what she told people instead of hello. As sweet as she was, my grandmother had a mean streak in her, and I bore the brunt of it. My grandmother told me I was scary; I was a punk. Maybe I was. I found out later on, I am also a marshmallow. It took a few years and a world of hurt to realize even marshmallows can get tough. Even the sweetest child can become bitter.

Chapter 2

Where's My Shine?

Girls like me weren't born out on the streets. You've got to realize we were raised, just like everybody else. My grandmother raised me. Took care of me as best she could. I turned nine years old, and in the middle of all that laughing, singing, drinking, hitting, I realized something crazy: all five of my grandma's kids left home early. They all left home at fourteen, fifteen years old. Nobody stayed in that house past that. My uncles came back to live with us from time to time, but my aunties were outta there. With babies. Josie, Suzie, my momma—all of them. My grandmomma did the best she could with what she had, but when she had a drink . . . I had to stay there with her, night and day, and be in that house with her, by myself, a young girl, listening to my grandma's angry alcoholic self. Listen to her sorrowful alcoholic self, when she was making her plans to die, talking about people from the past, making me validate my love for her. You know how drunk people are: "I love you; you don't love me like I love you. How much you love me? You love me, Brenda Jean?"

"Yes, ma'am," I told her.

"How much?"

"A sugar and a peck and a hug around the neck." And then I gave her a hug around the neck.

There were always other people around, other drunks. I was sitting on the couch, and all I wanted to do was shrink and get away. I could smell the liquor. I'm a kid, and I'm watching these people do what grown folks do. There was nothing interesting in this for me. I was watching them, and they just being inappropriate with each other. Even at nine years old, I knew they shouldn't be doing this stuff in front of a kid.

When I was young, the insurance man used to come over our house. Ma'Dea had bought some insurance from him. I didn't know this, but they had made some arrangement for him to come back later and have some drinks, and he came by with another guy with him. Ma'Dea set the drinks up. You know, looking back, I was kind of invisible to them. I can't remember how old Ma'Dea was at that time, but she was a good-looking woman. You know she wore those stretch pants with the stirrups from the sixties and those pretty little knit tops and they matched, and she had a neat shape and she had that red hair and a pretty smile. Brothers liked her. I remember I felt so uncomfortable. They were slow dancing, and I remember thinking this wasn't going to end well. My grandmomma had this boyfriend, Ike, but I never knew if they were on or off, on or off. I was sitting there thinking about Ike because I didn't like the way the insurance man was dancing with my grandmomma.

I had this ugly look on my face. They were dancing slow and nasty. Ma'Dea was drinking, and in order to keep me quiet, she done gave me the driest bag of potato chips I ever had. She told me go somewhere and sit down, and I obeyed her. I knew how to be invisible. I disappeared right there on the couch. *Poof*, I was gone. I was taught to never get in grown folks' conversation. I knew not to answer the door. "Bet not answer that door. What you doing at that door?" And if I said something, I got, "Don't you hear me talking?

You gone get knocked into the middle of next week." I remember sitting around and having to use the bathroom, and I was scared to ask cause I know can't interrupt what's going on, and so I'm just holding it. Ma'Dea looked at me and said, "What's wrong with you?"

"I gotta go pee."

She got mad and said, "What's wrong with you? Gone and pee!"

Everyone who was in the house would tell her, "That's right. You got her trained. She know better." And I was trained. Trained to be a ho, before I even knew what that was. I was living a ho's life: I knew what I was supposed to do and what I wasn't supposed to do. But I was still a kid. Not that I didn't get into trouble, but I was still a kid.

I remember one time, Ma'Dea was sleeping on the couch and I saw some spirits. I don't think it was my childhood imagination, I think it was some real spirits. They weren't unfriendly, but they just came and looked at me. It might have been my mom. Where we were then, the living room was in the front and you had to walk all the way down the hall, past the bedrooms, past the bathroom to get all the way to the kitchen. The kitchen was way in the back and didn't nobody have lights on, cause like folks say, "Don't be running up no light bill." You couldn't keep the refrigerator open too long when I was growing up. That was a light bill. *Please answer me why this refrigerator light is running up the light bill, boo-boo?* Anyway, I remember Ma'Dea saying, "Go get me a cold glass of water." But I wasn't really feeling me going back there in the dark. I didn't want go back there by myself, but Ma'Dea saw my face and said, "Girl, if you don't go back there and get me some water." So I went sliding down the hallway against the wall, and I got in there and I was trying to feel for the light. But I couldn't find it, so I opened the refrigerator and the fridge light came on. Standing behind the refrigerator door was a person in a long gown or a robe or something. I dropped the glass and ran back front, and I told Ma'Dea, "Something back there; I seen something back there."

"Girl, quit lying." But she went back there with me, and she cut the light on and she didn't see it, but I saw them. I'm a grown woman right now; I was not confused. Something was there and it was looking over me. I didn't know if it was a girl or a boy, but it was a spirit. When I was down or scared or lonely, I would think it was my momma.

My imagination wasn't just for conjuring ghosts. When Ma'Dea was asleep and I was bored, I found little-kid trouble. Ma'dea had these doilies all around, and I had a pair of scissors, and I decided to redesign all the doilies. I had nothing to do. I had already cut my doll's hair and that was not enough. I cut those doilies and then pieced them back together. I thought I had got away with it, but Ma'Dea was cleaning up one day and she picked them up and they started falling apart and she said, "What the hell is this? Brenda Jean, what is this?"

"I don't know." My eyes were as big as saucers. I didn't know if she knew I was lying or not, but I was so nervous when she was fussing about them damn doilies. I was about four years old. But my boredom ended soon enough. I went to kindergarten right across the street, Sumner Elementary School, and my teacher's name was Ms. Law and I thought she was the real law. She was tall, a big presence. I was a good student; I was a good kid. I could come out my front door and go right to school. It was real cool. There was a little store. And there was a cleaners. Learner's Cleaners, and it was a factory and everybody worked there, even Ma'Dea. Uncle Joe worked there for a minute, but he was always feeling on girls' titties so they fired him. He was a Casanova, especially with older women. He was always somewhere with his wang in somebody. And the husbands didn't do anything with him cause my uncle was a killer. Plus, these older women were hanging out with my grandmother. My grandmother cussed Uncle Joe out, "Leave them women alone; don't do this, these men gone shoot you."

But Uncle Joe was like, "Aw, I ain't scared of these boys. These dudes ain't gone do nothing to me." Uncle Joe was very frivolous; he was always doing something with some woman. Once, we had a house party, but we weren't supposed to, so Uncle Joe gave me a candy so I didn't say anything. And I never did, cause it was Uncle Joe and that was my partner. He went across the street and got twenty-five cents' worth of bologna and a loaf of bread, and me and him up sat up and ate bologna sandwiches together. Or he would get up in the morning and cook a can of biscuits and get some syrup and we would have that. The kids now want so much, but back then that's what we did and I loved it. Getting a fried bologna sandwich meant somebody loved you. We loved that bologna and that was the best bologna, too. Not this meat in plastic they got now. Back then was the good stuff. I was always talking to him, all day, every day, and he never told me to cut it out. One time he was in the bathroom, probably stinking it up, but I was standing right by the door and I was like, "Blah, blah, yippy hay, hay." He answered me every now and again. And I was like, "Blah, blah, middy, yippy, yeah, yeah."

My grandmother came by the door. "That's a damn shame. He can't take a shit by himself." I just followed him around and he let me. I loved my uncle Joe.

There was a lounge on Lake and Hamlin, and the lounge had some really good hamburgers, and a lady named Lea ran the place, and she ran into Uncle Joe and lost her mind about him. And next thing I know Uncle Joe was running it. He took money from the cash register and he was pouring drinks. It was his place now. I'm like, Can I get a job? And they gave me a job! To make the hamburgers.

When you walked in, they had a little grill area, and that was the area I had to stay in; I couldn't go near the bar part. I had to stay in the area and make the hamburgers and then go to the tables and give the customers the hamburgers, get my little tip, and then come back. Everybody thought that was cute. "Look at that little girl working the hamburgers and the French fries." I drank so much pop, they told me they weren't gone pay me. My grandmomma came down to get a little taste, and she asked around, "How she do today?" And they all said good. I was busy. I was washing dishes and flipping hamburgers. I was so proud cause I'm nine years old and I'm working, making my own little money at the liquor store/burger joint. I worked down there for a good month or so. I think I lost interest or something. It was no big deal, but for a minute I had a few dollars, and I could go up on Madison Street and go to the five-and-dime and get me some stuff.

That's where we shopped. For clothes, for shoes. We weren't having it no other way. For our little Fourth of July outfits, we went to the five-and-dime. Everybody had the same little stuff on. The shoes were on a nylon string, stuck together, and sometimes you got the white girls and sometime you got the blue ones—that's what we called those shoes: we called them girls. All that Nike and stuff, that wasn't in my neighborhood. Listen, you must have your dress shoes when we were growing up. Everybody wore those dress shoes to church and to picture day. You put on your ankle socks and you go about your business. I put mine on and follow around my uncle Joe anywhere he let me. That wasn't too far, because he was a gangster, one of the leaders in the Egyptian Cobras, which converted to the Vice Lords. The original Vice Lords. That's who he was.

Gangs back then were formulated to protect different neighborhoods. At that time Chicago was sliced up into communities and neighborhoods and every one of them—whether it was the whites, the Puerto Ricans, the Blacks—every one of them had their own gangs. I'm not sure about the other gangs, but my family was involved with the Vice Lords. They originated from the Egyptian Cobras, and they turned into the Conservative Vice Lords. Now, the Conservative Vice Lords were some brothers who dressed well and alike; they dealt with things. They were not selling drugs at that time, which was early on. I think they did some type of extortion; they were just running shit or they did some robberies and someone took off something from somebody. They also did something called "policy," and that was like the lottery, and they ran that around our community. The Vice Lords kept everything in order when it came to being on the streets. Stuff like that. But I was a little kid, I'm not sure what all they were up to. I had heard about some of the guys who did heroin, but that was far and between.

My family didn't really know guys like that. Most of the guys drank wine and sat on the corner. As far as I know, Vice Lords and the other gangs were about territories and guys who went to dance parties and fought fists with fists. I remember hearing about a zip gun a couple of times, but it was rare when a brother had a gun back then, because they were *men*. Maybe they had a knife, and when they were serious, they cut you. Lotta guys went to war with a baseball bat, and they could knock your ass out because they were some boxing brothers. I used to see how they dressed. Brothers were wearing the Ivy League look and were sharp as hell. My uncle Lee was one of them. He ironed clothes that came from the cleaners. Do you understand how serious that is?

You know, it took me until I was about nine or ten to figure out Uncle Lee was a pimp. I was so sexualized already. I was kissing this boy in the building. Nine and ten years old—and kissing. I remember seeing some of Uncle Lee's girls. He even had his trans. He pimped a trans. Her name was Sheba. She came over my grandmother's house. Ma'Dea knew exactly who she was, but it wasn't no problem cause my grandmother didn't discriminate. But Sheba was a well-known trans in Chicago at that time, cause you know they had the ballroom dance contests. I never went to one, all I got to see was Sheba preparing for them. She would sew and make all of her own costumes and stuff. And I would get a sneak peek of the costumes and the glam of it all. The glam was ridiculous. What I did know was that Sheba won all the balls. She was very extra diva, and she carried herself very reserved. She was like, "This is who I am and don't mess with me. Cause I'll cut your ass from A to Z." Grandmomma let me go over Sheba's house. She had wall-to-wall carpeting, gorgeous furniture; she even had a phone in the bathroom. She had that velvet wallpaper. This is still the sixties, and I ain't used to Black folks living like this. She was living large. She had a sewing machine in the house, made all her own clothes. Everything in her house was beautiful and extravagant and plush. That's why I liked to go over her house, and she would make me dresses and shirts, too.

All that time, I didn't know Uncle Lee was a pimp, and Sheba was one of his hos, but you know grown folks talking around kids and I'm hearing, "Lee gone get himself messed over, taking that thang's money and ducking." Uncle Lee had this bad habit: he would take Sheba's money and then tell her he would give her her cut in a couple days. But then he made sure he wasn't available. Sheba was looking for him and she was paying him well. And it was about a year after that that my uncle Lee got his throat cut. It didn't kill him. My grandmother said Sheba cut his throat cause he wouldn't give her her money. But my uncle said he was at a craps game, and they stuck it up and some dude cut him. Hmm. I think Sheba cut him. I was ten years old and even I knew you could depend on the truth from Ma'Dea. Ma'Dea told my uncle, "Sheba the one who cut your throat, and she gone cut it again, if you keep messing with her."

My grandmother knew all his business because Uncle Lee went back and forth from living with us to living with his women. When I went over Sheba's house, his clothes were all in the closet all nice and proper. He had places. But I guess my grandmother's house was his base and he didn't want to get too tied up with no particular woman. Two of my uncles came to the house and slept. Ate up all the food or brought something nice by and stayed. They spent forever in the bathroom. My grandmother be like, "Ya'll acting like sissies being in there for so long. Can't nobody get in there to do nothing." She cussed them out because they'd be in there for a long time, like women. Shaving and plucking. Both of them was way into themselves. We lived on Hamlin and Lake, right around the corner where I used to see the women working. Some of those ladies worked for my uncle. My uncle handled most of his business in our building. Our little place had a back door, a front door, a kitchen, and a little bedroom, and then it had a Murphy bed. The living room was our bedroom. We had talked to the landlord, and my uncle Lee had a little spot across the hall. I don't know why, cause my uncle never wanted to pay the rent. He never wanted to pay nobody money after he got it.

All of his ladies knew to take their cut before they handed it over to my uncle. Uncle Lee had this ho named Queenie, and she looked like Cleopatra or one of those Egyptians. She was so gorgeous—tall, Black, very dark. She had the first afro I ever saw on a woman. Long, pretty legs. She was the first girl I saw in miniskirts, and she wore those Nehru dresses. She gave me one of those Nehru dresses, but it was too big for me. It was a gown. She was very well kept and wore the latest fashions. Oh, I wanted to be stylish like that, and when I got grown, I wanted to handle my business the way she did.

Once, she was working a white guy and my uncle said to me, "Go on in there and get the wallet. Crawl in there and get the wallet and then bring it out to me while they are, you know . . . busy." And I did. I crawled in there, took the wallet, then I gave it to my uncle, and he took the money and he told me, "Now go put the wallet back in there." I was nine years old. And I did all that for ten dollars. Ten dollars was a lotta money back then. I wanted to go to Riverview, the amusement park, and Riverview was closing. It had the sideshows with the bearded lady and all that stuff. Riverview had a Ferris wheel and the parachute where you ride up and drop down real fast. I wanted to take a ride on the Bobs, the biggest roller coaster, and I was tall enough. Oh my God, he made me beg for that money. Uncle Lee made me beg for that money all day long. To get that ten dollars I had to cry, snot, and carry on. I was in my feelings, because I done went on a mission I still didn't understand. I went in there and stole the man's wallet and I didn't know why. I got a felony case and don't even know it. My grandmomma finally came out and told him, "Give her that goddamned money! Now you told this girl you gone her give that goddamned money, now give it! She been standing at your door crying over an hour." Why was he even holding on to that money, with his stanking ass? My grandmother said I could get on the Lake Street bus and I go from Western to Belmont to get to Riverview. Finally, I got the ten dollars; his ass was playing tiddlywinks. Even Queenie was telling my uncle, "Give that girl her money."

+ + +

That's what life was like with Ma'Dea. My grandmomma, cussing and drinking and cooking all the time. She could make something out of nothing. She talked to me a lot. Everybody else came and went, but

Ma'Dea was my always. Me and her were each other company. We had our special shows. We watched *Ben Casey*. *Creature Features*. I liked cartoons. TV went off at a certain time a night, 10:30. "The Star-Spangled Banner" played and the TV turned off, and either we played the record player or my ass went somewhere and sat down. And then we fell asleep, woke up in the morning, and she would make me some breakfast. In the mornings, Ma'Dea got the funny papers, and we would get in the middle of the bed, because I slept with her unless I slept on the pallet on the floor. I never had my own room. We read *Nancy*. We liked *Beetle Bailey*. See, every once and a while we had fun. I should have known even the little bit of good times that I had couldn't last.

Chapter 3

Suburban Bullshit

The alcoholic Ma'Dea; the mean Ma'Dea. Anybody in the family would tell you that she had a mean streak. She said horrible things that she wouldn't take back. When she sobered up, she would say, "I don't know what I said. But if I said it, I said it." It was like I lived with two people. I lived with the beautiful Ma'Dea and I lived with the Ma'Dea after too many drinks.

It had gotten real bad for us. Uncle Joe was dead. He got killed in 1968 by a childhood friend. Everybody knew Uncle Joe was a bully. The story was (and I'm not too sure how it goes because I heard it from the streets), this boy had been in my grandmother's house with Joe. Uncle Joe either wanted to take his money or his gun. There was a restaurant right on the corner of Pulaski between Adams and Wilcox. It was in an alley, and there was a little hamburger joint. Joe had beat on this boy before, and Joe was gone whoop his ass again. My uncle had deadly hands. He put brothers in the hospital. And this boy was scared. Joe came after him. My understanding was that the boy first shot Joe in the chest. Joe step back and said, "You gone shoot me?" Uncle Joe got up and he came back at the boy. That boy was so afraid, he shot my uncle in the head. Right in his temple. I remember going to view the body. That little boy cried when he told my grandmother, "Mrs. Myers, I was afraid for my life." He had a right to be afraid for his life. But that was a sad time for the family; it was a hard time. Lee was in jail, so he didn't get to go to his brother's funeral. My aunties came by, but they couldn't stay; they had their own families to raise. It was a hard time for everybody.

My grandmother played a lot of Marvin Gaye after the funeral. She just kept drinking and playing Marvin Gaye. "Too busy thinking 'bout my baby. And I ain't got time for nothing else." She played that record over and over again. She was messed up. Uncle Joe wasn't even thirty yet. He was maybe twenty-five? Something like that. He was still a young man. And Uncle Lee was in jail for God knows why. Robbing the cleaners, sticking people up. Uncle Lee was a fool. I had known him all my life to be in and out of jail. When the two of them, Joe and Lee, were out of jail, I was happy. I was always so happy when they were around. They spoiled me. They were so extra with me. Lee sometimes was a little bit mean, but he loved me.

But when Uncle Joe died and Uncle Lee was in the pen for a minute, I couldn't take the licks. "How did you get that bruise?" she'd ask me in the morning when she'd sobered up. "What's wrong with your eye?"

"You hit me, Ma'Dea."

"I hit you like that? You must of did something." We both were grieving Uncle Joe's death, but I was the one who had the bruises to show for it.

+ + +

One night Uncle LC came to our place to get me. At first, Ma'Dea started joking when Uncle LC said he was taking me home with him, but then she turned into this person whose anger veered toward me. "You bet not move," she said, pointing at me. "You ain't going nowhere." I started crying because I really wanted to go with Uncle LC. I loved being out there in them suburbs. You know, picking the strawberries, turning the flowers over. Just to get away was so good.

"Come on, Ruth, don't be like that. Let her gone." He turned to me. I was dressed, but I hadn't packed a bag. "Come on, Brenda."

"You sit down. You bet not breathe." Ma'Dea got real close to me and said, "I don't care nothing about your crying." And then she put her finger up in my nose and said, "Breathe on it. I dare you." I sat there, holding my breath. I started crying because of the emotional things she put on me. Just some real intimidating stuff for a kid. She was a good woman—I don't know why she put me through that.

+ + +

"Oh, come on, Ruth." She was headed toward the living room and he went to follow her. She probably wanted the hammer she kept under the cushions in the couch.

Halfway there, she turned on him. "Don't follow me, goddamnit." I still don't know how he did it, but Uncle LC shut her up in the bathroom. She was livid. Cussing. "When I get out of here, I'm gone kill your ass."

"Okay, Ms. Ruth." Then he turned to me. "Brenda, gone down to the car."

I heard my grandmother calling out, "You bet not move, Brenda Jean!"

Uncle LC looked at me hard and said, "Gone. I said gone." And I shot out the door.

I was crazy nervous, shaking in the car. We drove off. And while we were on the way there, Grandmomma was on the phone with Aunt Josie giving her an earful. Ma'Dea was telling Aunt Josie what she was going to do to me. "When she come back, I'm gone to beat her ass." So when I went in Aunt Josie's house, whatever was said, however it was said, Aunt Josie told me to come into the kitchen and asked me if she could look at my back. I had these extension cord marks on my back and these bruises. She shook her head when she saw them, and she told Ma'Dea, "You can't whoop on her like that."

"I can do whatever I want to do to her. I kill her if I want to." We didn't have speakerphones back then, but you could hear her ass all on the phone.

Aunt Josie hung up the phone and pulled my blouse back down. "Do you want to stay out here?"

"Yeah."

✦ ✦ ✦

I thought if anybody could protect me, it was Aunt Josie and my uncle. They were my heroes. It seemed like they wanted a better life for me. I couldn't take it anymore, and I told Aunt Josie I wanted to come over to her house. Auntie and Uncle LC had moved away from the West Side, to Evanston, Illinois, and they had bought a house. See, Uncle LC had two or three jobs. He worked for a trucking company for many years; he worked in security, and sometimes he was doing some stuff that wasn't quite legal. No drugs or anything, but maybe some merchandise. Folks brought in some unauthorized things and some state troopers had to get involved. Maybe it ain't a felony, but you might get caught cause you ain't got the right credentials. He was a jack of all trades. When he wasn't doing security or trucking, he was out in his garage fixing somebody's car. He worked so hard and we all were proud. Auntie and Uncle LC had two boys. Their sons had electric trains, electric guitars. They had nice clothes and matching coats. They were really blessed. I loved having to be a good girl at their house. They didn't need an extra kid in the house to feed. We girls are expensive. Now my aunt had three kids she got to do everything for. Another mouth to feed, an extra somebody to pick up after, another little person to worry about. Even as a kid, I appreciated that.

My life in the suburbs was great but traumatic at the same time. Going to school was fun; I had a ton of friends there. I was studying, learning stuff. But the boys started to hate me. I was cool as a cousin, but now that I was living there, I was coming in on their situation. So they were very mean to me after that. But I was coming fresh from the West Side. Neither one of my cousins could do anything to me, I used to whoop they asses up in that house. My auntie came home and my cousins would be raggedy as fetlocks. "What happened to y'all?"

I dog-walked they ass around the house. I was a squabbler. They were all scratched up, clothes all tore up. Hair here and there. Don't mess with me. I'm from the West Side. But here's the thing, I didn't know how, but they found out that I was claustrophobic. They used to lock me up in the closets. I was in there crying.

Claustrophobia is a strange thing. When you are claustrophobic, you panic. When you panic, the more you feel closed in, and as you go through the panic, the smaller everything feels. It closes in on you and you can't breathe. I used to be in that closet and couldn't breathe and I was trying to calm down. But then the boys unlocked the door and ran out the house. As we got older, they got bigger and they got stronger, and I couldn't whoop them both. They were always trying to start some stuff with me. Then they started to blackmail me. I wasn't strong enough to tell them boys, "Fuck, y'all." Thinking about it now, I should have said, I'm done with you punks. But they found out how to manipulate me. They made up lies. Like they saw me with a boy, or would tell Aunt Josie I was doing something she told me not to do, or say I was someplace Aunt Josie told me not to be. They used to manipulate me in that way because I didn't want to get into trouble. I had just left a house where you could get your ass beat into the ground if you were out of pocket. Aunt Josie never whooped me like that, but I thought if I misbehaved, she might.

Now Aunt Josie wasn't gone to kiss your bumps and all that. She wasn't a nurturing person, because she wasn't nurtured. Ma'Dea raised her, too. Aunt Josie wasn't nurtured, but I wasn't nurtured either. I was loved, but not nurtured.

+ + +

I was ten, almost eleven. I had started forming. I had titties and I had red spots in my panties, so I went and told my auntie, "I need a Band-Aid."

"What for?"

"Cause I cut myself, and I need a Band-Aid." Aunt Josie took me in the bathroom, she looked at my panties. She sighed—you know? She had all this stuff in her closet: the belt, the Kotex, everything. I remember thinking, *She had this all ready for me?* She was equipped for what was going to happen to me, and she stayed home that day and we drank hot chocolate. It was wonderful. I will never forget that. It was one of the reasons, later on, I felt safe leaving my daughters with her despite other dangers because I knew she could be so caring.

One time, I wanted to get a T-shirt, and Aunt Josie said, "Come here, Brenda Jean," and she looked at me and said, "This girl is busting out." She went out, got me some beginner bras, and she got me a girdle. I will never forget when that ugly-ass girdle showed up in my life. You know, back in the day, the rule was, you were not supposed to jiggle. Everybody was trying to hold that jiggle down. That caused me so much embarrassment in school. I went to a white school, and most of them girls had flat asses and wasn't nobody trying to saddle them. When I took my girdle off in the gym locker room, them white girls looked at me and said, "What is all that, Myers?"

And I told them, "That's my girdle."

"What?" They didn't even know what it was.

So the girls didn't understand why I wore a girdle, and the boys wanted to figure out how to get me out of one. But I wasn't really playing with boys, I was more laughing with the boys. I saw cute boys and thought they were cute, but that's it. I had crushes, but I wasn't trying to be with nobody. I got a ride from a boy named Bobby

Starks. Bobby had a reputation. I got out of his car in an alley once, and when I got out the car, my uncle saw us. LC got out of his car. And I walked right past my uncle. The look he gave me, I thought to myself, *Aw, he gone tell Aunt Josie he saw me getting out of Bobby's car.* But I just want to say, everybody wanted to ride in Bobby's car. He had a hot rod! I had rode in the car so many times before, with him and his girl. He had a legit girlfriend, Patsy. Bobby Starks was just really popular in the community. Older than me. I'm in junior high, they were high school kids. And I loved his girlfriend, Patsy; she was my girlfriend Regina's sister. The older kids used to think of us as those little silly girls. I didn't think Bobby thought anything of riding us around.

My uncle didn't tell Aunt Josie, but he pulled me aside when I got home. "I ain't gone tell Aunt Josie, but how old is that man?" I'm shocked, cause now Uncle LC was acting like Charlie and Dennis, my cousins—getting ready to tattle on me. I should have known it was about to get a lot worse.

+ + +

He started sleeping on the couch. I used to sleep in the living room. Bedtime, I used to have to go to sleep with *Perry Mason* and the TV news on, and should have been asleep, but they kept it on, so I kept watching. But then they cut the TV off, and Aunt Josie said, "Come on, LC." He laid on the couch, pretending like he was asleep and he couldn't get up. She went back to the bedroom, and Uncle LC was on the couch, and I was on my pallet. He just slid over and started moving his hands down my nightshirt. And I was real stiff. Scared to move. I panicked inside; I wasn't screaming but I was scared, crying, and I was tight, tight, stiff as a board. I made myself as stiff as I could. He made me feel nasty. My head was filled with Woody and the bouncy knee. And I was still tight, but he was forcing my legs open. I crossed my legs real tight, and I had strong legs, and I could smell his stinking-ass breath. He never penetrated me, but he had his penis out.

So now I felt like I got it, coming and going. I didn't feel safe nowhere.

Before, I was strong in that house. Charles and Dennis, they didn't scare me none. I was a fighter; I felt I could handle anything. But after LC did that, it became a nightmare to go to bed every night. My cousins were getting older. Dennis and I were friendly, but he was a growing boy and he could be tough, and Charlie, he was vicious, a hateful asshole. With everything going on with my uncle, I couldn't handle them under all of that. I had no defense left. The only thing that kept me from going crazy was school and my friends. In the middle of all that, I was going to bar mitzvahs. I was going to school in Skokie, and the community was totally Jewish. We got Jewish holidays on top of the other holidays we got off. I loved their ass for it. Run Kipper, whatever, I loved it. We was *out*! They went on amazing trips. I had little friends, and they were calling me. "Myers! Come on! We love Oscar Myers wieners! We love you, Myers!" Ah man, I was having a ball in Skokie with my good friends. But every night, I had to handle this nasty thing with LC. That situation with my uncle made me lose my power. He took everything from me.

Being put in a position like that from some creep, that takes you away from you. It takes your innocence away; it takes your choice. It takes something away from you that you can't never get back, and even if they wanted to, they can't give it back. It stops little girls from playing with dolls and ever thinking of being Cinderella. It takes the fairy tale out of a little girl's eyes. Every girl has a light in her that she keeps. You grow up, but you still have a little bit of fairy tale in you when you are raised in a nurturing environment. You think dreams can come true, but molestation snatches that away from you, and it is replaced with—how can I say how it feels? You ever see one of those scary movies? The darkness is coming around the corner and they see it? And it's right there and they want to get away from it and they can't? And the dark keeps coming. You begin to make all things dark; you begin to do dark things because you feel dark.

They take something away from you very valuable. Innocence is a blessing.

I listen to other women who lost their innocence by choice, afterwards, the next day, they felt a little "Yay!" They felt themselves, because it was their choice and they did it at a point when it was something special. But when it is snatched from you without your permission, it makes a sore inside you and it festers. That's how it was for me. The beautiful light in my eyes went away, cause my fairy tale's been broken. Maybe if the men knew that, when they took it, they wouldn't do it. But maybe they would. You got to be really sick and dark to do that to some kid, to some person who never asked for it. Uncle LC was sure like that.

The longer I stayed in that situation, the more I thought something was wrong with me. I thought if my mother were there, she could make LC go away or she could tell me how to be a good girl. I thought I was a bad girl. I thought even if we got caught or if I told, I would be the one who would get in trouble. I felt like the nasty one. All I wanted to do was go back home to my grandmomma. I had forgiven her almost as soon as I had gotten to Aunt Josie's. I hadn't lived with my grandmother for two years. Ma'Dea was the one who put a baseball bat on somebody if they tried to rob us. I needed that kind of protection. But Ma'Dea, at that time, was an in-home domestic. She stayed with white folks, and on the weekends, she went and did her thing. Sick as it was, I probably kept her more grounded. I went and saw her on the weekends, and she was living in the basement of these white people. They gave her this small room off to the side, and I stayed with her. I couldn't wander over the house, cause, you know, white folks were still seriously white folks back then. Everybody had a maid. Ain't that something? As if it was their right to have a maid. This was late sixties.

This woman my grandmother worked for, she looked like trailer trash to me. She was a waitress, but she had married somebody who had had a little bit of money, and I guess he was giving her some alimony. She had a nice house. That ex-husband paid for everything. I was young and I didn't know a whole bunch about white people, but even I could tell she was no class of white. I didn't know a lot about the world, but I knew what money looked like. I was already on top of that. When I was in the suburbs, them white kids used to invite me to everything. They took me on skiing trips. They loved little Brenda. Anyway, my grandmother used to take care of her boy. I liked to mess with him cause he was an asshole. My grandmother used to make me go out in the yard and go and get him to come inside.

"Tom, it's time to come into the house."

"Oh, I don't wanna come in."

I said, "It's time for you to come in."

"I'm not coming in."

I picked his ass up, and he was kicking and fighting me. And then this little girl saw me, and she started yelling back into her house, "Mommy, there's a little colored girl taking Tommy away!"

I took his ass in the house, and my grandmother said to him, "Didn't I say to come here?"

"Yes." He went to his room. Ma'Dea and I laughed as soon as he was out of earshot. My grandmother had his ass in order.

Our weekends were fun with antics like that, but my grandmother was lonely. She was lonely without me. I told her, "I'm going to come home." I never told her why. I wasn't thinking about going back to Ma'Dea's drinking and abuse. Anything was better than the situation I was in. I guess I thought I was thinking like a big girl. My grandmother needed me.

She was so happy. "You ready to come home?"

"Yeah."

She said, "I gotta get a place." And that's how we ended up on 3247 West Warren Boulevard. We were on the third floor. It was me, my grandmother, and we had a dog named Black Smut. A little cockerpoodle. I was so glad to be back. I had been out in Evanston for too long. From fourth grade up until almost eighth grade. I came back to Chicago when I was almost thirteen. Uncle LC started touching on me when I was ten going on eleven years old. You know, just about the time when my little figure started to show, when my little titties started coming out. And I was sure Aunt Josie discussed all that stuff with him because she didn't think Uncle LC was lying in wait for his little niece to sprout. He probably knew more about me than I did.

+ + +

This thing with him followed me even when I got big. He tried to come at me again, but I was older. I was coming from the streets. I guess he thought me and him had something. In his sick mind, me and him had a relationship. He knocked on my door like he was my man. I told him, "You need to get away from my door! Before I call your wife. My kids in here. This ain't this! What you doing?"

"Who in there?" he said.

"What you mean, who in there?" See, I wasn't scared of him then. Did I take his money? Yes, I did. Cause by then I was a prostitute. I'll take anybody's money. You goddamned right I did. And I fooled his ass and kept on moving.

This asshole talking about, "I'm gone come by later." You think I was there? How did that feel? You knocked on my door like you my man or something, cause you gave me a few dollars. Forget you.

I told Josie about all he did, not when I was little, but when I got grown. It took me a while to talk about it. All that molestation turned me into a really unbalanced kid who needed help. But we didn't help our kids back then like that. Grown folks turned their backs on us for things like being raped and being molested, being mentally ill. Things happened, and we had no defenses because we were children. We were expected to accept it, or we were told we were lying. No one believed our story. Boys and girls. When we spoke up against adults doing stuff to us or other family members doing stuff to us, nobody grown stepped up. Nobody wanted to be our hero.

When I told Ma'Dea, before she died, what kind of man LC was, she believed me. "I know he was a no-good motherfucker. He went at one of Aunt Josie's aunts. I believe you, cause he tried to have sex with

Onie and Chloe and he tried to mess with me. Josie didn't believe me. And when he tried to get with Suzie, she told Josie. And Josie didn't believe her." But years later, when I got up the guts to approach my aunt, my daughters had already told her Uncle LC had approached them, and she let them know then that she knew they told the truth. And she knew I told the truth, too.

+ + +

By the time I took to my healing and I saw him again at Aunt Josie's house, he was suffering. It didn't really matter to me. I saw him paying for his behavior in a way that I could have never made happen. Karma made it go around, baby. He was suffering. God, You are amazing. At the end, in 2012, I saw LC suffering and I thought, God is good. And LC wasn't in my head anymore, he wasn't inside me anymore. Jeremy, my adopted son, was there with me, and Uncle LC was using a wheelchair. He had gotten his leg cut off; he had got prostate cancer. He was just dying, festering inside his own body. He rolled around with a prosthetic leg. And then he took his leg off, and Jeremy was like, "Are you a robot?"

"Naw, I'm not a robot."

"Well, how you take your leg off?" Jeremy kept asking him crazy questions like that. You know how kids can be irritating? Jeremy was six years old and was asking annoying questions like nobody's business. He kept asking the same questions over and over again. Jeremy did that to him for about an hour.

Uncle LC had this look on his face like, "Somebody come and get this boy." You know them kids—*are we there yet? Are we there yet?* And I let Jeremy pester him. Finally, I said, "Come on, Jeremy."

As we left, I really looked at my uncle. Wheeling around with one leg and dying in his own stink. Uncle LC didn't control anything. He couldn't hurt me. He was paying for all the abuse he gave me when I was little and needed him most of all. And it was all happening without my help. He was paying. Unfortunately, my aunt went through it with him. He was awful, but she continued to be his wife. She

says now, "I should have never continued things as long as I did."
She got super sick taking care of his ass. He didn't like her. He was
mean. Just before they went down south, she retired. It was religion
that made her stay with him. She felt that "death do us part." God
ain't never told nobody to stay with somebody that's abusing you. He
never said stay with somebody that's beating you, cause "death do us
part." Whose death? Mine? That ain't fair. Our God ain't said that.
She regretted that: being with a creep. He died bitter and mad. It was
sad. He's been dead awhile now. Aunt Josie called me when he was
dying and told me, "Brenda, I know he hurt you. You know we don't
talk about this to nobody else." That's the closest she ever got to it.
Family secrets. But I don't feel like keeping secrets no more. It took
some good therapy to make sure he wasn't in my head anymore. "We
need to pray for him, cause he real sick."

I went to Keith, my husband. "You know Aunt Josie done asked
me to pray for LC?"

We had been married since 2005. Keith sometimes knew my
moods better than I did. He said, "What you gone do?"

"The only thing I can do. I'll pray to pray. Cause if I send Him
any other kind of message, He'll know I don't mean it. I'm gone pray
for God to give me a heart to understand. Maybe God will help me
forgive him because I can't do it on my own. I hope his foot fall off
and then we'll bury the foot and then we'll bury his ass later. That's
what I really want." Keith looked at me and just nodded. But God
is amazing. God will continue to bless you even when you can't sing
to the place where He is. He knows why you ain't there, because you
are not perfect. You're not feeling this. You're not that loving person
yet, you can't reach there yet. Later that night, I got on my knees
and thought, *You just have to let Him know.* "Listen, God, I'm only
human, and right now You have to forgive me for not being able to
be what You expect of me. I know You expect better of me, but better I can't show right now. I ask You for forgiveness. I am not able to
do it. I don't like him and that's it. I'm praying to You. I'm praying so
I can get to a place where I can pray for that man. Amen."

Part II

What's in the mirror
is not always who you are

Chapter 4

The Making of a Real Ho

You know what's funny? All that time I spent out there with those white girls, I never thought their kind of life was a choice for me. The way they made it would never be the way I made it.

Ma'Dea and I were living on the West Side of Chicago, and life was going back to what I remembered it to be. Old friends were floating back in. Ma'Dea was drinking vodka—a little bit, and a little bit more—and men from the neighborhood started showing up at our door with bottles in brown bags. As for me, after a while it began to feel like I had gone from the frying pan to the fire. Did I wear something that said *mess with me*? Did they smell it on me? There were several family friends who touched on me. They all were gnarly and ugly. Some of them were nasty, creepier than others. I gotta say, I kept their secrets because I didn't know what to do with them. I think today, how would it have been for me if I had had the courage to speak out? Uncle Lee was in jail. Would he have protected me if he wasn't in the pen?

One of those dudes was a guy named Cecil. He was thirty years old. He said he was a friend of Uncle Lee's. Cecil got at me over and over again. He used to come over with a pocket full of money and he slid Ma'Dea twenty, thirty bucks. To twelve-year-old me, that was a lotta money. He told her he been gambling and he didn't want to go home right now and he needed a place to lay down. Ma'Dea thought of him like a son. At fifty-two, she still really missed her boys. She told Cecil, "Gone and lay down on the couch." Or sometimes she would say, "Gone lay down in my bed."

Between my uncle LC and Cecil, I don't know who I hate the most. My uncle was just a vicious disappointment and turncoat to me, a traitor of the love I had for him, for the respect I had for him, for the hero I had made him out to be. He pushed all of that out of me. He broke so much love and affection that I had. He took my hero from me, which was him in a vile way. The violation he did was so deep. But Cecil.

After he molested me, I hated everything that was so supercool about him, the *Super Fly* part of him. I hated to see him; I hated to smell him. I hated his walk; I hated his voice. And yet with all of that, one time when he was molesting and raping me I had an orgasm. I remember hating my body for having that orgasm. I had never had an orgasm and didn't know what it was, but imagine you having your first orgasm with the man who's violating you. A foul son of a bitch. I rejected my body for a long time after that. I had sex, but I didn't allow my body to have orgasms. Sex was just a thing with me. It wasn't satisfying or anything like that. Because of the way I had the first one with him and I didn't like it. He knew he did it to me, too.

It made him feel more okay with himself after he did that. Like he was okay with what he was doing because I was okay with what I was doing. I hated all of that. Years later, when I was in therapy, my therapist told me it was my body reacting and there was nothing I could have done about that. I never knew that. Maybe if I had of gotten therapy earlier, I wouldn't have rejected and hid my body, cause doing that has an effect. It's like a toxin to you. After Cecil, if I wanted to have a good time or have some good sex, I had to be high on drugs. All at the same time, I was having sex with the neighborhood boys and Cecil was raping me. I decided I needed to be around a girl my age, somebody I could be normal with.

So I found a friend. I started hanging with this girl who lived next door, Gloria Brown. Gloria was my friend who I used to tell all my stuff to. She used to hear my grandmother beat me. Everybody knew what my grandmother did to me. I guess that was why nobody ever told her when I was ditching school and doing the things I was doing. Nobody ever told on me because they knew the ass whooping I got if they did. In fact, I used to hang out with older people all the time. One time this lady came upstairs and I felt so bad for her, cause she tried to say something about me skipping school and my grandmother was gonna whip her ass for coming to the door. I never felt so bad about somebody. My grandmomma cussed that woman out. But Gloria wasn't scared of Ma'Dea. At least she didn't act like it.

I hung out with her quite a bit. Gloria was sixteen years old and she had a baby and she was not a good example, but it was what it was, and I thought she was cute and she was. Looking back, I can understand why my grandmother thought it wasn't a great relationship for me. I was twelve years old. Gloria was older and she had been doing older things for a long time. Most of the girls in the neighborhood had. There was a girl named Lee Ann, and I used to say she going Ho-Ann. She had a nasty walk. There was a mixed girl who used to hang out with us, Ezal. She must have been only thirteen, like me, but Ezal was living with grown men. Mayola had a scar on her face, and she was about thirteen or fourteen. She got that scar on her face from sitting in a grown man's car, not messing with him or anything, just sitting in the car drinking and smoking weed and his wife came from around the corner and slashed her face. She hadn't done anything. She had been so pretty.

Me and Gloria used to sit on the porch with the baby, or sit on the fire escape, cause we both were on the third floor and the fire escape was on the front of the building. Men used to climb the fire escape to try to rob our house. Ma'Dea knocked two dudes off the fire escape. *Bam!* That man hit the ground and he got up, hopping and running. Folks knew not to mess with us. Ma'Dea damn near knocked him out. She said, "I got him." She went to the front door, opened it, and called out, "Come on back!" She turned to me and said, "Yeah, I heard him tipping up here. And when he stuck his head through that window, I handed that bat to his ass."

Our bathrooms, me and Gloria's, were tiny and right next to each other. I could sit in my bathroom, on the edge of the windowsill, and she could sit in hers, and our knees almost touched. She had little Terry, and we both be in the window, gossiping. Friday we'd be bored and she was like, "I'm bored." But I'd tell her, "Something gone jump off in a minute." It was Friday, folks gone start to drinking and then they gone fight; somebody gone whip somebody's ass. Domestic violence was entertainment in our community. People were getting they ass whooped. And if bad stuff didn't happen, we used to pull our own shenanigans. I used to make little Terry cuss. I tell him, "Say *motherfucker*."

"Mufa, mutha-fa, motherfu, motherfucker!" And we laughed when he said it. "Motherfucker!" One time Terry called my grandmother a motherfucker. She spanked his little leg. Gloria was so mad. I felt so bad cause I had taught him how to cuss. We were kids, man. We were kids raising kids.

Mayola lived over at Thirteenth Street, over there near Holy City where the Vice Lords were. Gloria started going with this boy who lived on the first floor; Mayola lived on the second floor, and so I tagged along. They had a singing group, and Bernard Page was in the singing group. Well, of course, when you have a girlfriend who has a boyfriend who has friends, that's how you hook up. So me and Bernard start talking. Bernard started coming over my house after my grandmomma went to work, when I was ditching school. We had sex all day in bed or on the mattress on the floor. You know how young people get it on, all stupid like? Just screwing each other, because what else is there to do? Sweating, screwing. He was sixteen; I was thirteen. Getting it on. Kids. I watch kids. That's why I know what they will do. People never believe kids will do the stupid stuff they do. But they will. I've never been shocked when I hear sixth and seventh graders getting blow jobs. When I was that age, I wasn't sucking nobody's peter but we were having sex. Eighth grade and having sex for no reason. I wanted someone to like me. I was looking for validation, and I found it with these little boys. I wanted them to tell me I was pretty. Those hookups were my comfort. They were hugging and kissing on me, and I needed that kind of touch. My grandmother hugged me, but only when she was drunk. You know, back then I really did believe in the white horse and shining knight. I thought maybe if one of those boys thought I was pretty enough, they could take me away from all of the trouble I was in. It would happen as fast as "Hi, how are you? Let's do it."

So I ditched school, and we went to the basement and did it. Or he snuck over Granny's and did it with me over there. I ended up getting pregnant by Bernard Page. But I had a boyfriend named Charles Mitchell who was in the navy, eighteen years old. He wanted to marry me even though I was young. He thought that was his baby, but I knew it wasn't. It was Bernard's baby. Bernard denied it. My grandmother told me, boys will deny anything. I didn't think that was going to happen, cause me and Bernard was cool. He was my boo. I didn't think he would take me to court, but he did. He took me to court for a custody hearing. He was there with all these guys who testified they had had sex with me, too. Out of all of those guys, I had only been with one of them. But I guess they were backing up their friend.

He told me, in front of my grandmother, he didn't think I was having his baby, and she turned to me and said, "See? What I tell ya? But it's okay, because we know whose baby it is, don't we?" I didn't answer, so Ma'Dea answered for me. "That's our baby."

When we got back home, she started taking care of me. I was thirteen years old and seven months pregnant—going on eight—when I told Ma'Dea I was pregnant. The milk was just squirting out my titties; I had toilet paper all in my bra. She was mad for about a week or two. Real mad. She didn't talk to me. And when she did, she said some real horrible things. "I guess you gone be like them other bitches on the street, just have them babies and squirt them out. Like one of them dogs." She said all kinds of crazy stuff. She was just angry. "Take out the garbage, cause that's all you good for now. You done messed your life up." And I think she was so mad, cause before I told her, I would just lie, lie, lie. She would look at me and say, "Brenda Jean, something going on with you? You pregnant?"

"No, ma'am."

Later, she told me, "Your momma was woman enough to sit me down and tell me she was pregnant." She just wanted me to be honest, and I had lied. I didn't know why. I had some issues. My issues were on top of my issues as a kid. I couldn't be honest with her because first of all I was intimidated by my grandmother, and second of all, I just didn't feel like I could talk to her like that. I could tell everybody in the neighborhood about me being pregnant, but I couldn't talk to Ma'Dea about it. She was mad about that, too. "All these people walking around me. They know my baby pregnant." She cussed Gloria out.

But Gloria told her, "You can get mad at me if you want to, Ms. Ruth, but it wasn't my place to tell you. It was Brenda's place to tell you." That was the truth. So Bernard Page was an asshole and is still an asshole; to this day, he hasn't confirmed that he's the daddy. But one day after school, when my daughter Prune was five, he followed her all the way home from school. I was waiting for her at the window. Prune called out, "Momma, this man following us!" And I saw who it was and I went outside to them.

"I saw this girl and asked her if her momma was named Brenda. And she didn't answer. This your baby?"

"Yeah, Bernard."

He looked at her and said, "Right."

+ + +

I was the neighborhood girl who knew what I could tell and what I should keep secret. Just like I waited to tell Ma'Dea the truth about me being pregnant, I knew I had to keep secret that Cecil was messing with me. He was coming by our place, like a dog with a bone. The minute Ma'Dea stepped out the room to go get a drink, he would antagonize me. When I was pregnant, he would say, "That's my baby, ain't it? I know that's my baby." I remember him once grabbing me by my hair when I was real pregnant, like eight months, and raping me. The whole time I was trying to have little boyfriends, he did that to me. I had too much stuff on me.

I was pregnant, a kid, I was getting raped all the time. Ma'Dea ain't making it easy because she's so disappointed in me because I'm about to have a baby. The hole I was in just kept getting deeper. Everywhere I turned I felt like I was less than a piece of shit. I was less than a piece of shit because Cecil was coming at me and raping me; I was less than a piece of shit because I was having babies and breaking Ma'Dea's heart. I was less than a piece of shit no matter what I did. The only peace of mind I had was when I hung out with my girlfriend Gloria. She used to really talk to me. "You gone make it. You'll get through."

Cecil's drug addiction had progressed, and I was working. Ma'Dea wasn't. She was watching Prune while I went to work and tried to go to school. Ma'Dea was getting an aid check. Cecil came in one Saturday, and he wanted fifty dollars. He told Ma'Dea if she wrote him a check, he could get her a TV. And Ma'Dea said, "Alright, Brenda, go with him." So we got in a cab, and I somehow knew the whole time what was going to happen. Some shady things were going to pop, and the only question was, what was I going to do when they did?

"I'll be right back. Okay?" Cecil got out of the car.

I waited and waited. And waited. But he never came out. When I went to the door to ask where Cecil was with the TV, them people said, "Cecil went out the back door, baby." But I never regretted losing that money, because when he took it, he could never come to our house again. I was so happy.

I went back home to Ma'Dea and told her, "He went out the back door."

"I'll kill that man if I ever see him again." She meant it. That's the kind of person she was.

She didn't talk nonsense, she handled nonsense. Ma'Dea's sister, my aunt Ola, was like that, too. Ola had a husband named Marvin, and Marvin was molesting one of my little cousins. Jackie turned not right. When she was about five or six, she sat and rocked in place and didn't nobody know why. She didn't play around with us; she would sit and stare. You'd talk to her and she just look past you.

She was like a deer. "Jackie. Jackie! Don't you hear me talking to you?" And Jackie had a fever or something and went to the hospital, and them people told Aunt Ola, "She tore up down there." He had done something to her. She was traumatized. So we all went back home, and Marvin was in the big chair looking at the TV. Aunt Ola went in her house to the dining-room table, and there were some scissors right there on the table. She picked the scissors up and walked over to Marvin and stabbed them down his neck and then called the police. "Come get this man out my house." Aunt Ola lost her mind for a few weeks. But she got him.

That's how we dealt with the trouble back then. So I have no doubt that my grandmother would have killed somebody if she knew about me. And then she would have gone to jail forever. I know my grandmother wouldn't have been one to say, "Oh, that didn't happen." She would have cold killed somebody.

So Cecil was out of the picture. And pretty much for me, I was controlling things. I'd had a baby. I was hanging with older girls, older guys. Sometimes adults. A lotta times adults. My grandmother was questioning everything and everybody who's coming through the house, cause she knew I was laying down with grown-ass men. She ran a couple out the door, when she told them how old I was, but most of them didn't care. They just wanted to be with me cause I was so fresh. So that's kinda what I was doing. I was messing with a lotta *Super Fly*–type brothers who had nice cars, or guys who had good jobs, like bus drivers and men who worked at Chrysler or had them good-ass Ford jobs. Steel mill brothers. They liked my ass. I was young—I was thirteen, fourteen—and I was gorgeous. It's not until you are old that you realize how pretty you were. You remember being beautiful when your body starts falling apart. I was very pretty. I couldn't walk down the street and some dude damn near ran into something. That was the kind of body I was handling. Like, if it were now, I could give them Kardashian girls a run for their money.

There used to be this place called the Garfield Organization on the West Side of Chicago, led by a man named Doug Andrews. He was a community activist who was in politics. I met Doug on Madison Street at Guy's shoe store. A lot of brothers hung out there— newspaper guys and dudes like that. Guy's was like the unofficial meeting place for a bunch of political Black guys and businessmen. They used to come through the back, and the man who ran the shoe store—whose name was really Guy—would let them sit down and have a beer. They would talk about the community and all the issues that were going on. I went in there one day, and I was introduced to Doug Andrews. He was actually doing good work in the community. He saw me. I was young and built like a brick house. I had potential. But what kind of potential? I didn't know. But Doug knew what kind of potential he wanted me to have.

This guy looked at me and was thinking, *Shit, this girl can make me some money*. Doug was saying to me that I didn't need to hang out with these greasy men who were taking my money. If I was smart, I could hang out with him and I'd be able to keep my coins. It's not like I charged anybody, it was more of a situation where I let the guys I was with know I needed a little money to get by. I would get a look on my face and then they would ask what was wrong. "Oh, I don't know how I'm gone make rent this month." Stuff like that. And then they slipped me money and told me not to worry. I didn't know what they were going to give me until it was time for me to go. There was some times when I'd spend a whole day with a guy and walk away with nothing, and I thought, man, I should have asked for money upfront or I should have been more clear. But I guess I wasn't that bold yet. Trying to pick the guy who was going to be the most generous was all a part of the game.

Doug didn't want my money, but he had dudes who wanted to be entertained. He told me, "We like you, Brenda. You don't need no pimp. You can just hang out with me." You know, men who did things with girls or young men were not considered bad guys. They were just thought of as men who liked a taste of the outlaw. So I started going to the Garfield Organization because it made me feel important. I would ask for Doug, and he would tell me to come on back to the office. The funny thing about Doug was he never tried to get in my pants. But he had ideas of who I could get with. A couple of weeks after I met him, I was working down the street from Guy's shoe store, at this furniture shop. Guy came into the furniture shop and said, "Brenda, Brenda! Doug and Stu Gilliam are at my shop and they asking for you." They were over there because they were promoting Burger King. They were going to build more Burger Kings in the community so that Black people could have jobs.

I ran over there. "Hi!"

Doug said, "Yo. That's my girl over here. That's Brenda. We call her Turtledove."

And Stu Gilliam saw me and said, "Hey. Well, alright now." He grabbed my hand and put me in the limousine. I get in the limo with Stu Gilliam and Hilly Hicks and Doug and some other guy. We went riding to a few more places. We ended up at the McCormick Place, and we went upstairs and I sat there while they did their radio show. And that was just the beginning. Doug would call for me when celebrities came to the city, and he made sure I was with them.

So I was sleeping with the neighborhood boys and the neighborhood men. I was getting down with the celebrities. It wasn't like I was a prostitute; I was more like the go girl. And wouldn't you know it? I got pregnant right behind Prune with Peaches. The daddy was this dude who worked for Pepsi-Cola. One of these good-job brothers named Spoon. He was in his thirties—really sharp dresser. Nice car, smooth talker. He was Gloria's man's friend. Gloria's man was named Mac, and Mac and Spoon were friends. Looking back, I realize Gloria brought a lotta nonsense in my life. But I liked him. It wasn't like we was *close* close, but I liked Spoon. He was just a cool-ass dude. I liked him, but I didn't think I was gone get pregnant by Spoon's ass, though. I had just gotten my six-week checkup. I hadn't gotten my birth control together or nothing. And he was loving it, cause I'm a young-ass girl and cute as hell, and he was infatuated with all this. I never told Spoon Peaches was his baby, I guess because of what Bernard did to me. But as soon as Peaches came out, I knew whose she was. Spoon's.

Everything about her, he was, too. He walked like a duck, with his feet sticking out. So does she. On her face is some of his features mixed with mine. Spoon knew when I got pregnant, but he didn't think it was his because I was with a lotta men then. Nobody was confused about what I was doing. I wasn't either. That's why my grandmother said to me, "You come in the house with all kinds of men. Old, young, light brown, black, green. Cadillacs, fast cars, motorcycles. Goddamnit, you ought to let some of these men give you some money. You should never come in the house without Pampers and a gallon of milk. And get me a pack of cigarettes, goddamnit. All these guys pull to the curb and blow for you." So what was she telling me? Maybe she was trying to say, stop laying up under these men and get a good job. Straighten up. Find a decent man and settle down. But I took it literally. I started asking dudes for favors. Now when I climbed those third-floor stairs, I had bags in my hands. A few dollars in my pocket. I hadn't really learned how to ask for money yet. But that was coming.

Oh, if someone could have directed me the right way. I spent a lotta time with nothing men. If I could have had the right director, manager—somebody putting some real weight on me—I could have been so much more. But my grandmother could have never been it, because she only saw life as one way. She never saw me as someone who could get rich. She had only struggled, so she only saw life as this struggle. And all those struggles caught up to us.

+ + +

Good Friday, 1973. I was fourteen, and I was going to change for good. Prune, whose real name is Ernestine, was a year old. Peaches, who I named Ruth after my grandmother, had been born four weeks before. I was going out with older men, doing a hustle here and there. Just being real cute and getting a couple of things. That year it changed. I went down to the street to turn my official first trick. That day. That day we had no food and the Aid to Dependent Children check didn't come in the mail. We used to get a check, and we got a little food-stamp book to go and buy groceries. Soon it was going to be Easter Sunday. We didn't have nothing to eat, and usually when we were like that, we called Aunt Josie to give a few dollars to hold us over, but you know we had two kids in the house and we got Ma'Dea and we got me, so how much could she stretch us? Aunt Josie could throw us a bone every now and again, but she couldn't float us all the way. Ma'Dea was talking a lotta shit about me and how I had brought us to a point to where we couldn't make it. She told me, "I ain't never had to depend on handouts. I ain't the one who need the welfare, you the one who need the welfare." But she *was* the one who needed welfare. But I didn't need the welfare because I got a friendly coochie. I was fourteen and jumping from this bed to that one, but Ma'Dea was the grown-up; she's really looking at cupboards that were bare. I didn't want my babies' Easter to be not right. I wanted Peaches to have the prettiest dress, and Prune to have the prettiest dress, the biggest bunny rabbit. They both were so beautiful; I wanted them to have little slippers to run around in. I thought to myself, *You got to shit or get off the stool.* The pressure was on. After Ma'Dea told me all about how the babies got to eat and we didn't even have a cup of rice in the cabinet, I went and asked a girl in the neighborhood who I knew was a prostitute how to set up my situation. At first, she told me she would show me, but I would have to see her man. But I didn't want to choose her man. Her man's brother and I used to go together. I didn't want to get that messy. She understood, and she told me where to go. She didn't tell what to charge, but I had read enough books and magazines. Donald Goines. Iceberg Slim. *Hustler*. Xaviera Hollander, the lady who wrote *The Happy Hooker*, she was giving lessons on how to be a grand ho. After reading her, I thought all hos got a hundred dollars. That's the kind of money I was looking for. So I took the train and transferred over there at Grand, Clark and Division, and started my little prostitution thing right there.

It was night. I hadn't learned yet when to come down and when not to. I was playing a dangerous game because I was new at it. And because I was fresh, nobody had caught me. If I had been a regular girl, who knows? There was a lot of police presence and there were a lotta guys out there. I found out the first night, getting that hundred dollars was not what happens in real life. The first car I got in and I asked for a hundred dollars, he said, "Honey, I'm not trying to buy you; I'm just renting you for a minute."

I looked at him like he had lost his mind. "Well, how much you gone give me?"

"I'll give you forty dollars for a BJ." I had no idea what a BJ—a blow job—was. I was still a baby in some ways. And even though I had read about a woman sucking on a man's penis, that hadn't come up a lot with me in my community. We didn't really do all that in the hood. I had had my cootie eaten two or three times, and it wasn't a good experience. It was like they were trying to chew my clitoris off. You need to know all of this to understand what I did next. I started to blow on his penis. And he said, "What the fuck are you doing?" I looked up at him. "Just suck my fucking dick, girl."

"Oh." And I did it. But I wasn't prepared. Nobody had told me about a condom, or what to do toward the end. So just as he was about to explode, I pulled my head up. And it went everywhere.

"Are you that new?"

"Yeah." And I started crying.

"Stop crying, stop crying." He reached into the back seat and got a towel and wiped himself. "Stop crying. How old are you?" I told him and he said, "Ah! I'll show you how to do this shit." Funny how he didn't tell me to go home. He liked the fact that I was fourteen years old and gave me another twenty. I learned then that guys picked me up because I was fresh. They were giving me money hand over fist. They liked the fact that I was new out there. I got out the car, and I felt a little sick to my stomach. I stood there with the taste of him in my mouth and tried to spit it out the best I could. It was too late for me to turn around. I wanted to, but I didn't know how to. I only had sixty dollars and that wasn't enough. So I took a deep breath and started looking around for the next car.

I got into the car with the next guy. He was Italian, and he did give me a hundred dollars when I asked. I was still stuck into the hundred-dollar world. And the only reason I got the hundred dollars was because I told him I was fourteen years old before we got started. I wasn't the only girl my age out there either. I knew this pimp whose whole stable was minors. I mean, seventeen was old for him. His name was Larrod. Forty years old and a short little dude. He used to wear the pimp suits. Everybody used to talk about him. Thirteen, fourteen, fifteen was the average age for his girls. He called them his hos and bitches. Somebody killed him and all his girls. Nobody was left in the house alive except a three-year-old baby. Some cold-blooded shit—they killed everybody. Shot them all in the head.

In the beginning, I stayed away from situations like that. I just went out there to prostitute. And the tricks taught me how they wanted to have sex with me. All I had to worry about was my wardrobe. I bought this new lime-green skirt and top, which had puffy sleeves. It was from this store called Three Sisters, and you could get an outfit for $3.99, and I wore my hair in afro puffs, but I got a wig.

The kind we used to call a "gypsy wig"—it was a long, wild, curly wig that hung in three layers—cost seven bucks, and I put that on. And these horrible shoes, these cheap shoes. I still remember those shoes. They looked like patent leather, but they were like rubber or vinyl or something like that, and they made your feet sweat and stink. Even the heel was made of it; they didn't even have the respect to put a real heel on the shoe. When you walked, they scrunched. But I was out there, ready to take that direction. I wonder sometimes if my mother was looking down on me saying, "Baby, my baby." I wonder if she was watching me and cringing. I had made like four or five tricks that night, and I made almost four hundred dollars. I cried through the first two. I had been with other guys and had slept with them, but it was more like a date before. You know, old men sniffing up my ass and liking me. But this was like impersonal, grimy in the car. I didn't know how to talk them into going to a hotel. I didn't think about all that. I made that money and went home, gave it to Ma'Dea, and she never asked me where it came from. One time I gave her five hundred dollars. All hundred-dollar bills. She didn't ask one question.

Chapter 5

When the Gorilla Pimps Want You

I went out there on the weekends. I didn't go out during the week, because I would go up to Madison Street and work in the furniture store. I was a part-time prostitute. I took some money to Sears, and I got the cutest dresses for Prune and Peaches. I got Peaches a bunny, and I put it in her crib. Oh, she was so beautiful, and her diaper always sagged on her little poor self. She was a little bitty thing, and the little diaper used to just slide on down and hang on by her hips.

I had been out there for a month. Then I ran into the pimps. Big gorilla pimps. I thought I knew the streets. I thought I knew how to be hard. But when the gorilla pimps wanted me, I got caught up. They told me I needed to have representation. "Your man need to be out here." See, if you can produce a man, they weren't gone go up against some brother and just do you like that. Dealing with the outlaws, that's what they called it. You couldn't be no woman out there working without a man representing you. When you on the streets back then, and your man was asked to appear, your man had to take a rag and peer on they ass. "That's mine, man."

"Oh, I just wanted to know. You know how this game is."

Brothers wanted to know who they need to bow down to, who they need to back off from. That's why assholes could step to you with that protection nonsense, cause there were fools out there who thought you were an outlaw, and then you would be under pimp arrest. Pimp arrest. I didn't know anything about working massage parlors or anything like that. I knew just what I knew: girls worked that area, I saw it, and if them hos could get some money, I could get some money. I figured out how to be a prostitute from seeing what was going on outside and from blaxpoitation movies. That's no bullshit. I was really influenced by *Super Fly* and *The Mack* and *Get Christie Love!* and *Cleopatra Jones*. Pimp pictures turned on all that. *Willie Dynamite*. All that was impressive to me. Sick clothes, sick life. Hos getting money, being a bottom bitch.

The first time I ever heard of a bottom bitch was in the movie *Truck Turner*. Turner was played by Isaac Hayes. It was about this pimp getting murdered. His bottom bitch was played by the woman who was on *Star Trek*, Nichelle Nichols—Uhura. And what I learned from that movie was that the bottom bitch actually ran shit. Because when the pimp got murdered, all the hos turned to Dorinda, and she told them, y'all gone do this, y'all gone do that. And I liked a statement that she said in the movie: "I haven't had to sell my pussy since I was fifteen and found out I could sell other bitches' instead." That laid me back. I thought that was so profound. That was gangster. So I wanted to be the bottom bitch; the one who didn't have to do the work. The one who just did the handling. She's in control. And the only person she takes orders from is the pimp. I didn't know about the loneliness. I didn't know about the responsibilities that you take on as the bottom bitch. Not only do you take on the control of the stable; anything that goes wrong, you're the one who goes down for it. You are responsible for everything, but you don't get a dime of his money. You are doing it all for him. And before you know it, you become a little him. I thought like him; I acted like him. You did things that he would do when he wasn't around. And it becomes hard, because some of those things you don't want to do. A bottom bitch was the best that I could see and reach for at that time. I didn't know anything else to reach for. I didn't realize that I was reaching for the lowest part of my life.

What came with being a bottom bitch was losing your identity, becoming an awful person for the love of money. Even when I finally made it as a bottom bitch, it never made me happy. Because I knew when I left, everything he had would fall apart, and that's a lot to put on somebody. That's a lot of pressure. Pimps would come looking for blood if you left. You weren't a bitch who could just run off. Leaving interrupted his lifestyle. Not only would your pimp be looking for you, other brothers would be looking for you, too. You worth fifty, a hundred dollars if some guy found you and brought you back. I know all this now, but back then, when I first got started, the movies made it all look really glamorous. It looked powerful. And when you are in pain, you are looking for some power and control. How can I be on top? How can I be the boss? So yeah. I watched the movies. I read *Hustler* magazine and took notes. *The Happy Hooker*, she was talking about making hundreds and hundreds of dollars and basically giving the ABCs of hoing. The rest of my learning was self-taught, and it was a hard education.

But before I got to all that, the gorilla pimps got me first. A gorilla is a pimp who uses force and abuse to control his women. These aren't men who are smooth and play the boyfriend part in the relationship. It's all about fear. Gorilla pimps are brutal. And they can get creative with their violence. These pimps, they weren't handsome; they didn't have no swag. They were just some country-ass punks, and the only way they got hos to choose them was to snatch them, cause they had nothing else for a girl. They had to kidnap.

I never knew what kind of relationship those two assholes had between them, but it wasn't healthy. One of them was really dark, and he had this half-ass perm, a nappy perm. He was always putting rollers in it, and it never quite looked right, cause he had that real fly-up-and-away hair. He had a crooked tooth in the front of his mouth, and his hands were real big. When he hit you, it was like *ah!*, it just took over the whole head. The other asshole had a little bit of a gut. Brown skin and a ponytail. They had a Cadillac. Dark blue, and they kept it up really nice.

I had only been out there for three good weekends when they grabbed me. I was standing in the middle of Clark Street. I had just gotten out a trick's car in the middle of the block when they rolled up on me. Had I been on the corner I would have been around more people and they wouldn't have got me. But in the middle of the block, it's dark with no streetlights. Two o'clock in the morning and nobody was around. And when I got out the car with the trick, I'm walking fast to get to the corner of Clark and Division. But one of the gorilla pimps is walking super quick behind me; the other one is rolling down the street on the side of me. I see the play, but I can't get away. And then the pimp behind me jumped and bust me in the head with the pistol. I was shocked because I didn't know pimps wowed out like that. My uncle was a pimp. He never pulled shit like that. I didn't know yet that stuff like that happened out in the street.

They grabbed me and shoved me in the trunk. *In that trunk.* I don't know where to put that. To this day, I don't know where to put that experience. I was screaming and bleeding from my head where the dude had hit me with his gun. There was a blanket in there and a metal can, a tire jack handle. It was a huge trunk, and I remember getting jostled. A roll of tape bumped into my thigh. The only thing I knew was when we were moving forward and when we took a turn. God, I tossed around and around. I was paralyzed and scared. It was like being in a grave. I peed all over myself in that trunk.

They took me to a cornfield and did Russian roulette to me: they took a pistol out and put it to my head. It was not the last time they did that. They used to do that for entertainment. Me and the two gorilla pimps were all in one hotel room. I could tell they had been snatching up girls for a while, going back and forth with some girls. Playing tennis back and forth with a bitch. It was just me at first, but then they got another girl. It was just two girls at a time because a whole lotta girls was too many to watch. I don't care what you say, a gorilla pimp ain't gone keep a ho long. Too much food involved. Too much fear and intimidation and physical brutality to keep up.

They would send me out to get tricks from the trucking stations. The only time the gorilla pimps came off the major highway was at the truck stops. They would go with me. They would pull into the truck stops and park in a particular area. At that time, police weren't messing with pimps doing business. They put me out the car and told me, "You work this side and this side only. You just work up and down this lane. When you get to the end, work yourself back down the other side." They watched me closely. Some of the truck drivers knew the pimps I was with. I found that out because one time a truck driver walked up to the pimp to complain. I had cried the whole time I was with him because I had gotten beaten up before they put me out there. I was still upset.

The truck driver walked up to the car and told them, "I want my motherfucking money back. That bitch cried the whole time."

"Okay, partner. You want her to do it again? Cause there ain't no refunds, but she'll take care of you." But the gorilla pimp was looking at me like, you know I'm going to hurt you when we get back to the motel. So when I got back to the room, they beat the snot out of me. To me, that validated every threat he had ever given me. They had told me, "I know everything you do. I got people every-where." I felt like even the customers were in on my kidnapping. I didn't know what was going on. Was the truck driver their friend? That just happened one time, but that was enough to keep me scared about running off. They found shit for me to get into. Sometimes they dropped me off on a street corner to work, but I didn't like it. The truck drivers knew what the girls were doing. They were dating us really fast. You could get your money quick. But standing on the corner? It was dark and scary and you could be out there for hours and not make enough money. So the truck stops was where those gorilla pimps really got their money's worth out of me.

We stayed on a major road; I knew that much. Sometimes we would find a spot and we stayed because I made money there. I mean, these guys weren't the brightest, but they knew where the money was. We worked between five or six different truck stops. When I came back to the motel from hoing, they felt like they needed to terrorize me some more. They were big on anal rape. They were big on doing terrorizing games. Make you intimidated and keep your thoughts off of planning what to do. Keep you locked up, tossed up in fear. In the beginning, I was trying to figure a way out. But those were the things that got me beat up. Bad. Every time I tried to escape, I got caught and punished. I kept thinking, *If I could be out of this room, if I could get out of this cornfield, I could get around people who would save me.* Every time I tried something—not showing up at the Cadillac at the end of working the truck stop, asking somebody for help—it just all went bad for me. No one was willing to step into a situation that looked like it was just between me and the gorilla pimps. I thought about my kids, but I also thought that somebody was looking for me. Ma'Dea would find me. And I thought if I could just stay strong, I would be found. I didn't know that people don't look for little Black girls. They didn't then, and they don't now. So many missing Black girls. Nobody looked for us. I didn't know that back then. All I knew was being lost was a lot for a fourteen-year-old girl to hold on to. All that pressure gone bust a cap. I'm talking about me and all the girls they did this to. My pressure valve was going to burst. So many petty-ass mind games to throw me off and keep me unbalanced.

I made all their money, and I'd come home and they'd say, "You can't eat."

"Why can't I eat?"

"Cause I said so, bitch. And who am I? Who am I?"

"God. You run this show."

"Bitch, gone somewhere with your simple ass. Go sit down. You don't know what you need."

So not only are you sitting up there confused, tired, you got to go to bed hungry. I hadn't been hungry in a long time, but I cry if I get that way. I mean really hungry and there's no food. I get desperate. I was with them for five, six months. There had been opportunities for me to get away, but I didn't see them. Or maybe I was too afraid to take them. I needed someone to rescue me. To say, I got you. I needed somebody like that because I didn't have the courage.

As part of my seasoning, they had me in Indiana. For me, it might as well have been in New Zealand. They had me at unfamiliar truck stops and little sleazy hotels. I'm talking Motel 6 would have been an upgrade. Side-road motels with rusty-ass showers. They locked me in the closets, and mold was growing out the carpets, to let me know there were consequences to my behavior when I didn't follow their commands. "If I ask you something, I need a response right away, bitch."

"Well, I thought . . ."

"Bitch, why you thinking again? You don't think. *I* think. You do what I tell you to do. What was you doing, thinking?" How brutal is that? To take a person's will to have a thought in their brain. You begin to question even thinking about something. Someone has cut that down to: You don't have the ability to think. I'm going to do the thinking for you—"that's why I'm here, bitch." "If you stop thinking and do what I tell you to do, this would be beautiful." So you begin to believe things would be better for you if you just go along and do what you supposed to do, and some kind of way you might be happier or at least you won't get consequences and that will make you happy. You do things to make them happy. After the rape became no more rape to me, it was just part of the formula, they actually stopped raping me. In the beginning, they raped me all the time. Together. Separately. The crying, the begging, it was a part of how they got off. Knowing that they were brutalizing me and messing me up; I was in pain, hurting me was okay. But it became so normal. And I'll tell you something about myself: I can adapt to a bad situation fast. It was one of my survival instincts. You learn on the streets: you either get it or you get got. I would get to the motel with my money, or whatever they were okay with, because I couldn't come back to the hotel until they were okay with it, but there was a possibility that I was still going to get jacked up.

I didn't know what was going to happen whenever I got to the motel room. Where they going to let me go to sleep? Was I going to get a hamburger or what? If I got a hamburger and was able to go to sleep, it was a good night. And that's only because they had some other shenanigans going on. Other times, I could expect the brutalization and it didn't even bother me. I was being raped and not really screaming, not begging and stuff no more. It became a part of the program. It just became, "What you gone do now? How you gone be tonight? Let's do this so I can go to sleep." That's why they went and got another girl. I was no fun anymore. I was doing what they wanted me to do because I was tired of getting beat, I was tired of being brutalized. And they couldn't find new ways to bruise me up or for me to be sore for three or four days. They wanted me to go get them some money, alright, but it's hard for me to get it because they brutalized me so bad. I was sore, I was hurting. I needed medical attention, but I wasn't getting it and I still had to get their money. What they were doing was tearing me down. And I detached myself to deal with it, cause if I detach myself, you can't touch me. A part of me that got into the game could do that. So it was no fun anymore for them.

The other girl was about my age. I think her name was Sharon, but nobody called her that, they called her "bitch" and they gave her the street name Sparkle. My street name was Liza. I got it from a soap opera: *All My Children*. Liza was a trip, so I was going to be a trip. I loved Liza, and I adapted to that name. You become those names in your own mind because you saw those people and you wanted it to be you. I just connected to being people I liked. It helped me disconnect. It wasn't Brenda doing those things, it was Liza. Brenda didn't have to take the abuse, Liza did. Things that were going on, they were happening to the alter ego I had adapted. Brenda couldn't have went through all that.

By the time Breezy came, Breezy was a mess. Breezy was created by all the other names, and that ho was something else. She was her own reality show. I was on *That's Entertainment!* when I was Breezy. I used to have costumes when I was that ho because it had become a game. And I had to be the star of the game. I was the star of whatever was going on. That's why sometimes people wanted to hurt me. I did this too well. I was always hearing, "That bitch think she something."

I don't know what they think they thought I was, but I *was* something. I was surviving. I became a chameleon to deal with the situation. I became so desensitized to rape, that I had a rapist turn around and pay me. You think I'm playing? I had a rapist turn around and leave me alone, cause there was no sense in raping me given the way I was acting. It wasn't even rape. I didn't give in to what their plan was; I made a new plan while they plan was on top of me. I wowed out with the dude who came to harm me and flipped the script, and now I'm hanging out for two, three days with this monster. But by then I was controlling this game. I was actually enjoying this terror and crazy. It started off dark; it started off with him having something on his mind and I had to change his mind. I remember one time, I told this rapist, "Why are you raping me? This dick is so good. I'm gonna come." I was just playing him. And, well, he just got up. He was trying to have something from me, and I had to get it off his mind. I sat up and he looked at me and I said, "You want to do this again?"

He backed away, snatching at his clothes. "I'm good. We're good."

"Sure you don't want to go again?"

"Naw, I gotta go." He was trying to get away from me now, because damn it! I can't just let you keep on doing this to me. I gotta flip it; I gotta do something with it. I gotta take control. No matter what happened to me on those streets, I had one big thought: *I'll fix your ass.* At the same time, I was fixing me, because if I didn't, the horrible in me might get out. There has to be a good ending for me, I thought to myself.

+ + +

But before I learned to turn into something horrible to get me out of trouble, I had to live a horror. This was the course of business: the power, the control, the brutality. The unlawful holding of a human being, the slavery piece, the brutalizing piece, all of that happened often.

In Indiana, I had learned folks in general don't want to help. People have an ugly part in them. They just don't want to be involved. People can literally watch someone get stomped to death because they don't want to be bothered with it. Most folks looking, hoping somebody else will call the police for help. But by then I was thoroughly beat. I watched people looking at me get a beatdown. I wondered what they thought I was saying to myself. *Well, let me just pick up my ear that just fell off and go home. Let me pick my body off the ground and go home.* That was what they all thought?

But as soon as I learned that lesson, God was ready to teach me another one. Out there, in places where you were lost, there was a special kind of somebody, a special kind of people who would step outside their comfort zone to rescue or help somebody. I know that from traveling the world and being in situations where if it hadn't been that kind of somebody out there, I wouldn't have made it. The majority of people didn't give a rat's ass about me. They saw me sitting up in a diner or a truck stop with these two horrible-looking assholes, tears running down my ears, looking very uncomfortable and frightened.

The waitress looked in my face and said, "You okay today?"

"Yeah, she okay." Punk-ass ponytail leaned in too close to me and put his hand around my waist.

"Alright, then."

Nobody got outside themselves and said, "I'm gonna call the

cops." That was what I thought somebody would do. I was too scared to move. I was gone to spend the rest of my life in Indiana in cornfields and truck stations.

But then this big fat hillbilly redneck turned up to be my special kind of white man.

I had hopped into his cab, and we started to do our business. I don't know. Maybe I had had too many bad days or maybe I was extra sore. Whatever was going on with me just came out. I started crying and I couldn't quit. I told him everything: how these gorilla pimps had kidnapped me and had been raping me, putting a gun to my head for fun. I didn't even know where I was. I had two little baby girls at home. The last time I saw my youngest, she was just one month old. I had people looking for me in Chicago. My grand-momma had probably lost her mind with worry. He said, "It's a god-damned shame. We're gonna get you outta here." And he pulled out the biggest pistol I ever seen. "I'm gonna shoot anybody that come round here." He still had his entire racist mentality, along with his big-ass heart. But the goodness in him—*this shouldn't have to happen to nobody*—overstepped his beliefs about Black people. And God or my angels were working on his ass, so he could work on my behalf.

So that big fat white guy drove me all the way back to Chicago. In an hour or something I was right in front of my grandmomma's house. Maybe I was in between Indianapolis and South Bend all that time. I hated leaving that second girl. She and I were trying to flee together, but she wasn't around, and I couldn't just turn down that white boy and wait for her. Me and that girl hadn't made a plan yet, but we had said together we were going to make a run for it, if the space opened. We were both fourteen and we looked like sisters. And she didn't get beat as much I did because I was there to show her the ropes. Before she stepped out and did something wrong, I would warn her, "Don't do that. You'll get a beatdown." But now I was in this white guy truck and she was nowhere around. I couldn't ask him to stop and look for her. When was I going to have another opportunity like that? We listened to country music all the way there. He dropped me off right at my front door.

+ + +

I got home and Ma'Dea said she wasn't looking for me. She told me that. She was that type of person to say something like that, but I couldn't hear that right then. She said it with conviction and I couldn't take it. I was coming off some serious shit. I was looking for something that Ma'Dea didn't have—nurturing. I had been kidnapped for five months and was planning to come home and get some nurturing, gone upstairs, cry, and sit with a blanket and tell her what had happened with the men. How I survived and got out of it. I thought she would be proud of me because I got out of it. *I was tough and I didn't lay down, Ma'Dea.* I just wanted to eat and lay down and hold my babies, but that didn't happen.

"Yeah, I wasn't gone look for that bitch. Motherfucker just show up, like that." I understand what she was saying now. How she probably said those things to protect herself. It was just the kind of hurt shit that I carried for many years without an understanding. What I say about her even now is through a lot of growth and development and wisdom and being on the outside looking in on how it happens. I realize that somebody who loved you that deep didn't really mean the things they said. They didn't know how to deal with you; they didn't know what to say to you. They didn't know how to talk about your hurt.

When I say now I know where my grandmomma was coming from, I mean it. But back then, all I was thinking was *Damn. She couldn't mean what she just said.* It broke me, broke my heart. I took two steps at a time up to the third floor where our apartment was. I was so excited about getting up those stairs and getting home. I could hear voices coming from our place. Ma'Dea had a loud voice, you could always hear her. She sounded so good. I knocked. And when she opened the door, we just looked at each other. I looked beyond her shoulder and could see my kids playing on the floor. I took a step inside, but Ma'Dea's voice stopped me cold. "Well. Well. Look who finally showed up. Ain't this a motherfucker." She said such mean things. "Oh, I guess you gone just come home. Take your ass back out there for all I care." Tears started rolling down my face. She turned away from me and walked further inside. I followed. I could tell she had been drinking. She lit a cigarette and just looked at me. I wanted to say, "Ma'Dea, let me tell you . . ." but before I could open my mouth, she started. "Your motherfucking ass left me with these kids. Your ass been laying up with some nigga; you ain't shit." Nothing came out of my mouth. "I told you I wasn't going to chase after you in these streets. I got these kids and that's why I never looked for your ass." That hit me so hard that she cut me off from explanation. It was like she threw a brick at me. I just stood there and looked at her. As she told me off, called me names, telling me I didn't care about my children. I didn't deserve the kids. And those were valid things to be said, but first she should have let me tell her what had happened. But the alcohol didn't let her. She just went on and on. Into the middle of the night. She was drinking all the while. The kids were grabbing at me and trying to hug me, and then Ma'Dea would yell out, "Don't be grabbing at her; she ain't shit." The verbal whooping went on for a while. Ma'Dea wasn't the kind of person you could talk back to. If you did, she would pick up a piece of furniture and take a swing at you. So I just sat there and let her have her say. I had just gotten out of a nightmare, and it felt like I had landed in another one. I had just left this place where if I said anything, I got beaten up by two gorilla pimps or chained to the radiator. My mind was still in that place; I hadn't moved past the motels and the truck stops. I had learned the best way was to shut up and shut down. I didn't have the courage to stand up to Ma'Dea and speak my piece. You know, looking back, I was as much of a kid as Peaches and Prune were. I sat there on that couch and took my lick because that's what a child is supposed to do. I think if I would have voiced myself more, things would have been different. But back then I lost my voice a lot of times. I just couldn't speak up for myself. Maybe if I had, Ma'Dea and I could have had a real conversation. She could have heard where I was coming from, and I could have heard the same. Instead, it took a lifetime for me to really hear where my grandmother was that day. She was hurting because my kids were hurting. And who was there when my kids were hurting? She was. She was hitting back at me on their behalf even though she didn't know that's what she was doing. Peaches was just sitting up. And Prune was walking. Ma'Dea told me Prune hadn't really ate or slept the last five months, cause her momma wasn't there. Ma'Dea was angry. These babies were suffering. And from where Ma'Dea stood, it looked like for no reason, I got lost with some man. She didn't know I had been kidnapped; she just knew I was out with some dudes.

Still. I couldn't take those kinds of licks. Not when I had gone through what I just went through. Ma'Dea's abuse was almost as bad as the physical abuse I just escaped from. I didn't want to leave the girls, but the pain Ma'Dea kept heaping was breaking something inside me. I couldn't function. I wasn't sure I would be able to put myself back together later on. One week later, I left. I didn't pack anything. I just walked out the door.

Part III

Fake love can never own you

Chapter 6

The Beginning of the Lie

It used to be, pimps didn't let they hos come out looking any kind of way: unkempt looking. Clothes on for two days. If they got a fresh ho, they'd take her home, bathe her. Cause if she ain't looking like money, how she gone make money? Sometimes back in the day, girls would choose a man, get with a pimp, cause of the way he keep his hos. New girls like me would be out there, looking around at the hos on the stroll, thinking, *Oh, that brother dress a bitch. Oh, I like that. Let me find out who you with. I'm gone get with your man.* Simple as that. Nobody do that anymore. The whole concept about how we do it is different.

Today, most girls out here making a lotta money work at the escort service. There's more money for girls online. The internet has become huge in the game. Girls are using the chat lines and websites. All you need is a phone nowadays. Instagram and all that stuff have a part in human trafficking now. But what folks don't realize is that all this social media has increased the murders of and violence against women. Now girls are picking guys from social media, from a profile or from a couple of conversations on a chat line. You don't know who you are dealing with. And people have more access to you. These men have more access to you, before you get to them. Before, you had to create a book; you had to have phone numbers; you had to have word-of-mouth advertisement. But today, even pimps have found their way to social media. Hashtag #DoYouNeedAHo. And girls get into this lifestyle because they think it's less static and stress than the streets. They think to themselves, *It's just sex.* They think sex is sex, it only last for so long. When you get involved with something like this, you rationalize it: fifteen minutes and they're done. It's quick and its more money than I can make on a job.

They don't think they could be hooking up with a murderer. He could have mental health issues. He could want to disfigure you. Those are the kinds of things girls don't think about, up front. Most of these girls think, *That won't happen to me.* But this kind of stuff happens to regular women; so chances are even higher that this is going to happen to a prostitute. Right now, human trafficking and prostitution in our country is bringing in as much money as drugs. But careful—don't think it's just about money. What folks don't know, having a pimp or not is never just about money. Real hos who talk about getting the money? It's never just the money. The players change, but the game is still the same. It's about slipping in at all the wrong places. Getting into dangerous situations and getting out of them. That's exciting. That's what you want. But you want something else, too. When you grow up—molested, abused, avoided, traumatized, and left out—you want somebody to love you. And you gone find it, some kind of way. I'm an old bitch. I looked for nurturing. I wanted to belong to somebody who'll say, "You mine. I love you, bitch." I didn't care if they called me "bitch." "Bitch, I love you. I do this shit cause I care."

"Okay, but let me get my eyeball off the floor."

So it's never just the money. It's about the search for someone who can love you. He wanted to be yours, and you want to be his.

It's so crazy. A pimp. A prostitute. You're trying to find where you belong, and you're trying to just find the right pimp for you.

There were the pimps who mentally and emotionally controlled you. They were the most dangerous ones. They were more dangerous than the gorilla pimps. At least you want to get away from the gorilla pimps. But those pimps with all that swag get in your head and play games with your mind and control you completely, and you don't want to get away from them. You are in love with the control, and some days you have an epiphany, but you can't even get down with your epiphany because he has that much control over you emotionally and mentally. You can't go nowhere. And cause he got you—you don't want to be with your kids, with your grandmomma; you don't want to visit nobody in your family. If it's not a part of his rules, you don't want it. You'll choose him over everybody else. And you have no control over what you choosing. That's why I believe that Stockholm syndrome is really deep inside of all of us. And I mean prostitutes, women, anybody who finds themselves in love and can't let go.

I've heard some hos say, "If he asked me to take a pistol and go out there and shoot somebody, I would do that for my daddy." I've heard women say, "I'd die for him," and they were serious when they said that. And some have died—for that man. How do you mess with something so deep? People want to look at you and ask you, "Why didn't you just leave?" Because, check this out: Just like some white lady wouldn't leave her half-a-million-dollar home and her Mercedes and her spa and her good life, well, listen, that pimp was *my* half-a-million-dollar home and my spa and my good life. That was it for me. You dig? These ladies were no different from me, they were just from a different culture. Her ass got whooped in her own mansion, and that white lady still put up with all kinds of abuse and violence. Domestic exploitation is happening to this fancy woman and she still acts like a big girl and puts makeup over it. She smiled at the cocktail parties and told everybody what a great man he was, and her family didn't even know because she wore that smile all the time.

Now, I'm gone ask that lady: Why didn't you leave, why didn't you drive away? Cause you had a car. I didn't have one. You could have driven away. People are always so willing to handle unexplainable situations. Any person with a brain understood this life I led wasn't a choice. People don't choose this type of life. When I said to men that I liked it, they should have known I was lying so I wouldn't feel bad about me. Because I had to tell myself every day when I woke up that this is what I wanted to do and I'm okay with it cause I'm the coldest one and I'm that bitch; I was born to do this. I started saying the same thing that he was telling me. I say it to myself so I can stay in the loop without committing suicide. Cause I would have killed myself if I had of really realized.

Some girls figured it out.

I knew a girl; her name was Cookie. Cookie was sweet, she had been in the game for a while, and one time somebody had put something in her drink. She drifted off. And a bunch of men had a bunch of ways with her. You know what I'm saying. That kind of stuff could happen to you sometime. You had to make sure your friends were looking out. Hos be out on the track, talking shit, just out there showing out, but we were looking out for each other, too. Anyway, after that, Cookie wasn't right no more. Ms. Cookie didn't show up one day; we were like, "Where Ms. Cookie?" We like, "Oh, shit." So we go into the building we had been using to turn our tricks, and we start looking for Cookie, and sure enough she had strung herself up. We got in there just in time, and we took her down. We saved her. But later, she wound up succeeding.

When I work with these girls at Dreamcatcher, I remember Cookie. I know some of these girls are just like her, and they are still knee-deep in that mindset. Dreamcatcher was formed to mentor young ladies, twelve to twenty-four, because we saw that our young girls were in crisis. We didn't know how hard it was going to be for us to help these girls, but we've done a pretty good job helping the youth and women. We say twenty-four, but we don't turn down anybody. What we basically do is outreach to start relationships with these girls. Programs do not save people; relationships help save people. If we don't build relationships, trust, and understanding, we can't make a difference. All of us at Dreamcatcher can say, "I just came from where you are now," and mean it. "I'm out of it and you can be, too. This ain't some shit I don't know about." I've already been through the ABCs, and I know, if I grab their hand and they don't let go, I can get these girls on their feet so they can walk again. These girls don't know they already got what it takes to get through this. If you've made it through human trafficking and prostitution, you are a G. There is no way these girls don't have the ability to survive. That's why at Dreamcatcher we get so tired of people referring to these girls as victims. That's not a label that these girls want to wear for the rest of their lives. They need help and some basic 101 of how to start brand new. We teach them how to get on the phone and talk to somebody and get your needs met. We call social services for them and show them where to stand on line and get their driver's license. We help them get apartments. Basic shit. We teach them how to communicate in the regular world. "How can I keep this going, Ms. Brenda?" That's what I hear out on the streets.

These girls have so much emotional garbage inside of them, they want to know how to flush all that out. Just last week, I was trying to send this girl twenty dollars for food. These girls think they make the best decisions. They get on the phone with me and try to convince me they are so right in what they doing. "Let me go down here with no money and no job, cause I love him. I'm leaving a comfortable-ass house to support him on a whim." I know that's what they're thinking. But that's young love. That's what we deal with. Young girls. Young, dumb, and full of cum, as they say. The first thing these girls want to tell you is: I'm grown now; I had sex. "Ms. Brenda, I can do this by myself, but I'm hungry." Well, baby, you not doing this by yourself, if you asking me for twenty dollars. "I haven't eaten all day, but I got it going on down here." I don't mind it; sometimes I even love it in a way, because I've been exactly where they are. I know how much trouble you can get into trying to find a home and somebody to love, too.

+ + +

That's how I found Johnny Allen, my sweet daddy pimp. I was looking for somebody to say, "I love you, bitch."

I didn't have to look that hard. I had run into Johnny Allen along the strip on Cicero—the couple of blocks where they had all the bars and the lounges, the places where you went after hours for sex. The places where the night people went and looked sharp. Johnny Allen caught my eye because he looked like a straight cold businessman with an Armani suit on. He had this Don Juan look. Handsome Black man. Superfine. He was all blond—'fro, sideburns, goatee. And he smelled good, with a cold-ass cologne. He was always double-breasted up, always a mink coat. He was a fashion statement to me, and I thought, I need a brother like that; I'm sharp, too. I had graduated from ho school, and I had learned how to turn tricks with store owners, and they would give me brand-new clothes for payment, so my wardrobe is up here. I wanted to be with someone who knew I followed the rules, and that was what it was like when he met me. Johnny was one of those *I'm gone wine and dine you, bitch*. You wanted to be in his good graces. That's the way it was for me. I wasn't doing nothing but messing with them entertainers from the Garfield Organization, so his whole situation looked good. His hos were all laid out, and I thought, well, I want to try him.

Johnny had four girls. One was a famous ho; her name was Doris. She worked in Chicago on Madison and California, and she was the coldest flat-backer in that area. Nobody else was turning that many tricks. That country bitch had to suck up on a lotta wang to get five hundred dollars and some. She never got less than five. Big country yellow bitch. Tammi Terrell–looking ho. Thick ass. She worked on the worst ho stroll in Chicago. We called them cheap bitches, broke bitches, but Doris wasn't. They said her tricks were sitting there waiting for her. She was like, "Next!"

Me and Ma'Dea had made up with each other by then. My girls were staying with Ma'Dea, and I wasn't really up to no good. Guys was pulling up front and blowing for me. None of these dudes come upstairs. I was like, "I'll be right there!" Ma'Dea said, "You in *all* types of cars. What kinda trouble you getting yourself in?"

I had gotten a job at a store, a furniture store, with this Italian. The Italians ran a lotta of the furniture stores on the West Side. And this one guy named Joe Albert had three furniture stores somewhere in Jew Town. Jew Town (that's what *everyone* called it) was still popping back then. I was walking past, and he had this Italian assistant named Frankie, fine-as-hell white boy, rode a motorcycle. And Frankie said, "Come here. Come here, let me talk to you." So I went back with Frankie, and he said, "You want a job?"

I said, "Yeah."

He said, "Show up here on Monday at nine o'clock. Just tell them Frankie told them to tell you come in." Frankie's job was coochie finder, and the owner wanted my coochie. He had a thing for Black women. He had this cold Black bitch on the side, and her name was Pam. She was little bitty, and she was one of them sisters who looked like Robin Givens, the lady who married Mike Tyson. The bitch was cold. The only thing I had on her was age. That's how I learned that when a bitch was about to retire, she got less interesting. But Pam was the coldest because she was educated. She wasn't no fool. She played like Eartha Kitt; her voice was like, "I can talk to anybody." She had a commanding voice. I liked that bitch, but she didn't like me, and I was young enough not to care.

Every time Joe had me in the office, I was super sweet. Joe sent furniture to my grandmomma's house—yes!—and didn't nobody know where my bill was to this day. They put the fake paid bill and didn't nobody ever see it again. And his friends who had the men's clothing stores and the shoe stores were asking about me, too. I was so clear. I never tried to be indignant about what a man's intention was when they called me over there to do what I thought they wanted me to do. Listen, I barely finished the eighth grade, ain't nobody hiring me cause I was brilliant in that way. But in this way, I was the banana. Somebody told them to put me on the payroll, and it was totally up to me if I was gone get anything else out of it and often I did.

I tried to get everything I thought I could get. Gimme this, gimme that. I didn't even need it. You sell men's clothes, but let me see if I could fit that. I was taking everything I could get my hands on over to my family. I didn't care, just gimme, gimme. I was just a little gimme girl. I was fifteen at that point. Fifteen and rough. I had just come up out of five months of hell with two psychopaths. And lived. I was flipping them brothers on the West Side, individually. I sold myself out because they were sucking my poontang, and I was the cutie pie. And every man liked to have me.

I was making so much money, I decided to leave Johnny Allen. I choose him on a Thursday and I left him on a Saturday, but as I said, he was a sugar daddy pimp. He was so sweet. First real pimp I ever had. I liked belonging to somebody. I liked giving him my money. I was with him for less than a month, but being with him made my value high. Johnny Allen was just one of those wild ol' pimps on the West Side that made you have a little stature or caliber. You were a thoroughbred if you were with Johnny Allen. A bottom bitch, an everyday bitch, a fly-by bitch, but always a thoroughbred. And for a moment, that was all I wanted.

Chapter 7

Loving the Knockout

You want to know the real reason I left Johnny Allen? The real reason I left him is because my secret heart was still looking for a pimp who wanted to knock me out. Not knock me out in a good way. But knock me *out*. I used to sit on the fire escape with Gloria Brown and watch women get beat up on the sidewalk. I had grown up surrounded by abuse—from Ma'Dea, from the molesters, from the gorilla pimps. I thought I needed to be intimidated. Otherwise I wasn't gone act right. That was the girl I was; that was the girl I was growing up to be.

When Tommy Knox came along, he felt perfect. Like a knock in the head.

Before I met Tommy Knox, I had hooked up with the transgenders who were out west doing their thing. I was out there, too, like an outlaw. We were getting the tricks who came out from the western suburbs. I was messing around with different guys in the neighborhood just to have a place to sleep at night. I didn't have a pimp anymore. They took me under their wings because they liked me. They thought I was funny. And young. They knew I was a runaway; they knew I didn't have anybody to protect me. The transgenders invited me to their apartments and let me crash on their couches. We would have girlfriend parties where they taught me how to put on makeup. "Girl, let me show you how to put the princess on." They taught how to wear lashes and how to apply blush. They moderated my wig. There's a way you can put on a wig and make it look natural. "See, Ms. Thang? Comb that there, pin that here. That's how you do it. Now you got it." In the daytime we would watch soap operas and eat junk food. They let me go out and work with them, and I loved it because they kept me safe. These ladies could turn into a man at any moment. I learned that little trick from them. I got so good at it, I used to rob tricks with my voice. I would get in the car, all sweet and then, I CHANGED MY VOICE.

Those tricks freaked out, "You a man!"

"THAT'S RIGHT, SON OF A BITCH. GIVE ME MY MONEY." I knew how intimidated they were by transgenders, and how if you mess with the ladies, they would tear your ass off. So I used my man voice. I was like, don't make me get vicious up in here. First, I'd park him. I'd make him go drive in the alley, and I'd get him to park his door up against the garage or the wall, and these stupid-ass tricks— you should never let nobody do that. I got the only out.

Sometimes I just grabbed his keys, snatched them out the ignition, pulled my wig off, then I'd go into that voice and rob them. I'd throw the keys out the window. They went looking for the keys while I got away. You have to find your keys because you were not coming out that alley without your keys. My ladies taught me how to get over. Folks knew they couldn't mess with me.

So when I found Tommy Knox, I was ready. I was at a bar, and Tommy Knox was with this country guy from Tennessee with a gold tooth in the front of his mouth and his shoes were way too tall. He was wearing platforms. We used to call them stacks. They were the stupidest-looking shoes I ever seen in my life, cause only short assholes used to put on stacks. You know when they step out of them, they stood down there at your belly button, but the sweet daddy he was with, Tommy Knox, was a fine Black man, especially when he had his hats on.

He was light-skinned, with light brown hair, and he had a perm. He was tall and high yellow and slim. And the brother was a gangsta in his own mind. Every time somebody did something, he had some words for it. I met him at the bar, and we were talking and getting along. Next thing I knew, I was going home with Tommy Knox. He told that country dude he had come with, "I'm gone have to catch you late, cause I'm 'bout to get this baby."

I get in his car, and we talking, and he said, "Let's go to my place." "Okay."

"I got a couple of crazy girls, but they my friends. Don't pay any attention to what they talking about up there."

I laughed and said, "Okay." So I get in the house, and he had two women, Jackie and Cassandra. Cassandra's eye was black. Something was going on with Jackie's arm. I was looking at this scene, and no part of it was good, and what you think I did? I stayed! What the hell? Looking at those women and the state of beatdown they were in, did that not tell me anything? I'm telling the truth, I should have pulled out my running shoes and took off, but I stayed. I'm not making that up. When I think of it now, what kind of stupid-ass shit was that? Did that not tell me anything? Shouldn't I have asked for a cab or walked to Chicago Avenue and caught the bus? No. I stayed.

He immediately sent me to work with Jackie, and Jackie was livid. She said, "How old are you?"

I was looking at her and walking fast. "Eighteen?"

"Ooh, you lying your ass off. Your ass ain't eighteen. How old are you?"

"I'm fifteen." But she still looked like she was gone jack me up. "I'm fifteen, for real! I got two babies."

"Argh! You must be one of the dumbest girls in the world."

We went to the liquor store and got Richards Wild Irish Rose.

When you drink it, it made you feel like you could fight Godzilla. She was angry, and she wanted to go and get in a fight. All through the night, she would turn to me and say, "Dumb bitch."

Finally, I said, "Wait a minute. Why I gotta be a dumb bitch?" I wasn't no punk or nothing.

She turned to me and said, "Shut up, bitch. Young-ass, jazzy, jump-in-the-car-with-a-crazy-motherfucking P, young-ass bitch!"

I was like, "Huh?"

She said, "Yeah, you jump in the car with a cracked-up pimp and then you come in the house and see my arm broke and Sandra got a black eye and your ass ain't ran! Don't you see what's happening here? You a goddamned fool."

That's just how that went. That was how silly I was, and that's how I know my girls today. I know how stupid they can get. I was there for a minute before Tommy Knox showed me he was a sociopath who had psychopathic tendencies. He was a maniac.

Here's what I know: some pimps have to be the bitch inside of them. They have to be weak and hateful. It's some type of deep-down, incorrect relationship with a woman that has him twisted around. Sometimes pimps get lucky, and they fall in love with a real bitch who can handle them. But those women had to be some cold-ass bitches, because sometimes that pimp didn't want to love. Or maybe she loved him, but she wasn't no punk, and they came through that nonsense together, and then they found out that they really loved each other and knowing that they loved each other ate their ass up. Sometimes a pimp and a bitch turned out okay together because it seemed like it couldn't work no other way. Jackie loved Tommy Knox to death. It was something in their relationship that was like nobody else's. They were together for like thirty years. She knew what he needed, before he said so. He knew how to soothe Jackie before she bust a cap in his ass.

Tommy Knox was good at that. Tommy Knox knew almost everything about all his ladies. When I was with him, we had little apartments all through this two-story building. There were two apartments in the basement. There were four apartments on the first floor and four apartments on the second floor. All of them were kitchenette apartments. You would let the bed out the wall, and once you pushed the bed up, you had a little sitting area. Tommy and Jackie had the first-floor apartment in the front; we also had the apartments in the back. That's where he put me because he said I was the baby.

And I was a baby, and he treated me how I should have been treated. He used to call me Dirty Red. Most times he treated me like a kid. "Go sit down somewhere," he'd tell me. "Don't say nothing. Eat this." I was supposed to give him a hundred percent of the money, and then he would give me an allowance. But Tommy was difficult. He'd forget to give me the allowance, and when I asked for money, he'd give me a hard time about it. If somebody came through with food stamps to sell, he'd give us that and let us go grocery shopping. I always held back a little and spent it on records, soda pop, lunch at the diners. Jackie taught me to do that. She held back her money to get high before she got high with Tommy Knox.

I had been with him six months when I tore his car up. He had this Cadillac, and I'm driving it, trying to let everybody know this was my pimp's Cadillac. I jumped in there to move the car, but I didn't know how to drive. Stupid me. All the pimps who were there were looking at me like, "That bitch dead." The next day, Jackie told me one of the pimps said, "Man, we ain't gone see that bitch again." Another said, "Oh man, I know him. She dead. That bitch done tore that Cadillac up, man." Everybody knew what had happened in the whole ho/pimp game. I went to jail that night, and even the folks in there knew about it. "Ain't you the one who tore the car up?" I heard some wife talking about it from the cell: "This crazy young bitch decides she wanna be a truck driver and run into something."

Finally, I couldn't take any more. "Bitch, I hear you talking about me, ho! Ask me how much money I got, bitch, while you talking."

I knew I was in trouble, so I stayed on the streets working for five days until I had a thousand dollars to give Tommy Knox for the car damages. Nobody could get money like me. At least you could say I was the best street trainee in the world. Ma'Dea had made me tough, and Jackie got me street ready. Jackie was like a big sister to me. She told me how to act around Tommy Knox, and I learned not to say nothing out the way. Unfortunately, Jackie didn't take her own advice. She took whoopings for me. She even took the blame for tearing up the Cadillac. *Be quiet, girl*, but she loud-mouthed Tommy Knox in a minute. Tommy Knox always used to beat Jackie more than he beat me.

I mean, Tommy used to walk up to her and be like, "What's up bitch?" *Boom, boom. Boom, boom.*

I was on the steps crying. "Why you hit her?"

"Bitch, shut up and go upstairs."

I was crying, "He gone kill her. He gone kill her." I was the baby. I was just up there in my apartment, traumatized. But I was also loving it, loving all this drama going on.

Tommy was a drug addict. Jackie was a dope fiend some of the time, too. They nodded off: heroin, pills, syrup, Robitussin, anything that was a nod. They didn't care. But when Jackie stayed sober, we used to have all kind of adventures. Once, we were out strolling and we saw Mailbox Mary. I had met Mailbox Mary in jail. She was a white woman with brown hair. Mailbox Mary could have been in her thirties, but she looked older than that. We used to call her "crazy white ho" because, first of all, Mailbox Mary didn't have a pimp. She wasn't attractive, and the pimps called her a crazy bitch, too. Anyway, the hos found out about the envelopes and how she used to mail the money she made on the streets back to herself. She was this careful white woman. She didn't get picked up and put in jail like the rest of us.

We would be in the bullpen, and of course, there was always a power struggle when you were in lockup—there were the bitches that ran it and the bitches who got it. Say, for instance, if me, Jackie, and Sandra were in the bullpen together and another ho was there. Okay, that girl is not in our family. So when she went off to sleep, we would check and see if she had any money in her shoe or in her bra. We gone take that money. Because, in that bullpen, we are the aggressors. Now, if I am in the bullpen alone, I got to be careful. If I went in there by myself, I didn't go to sleep. If you did, you woke up with a shoe heel in your head. They were wearing those platforms back then. You'd wake up, and a girl would have bust you in your head. They would steal your money, your brand-new boots. Anyway, Mailbox Mary would be in jail, and it was crazy. She'd be standing up in the corner; she knew better than to go to sleep. She was tall as hell. And girls would be getting mad. "Sit down, bitch, you making me nervous." And Mailbox would just fall down in the corner and say, "I ain't falling asleep around you bitches."

If we thought she was asleep, we would sneak up on her. But she was playing possum. She'd start screaming, "AHHH! Guards!" And then the guards would come and they would put her in a bullpen by herself. Then in the morning, when we all went to court, bitches would throw their old bologna sandwiches at her. Mary would be in the corner hissing at us. So one day, me and Jackie were on the North Side and we saw her. We were going to catch her before she got to the mailbox. Mailbox Mary took off. Down the block, *vroom*, around the corner. We couldn't catch her. That ho slammed into the mailbox and slapped her envelope in.

You know, everybody talked shit about her. Some hos said Mailbox made a lot of money. Some hos thought she didn't make that much, but they underestimated her. But no matter what, Mailbox was out there. She had her regulars. She was out there for something; she wasn't just out there to get abused. I'll tell you what: she knew how to get that money to that mailbox. And when I start thinking about the relationship between prostitutes and pimps, I stop thinking that Mailbox was a dumb bitch. Maybe she was the smartest one of us out there. Maybe we were the dumb ones, because no one was taking Mary's money. You could count the times when someone found money on Mailbox Mary. That bitch always made it to the mailbox. Jackie and I had to find other things to do besides spending all of our time chasing after the lone white prostitute.

One time, we were working and ran into a hotel on Lake Street. We ran through this hotel if the police were hot, and we walked down the hallways to see what was happening. We would see a door ajar, open it up, and peek in, cause we were always in them hotel rooms. Try to catch somebody sleeping. There was a white lady knocked out across the bed. She had a mink coat on the chair, and there were two-gallon bottles, like the kind they have in the pharmacy, of syrup, and a whole bunch of other stuff. She had come there to buy drugs and Lord knows what all. She had a lotta money, too.

We stole the money, the drugs, the mink coat, slipped out the back door, and went home. Jackie and I stood at the front door, and I made a decision. I had never tried this kind of dope in my life because I was taught that out in the game, you never wanted to be a drug-addict prostitute. I didn't even work in the vicinity of them. I still thought I was going to be something important. I thought I was going to run into this fantastic, rich-ass trick who was going to take me away from all of this. And I would be a kept woman somewhere. I would have everything I need. But at home with Jackie and Tommy, I wanted to fit in. All the time, I was left out. Everybody was nodding and getting high, and it seemed like they were communicating. They were down there nodding, and all I was doing was staying in my room listening to music. I was left out, even though I was the money getter. So this time, I stood at the front door with Jackie with all our treasure and I thought, *Y'all not leaving me out this time.* And I drank syrup with them.

At the end of the week, my back was hurting and I told Tommy Knox, "Something's wrong with me. I can't describe it." I told him how I was feeling.

"Bitch, you got a habit." He closed the door on my face.

I stood there in the hallway thinking, *What?* I went up to my room. It was Tennessee's, the country pimp, old place. He and his woman had the upstairs front apartment. Tennessee was country, but they had everything laid out up there with a whole seventies look. They had shag carpet, the beanbag, the beads separating the kitchen from the living room, the crushed velvet bedspread. It was funky; it was cool. Tennessee and his woman left town, and I asked the landlord could I get that apartment. I was glad I did. I loved it up there, my little own seventies domain. I spent a lot of time up there by myself. I opened the door, and I started crying, cause I felt like, I guess, a dope fiend. This is how it feels to be a dope fiend? I needed some more syrup, but I wasn't gone let my body do that to me. So I took a laxative and I drank a lotta apple juice. That whole weekend I didn't come out and make any money cause I was up there messed up. And Tommy was downstairs, high as always, so it wasn't like he was keeping tabs on me. I was upstairs in my little apartment, kicking it.

Jackie started doing as much dope as Tommy Knox. I loved her, but that bitch was a professional nodder. I used to be working with her sometimes, watching her back, and I was thinking to myself, why this bitch taking so long? One time, I went back there and there she was nodding off on a trick's schlong. And the trick was sitting up there in the car, looking like, *Come on now.*

He looked at me and said, "Wake this bitch up! This ho's done went to sleep on my dick."

I started tapping on the window, "Girl, wake up! You spose to be dating this man!" Jackie tried to wake up, and I got her out of the car.

Every time she pulled that stunt, I got her home some kind of way. But Jackie couldn't get too high for me. She was my girl, my big sister. And I was a little girl. She protected me. She could sing, too. Jackie Webb. Everybody in the game could tell you about Jackie Webb. Back in the day, they knew about her.

Jackie and I used to be together all the time, getting into this and that because I still had connections to the stores on Madison Street. Madison was still the ghetto shopping area for the West Side. Now it's a bunch of beauty supplies, but back in the day it was shoe stores and Three Sisters, Learner's Shop and Goldblatt's. Stores that were bustling and we bought everything from them. Everybody went to Madison at the first of the month to spend money, and folks were selling stuff out of the trunk of their cars. Folks selling bootleg shit and socks and whatever your pleasure. There's a hot-dog stand here and there. People would be piled on top of each other. Somebody would tell you that was thirty dollars, and when you walked away, they would say they would give it to you for ten. That was the beat of Madison Street. I could go up there without a dime and come back with bags. Jackie and I used to go—she used to wake me up early in the morning, cause she dug the fact that I had these connections and we could go up there and shop. "Let's go up there on Madison," she said.

"Alright. I ain't seen them in a while."

I had one named Bob who used to work at Bakers shoe store. We used to load up on shoes. I had a good Korean guy at the wig store. And the dude wasn't my trick, it was just that I could go and talk him out of anything. Sometimes he just gave me free wigs to get me out of his store; I was talking so much slang. His name was Mr. Kim; he was cool.

On this particular day, we were kicking it. We had got our little outfits and we were sharp. So we had decided to go out in the streets. Let's work early. Tommy Knox didn't really care. He didn't know if we were in the house or not. He was in there nodding with that fatass Teko and that old man Fred. Oh my God, let me tell you about those two. Old man Fred: he looked like something out this Snoop Dogg movie. Old-ass dusty dude. He was a pimp, and he had one bitch, and she never made any money. She was always locked up. The only time he had money was the first of the month, when they got a check from the government. He was a leech. If Tommy got to snorting, Fred snorted with him.

The other dude was this big fat Yogi Bear type, Teko. He used to nod standing up. I remember him because my job was to make sure they didn't burn up the house. All of them would drop their cigarettes when they nodded off. Tommy would wake up and the mattress would be on fire. The mattress smoldering—that's how their nod was. They left me to take care of it because I didn't do no drugs. Milkshake and a hamburger and I was tight.

When they got around Tommy Knox, they got into his mentality. They wanted to say anything to us. I was glad when Jackie looked at them and said, "You can't just say shit to me. You ain't Knox, man." She just cussed them out real bad. "You stanking-ass, ugly-ass punk. All you do is hang around here and hold his dick while he nod off." Of course, then Knox got up and knocked her down. "This disrespectful, bitch."

But Jackie said what she needed to say.

+ + +

So that's where I lived. Living and loving it up with Jackie, but Tommy Knox was always there to remind me how harsh it was. The longer I stayed, the worse he got. It was like he couldn't help himself. I will never forget the first time he beat me with that half a pool stick. Right in front of me, he sawed it in two and wrapped it in black tape. I was in there talking to him. I could detect there was some sinister thoughts going on, but I was just thinking this brother high and talking. But when he got through taping that pool stick up, he said, "Come on in the back, Red." He took me in the back apartment and started beating me. He stood in front of the door so I couldn't get out. I was trying to protect my face and my body with my arms. He beat my arms up real bad. I had so many bruises on me. He had me take my clothes off while he beat me. Then he locked me in the bathroom. I climbed out the window and ran to the neighbors' house and knocked on the door. It was a couple's house and the husband came to the front. I didn't know them.

I was naked and I was knocking on the door. "Can you help me?" He stared at me; then he looked back into the house.

I heard his wife say, "Who is it, baby?"

"It's a naked woman from next door."

She came to the door and let me in.

I said, "Could you help me?"

Tommy Knox beat me with that pool stick because that was all he knew. He used to beat Jackie like that, for no reason. With Sandra, he went over to her apartment across the hall sometimes and just tighten her up, just *whoosh, whoosh, whoosh.* He was brutal with women. "I can't stand funky bitches," he used to say. "I don't give a shit about a funky-ass bitch." And yet he had hos.

We had no self-esteem, and we allowed him to talk to us like that. But after I went through that, I knew it was time to get out. I just didn't know how to do it. Something needed to push me out the door. I was just as shocked as anybody with what went down next.

+ + +

Jackie got gang-raped by gangsters. Jackie had a smart-ass mouth. There were a whole lotta smart-ass-mouth bitches out there, but sometimes you don't realize who you talking to, and you ain't spose to be talking to everybody that way. Gangsters were out there hollering at Jackie; Jackie hollered something back. Out there in Lake Street. Lake and Central. There was a lot of traffic up there. The el train was coming through. Then them dudes heard Jackie saying, "You faggot motherfucker." The whole gang went around the corner and snatched Jackie in the car, and they took her to an alley and raped her.

After them gangsters were done with her, she ran back to Tommy Knox, who was off in the back nodding off, like always. Jackie told him, "You need to do something and fast." He said, "Let's go round these punks." Not "Let me go bury these brothers," but "Let's go round these punks."

So they ganged up—old man Fred and Teko and Tommy. They went up there and shot out the gangsters' car with a .22. I mean, with a .22? That's a little-ass gun. What they should have done was went out there with a BOOM-BOOM gun, make a building shake. After it went down, that .22 was all the neighborhood talked about. I mean everybody was saying, "He did a drive-by with a .22? What kind of mess was that?" I was getting an earful. On the ho stroll, when I went to jail, everybody was talking about how somebody shot up the gangsters' car with a .22 and the gang was out there looking for the dudes who did it.

Now, there were three dudes with the same kind of car. Tennessee, who had come back, had a steel gray Coupe DeVille, and so did Tommy Knox. And so did one brother up on the set. But Tommy's was a Coupe DeVille with black trim, and this dude's was a Coupe DeVille with silver trim. But the homies didn't know the difference, so when they all hooked up, they ran into that boy instead of Tommy Knox and they killed that boy. Tennessee moved out the building that evening and left town, cause he had the same car, too. Tommy never did anything about it. All he kept saying was, "That funky bitch should have never said anything to them dudes. I'm 'bout to get killed over a funky bitch." That's how he backed down off of them. He got mad at Jackie.

+ + +

So I was like, I'm going to leave Tommy Knox. I was with Tommy a year and a half. Jackie was his wife, and I was the moneymaker. She went out with me, but I was a young bitch, tearing them off. I had five-hundred-dollar days, thousand-dollar days. If I rob the right white boy, I came home with five thousand dollars. Jackie and Tommy Knox went from just buying bags to buying spoons to buying halves, because that was just the way I worked. I could have been a stock-market bitch or something like that with my work ethic.

With all the shenanigans, I wanted to get back in touch with my family. I started slipping between family and the game. I had started to get close to my dad. I had been seeing him once or twice a year since I was a kid, but when I lived with Aunt Josie in Evanston, she would let me go over his house on the weekends. When I was out in the streets, I would stop by their house to visit. My daddy kind of knew I was hooking, but he was the kind who didn't ask questions that he didn't want to know the answer to. He didn't like my lifestyle, but they had their own troubles, so they felt they couldn't judge. On any given day, when I couldn't take any more of Tommy, I went over there with my daddy and my brothers. Jethro, Jerome, Wiley, Terry, and Todd came and got me when I was in tough situations. I was making regular appearances over at my father's house, so they were getting to know my wife-in-law, Jackie.

✦ ✦ ✦

Tommy Knox came out of his nod and realized I had been missing for a while.

"Somebody at the door for you," my brother Jethro called out to me. It was Tommy.

I went to it. "What's up?"

Tommy leaned in. "Come on out and talk to me."

"I ain't got no clothes on," I said. "You gone have to talk to me in the hallway."

He didn't make a move to come inside. I knew he was teed up. I stepped outside on the porch and looked back to the house. My brother Terry came to the door, cause me and Tommy Knox out there talking.

"You serious, you don't want to fool with me no more?"

"Don't, Tommy." Without my knowing it, I had walked down a couple of steps from the porch. I took a good long look at Tommy Knox and all I could see was Jackie and her gang rape, the pool stick he used on me, all the dope. I turned around to get back inside. "Bye."

"Bitch, get your ass down these stairs." And *pow!* He bust me in the head with a pistol.

"Daddy!" I screamed. I made a distress call. *Boom!* All you hear was footsteps. Jethro, Terry, Wiley, Jerome were hitting the door. My brothers were running down the street chasing Tommy Knox.

I called out to Terry, "Terry, get him!" and my brother's pistol went *ka-ka-pow* as Tommy was making that turn around the corner, his coat flaring up behind him. That's what caught the bullets.

So of course, I went by Tommy's the next day to see if he was okay and that he was still alive.

He showed me his coat. "Your daddy gone have to get me another coat. He shot my coat up." He turned to Jackie and said, "She got some real wired-up family over there. Her daddy be running around with six-shooters and everything. Brother named Jethro. What kind of name is that?"

Tommy was talking about he shot my brother in his ass. I told him not to get too far out on that kind of rumor. See, Tommy didn't know Terry. Let me tell you about Terry. Terry was good-looking, fine as hell. Hazel eyes. But he had a short fuse. Before he went to California and went to jail, he told me, "One time, there was some people over there in Jackson. I was in the park, and I was waiting on somebody to come by so I could get 'em." He hid in the park, in the middle of the projects, ducking down, waiting on prey. "I saw you and your girlfriends come outta that building. Y'all all had fur coats on and y'all was looking good, and I was mad at you. And I thought to myself, I should go over there and rob all your asses. But I let you alone that night." I was like OMG! My brother was thinking about robbing my ass! And I had only owed him five dollars.

+ + +

That's who Tommy Knox was trying to talk big to. I knew if he pushed it, he was going to get jacked up. Somebody needed to protect Tommy from himself. That might as well be me, I thought. I went back over to Tommy's after that shootout because I felt like that's where I belonged. I didn't belong anywhere else except with those people. It sounds crazy, but we were a family over at Knox's. What was happening to them was important to me. Over at my daddy's house, babies were crying, kids were going to school—that didn't feel real. If I stayed for too long, somebody would have gotten around to asking when I was going to get a regular job. That was square life. I was a street person, and I wanted to be around street people. I needed to get back to the family I knew best. It's a street family, but it's a family. You form allegiances to them. They become as important to you as your own personal family. That's what I became when I was with these pimps. Tommy was the head of the family, and Jackie was a sister to me. And I worried about Jackie. Jackie was the best friend I had. Would he take all this mess out on her? It didn't matter that she was a dope fiend. I loved her. I wanted to get Jackie out. And even if I didn't know it, I needed to get me out, too.

Chapter 8

The Gangster Pimp

A couple of months later, I was on the street with Jackie, just talking, drinking wine, or whatever, and a car pulled up with Jackie's old friends off Poke Street in it. And Coolie was in there, too—Jackie had just been telling me about Coolie, how he'd just got out the federal joint. "Who's your girlfriend?" he said to Jackie. He had this beautiful smile. He had lips like James Earl Jones. Super-soft lips.

I was just standing back there smiling, I didn't know what to say. I was young. Sixteen. I was still a baby.

Coolie was light-skinned but on the brown side of all that. Even sitting in the car, I could tell he was muscular. About five eleven, with a husky build. I could see he was interested in me. Everything Jackie had been telling me about him was really exciting to me. She was telling me about what a sweet brother he was, but that he wasn't one to mess with. That was a known fact. She had told me little stories, some nice and pleasant stuff, but I also got from her that if I got with this man, wouldn't nobody mess with me. If I got with him, he'd be my protector, cause didn't nobody fool with Coolie.

I knew it was time for me to separate from Tommy Knox. I had been with him for almost two years. Everything about him was so raggedy. His pimping was raggedy. Two or three other pimps had moved into our building with their hos and disrespected the neighborhood. We lived on Parkside, two blocks west of Central Avenue. Yeah, we worked out of that place, but we were discreet with our tricks; we respected the neighborhood. But these new hos turned the neighborhood into a ho stroll, a track. Eight to twelve hos were standing right where they live, turning tricks, ripping customers off. So if somebody got robbed, they knew where to come back. That was a whole deal right there; it made me feel unsafe. What if somebody ripped somebody off and they came back shooting at the building? And the whole business was starting to depreciate because bitches would underbid. Everything was just going downward.

I was looking for a way out. So I started making money and stashing it. I gave Tommy some, but I kept on saying, "It's slow; it was a bad night." I found out Coolie lived around the corner on Ohio, like two blocks away from us. I found that out from Jackie. She was real mad at me when she found out that I went over there. On this particular day, I told Knox I was going to the cleaners. See, I had this rabbit fur coat that I loved. This was when rabbit coats were in. It was a three-quarter-length coat; I thought I was styling. Later, when I got with Coolie, he threw that coat away, cause he thought I had graduated to fox and mink. But I thought that little funky coat was the bomb.

So I told Tommy I was going to the cleaners to get some clothes out of there. I had to get out of the building fast before somebody said, "Take my shirt, take my pants." Coolie didn't know I was coming. He didn't know anything was going on. This is what I did: I had my little bag, I took it around back, and I set it by the back door. Then I went around the front and rang his bell. "Who's that?" He looked out the window and said, "Hey! Cutie pie!" He had company and he was talking to his friends. "Must be Christmas, cause I think I got a Christmas present down here." I was blushing. I went up the stairs and he said, "What's up, baby?"

I whispered, "Could I talk to you?"

"Yes, ma'am, you can. You can talk to me anytime." He had all these locks on the door. He locked all the bars behind me. From his living room to his dining room, all you could see was a bunch of men up in there around the table, and they were shooting craps. Tyrone Davis was there, all the big drug dealers.

This one drug dealer named Big Al, big ol' teddy bear, looked at me and said, "What you got there, Mr. Coolie? You got Christmas?" I was a little sweet thing, and everybody was like, *hmmm*. All the guys had a little statement about me coming up in there.

Coolie said, "Let's go to the bedroom and talk." I went in, and I sat down on his bed. He started chopping up some white rocks. It was cocaine. "You want some?"

"I don't do that."

He said, "Oohh. That's nice. No shit?" He ain't saying it, but he was happy I didn't do drugs. "So what's going on?"

"Well, I was thinking you and me could do something together."

"Ah, yeah? Really? And what make you feel like that?"

"When I met you, it was just something about you. I done heard Jackie talking about you. And I felt a drive to come here."

"Okay. Okay." We start talking. "What you do?"

"I don't do a whole lot of nothing right now, but you know what I do. But I'm open to whatever." We were just talking. He asked did I have kids. Asked about Ma'Dea. He was asking all these great questions, like he couldn't wait to figure out who I was. It was almost like we were two girlfriends talking. He was so different from Tommy Knox.

"How old are you? For real?" I was going to be seventeen. I hadn't made it to April yet. He wasn't intimidated by that, cause

Coolie liked young girls. I found that out later. There was a little pedo in him. But a lotta men had that. Cause it was all about power and control. Get you a young girl and you can train them, almost like you can a dog. Now that I think about it, it's almost like, *Train me? What?* But at the time, it was the thing to say. That's how conversation went about women. Get them young and train them into what you want them to be. And you have her where you want her.

"Well, where your clothes at?"

"They on your porch."

"Where?"

"Out on the back porch. I didn't know if you was gone say yes or not." Coolie started laughing and I said, "Oh, and I got something else for you." And I went down in my panties and I pulled out a wad of money.

He said, "You had this really thought out, huh?"

"Yep. You didn't think I was just gonna come here empty-handed?" I probably couldn't work for a couple of days until he got everything squared with Tommy Knox, because basically, I still belonged to Tommy Knox.

Coolie smiled—he had this great big ol' smile—and we went to the back door and pulled my little bag in. He ended up throwing all those clothes away. Then he had somebody go get me something to eat. And I said I really want to take a bath, to be fresh. He gave me a towel, all kind of stuff.

He went back out, and he was gone for about an hour; then he told his friends, "I got some business to take care of."

All those guys were cracking. "Yeah, yeah, now you wanna put us out!"

I was excited. I could hear what was going on. Sounded real positive, sounded like I was the conversation. I liked it.

Them dudes were drinking, snorting cocaine. Lotta pistols in there, everybody had a gun. Some of Chicago's finest. Some of them were well-known criminals, some were celebrities, some of them were politicians, and yes, some of them were police. It was hilarious. They were all sweet guys, all old middle-age men; they all became protectors of me.

One of them was Coolie's brother, Cicero. Cicero had ties with the old Chicago crime family, people like Sam Giancana. Cicero was Giancana's boy, the Black guy for Giancana. He ran policy for Giancana for years before all of that gambling faded out, and he had connections on other crimes, too, like if they were going to do a job or do something illegal. I don't think there was too much drugs going on from them. I think they were getting their drugs from the Herreras, from Mexico. The conversations I heard at Coolie's were stories I would hear later on, on TV news or reading the paper. Coolie started me reading the newspaper. He said you had to read major news every day. "Read the news and current events so you'll know what going on in the world. Plus, it heightens your conversation. You don't want to get around people and not know nothing. You won't have nothing to talk about."

He didn't let me work at first. He took me to the doctor. There was some things going on with me that hadn't been taken care of, cause I was with a pimp who didn't care. I had a little thing with my cervix. And I had a STD. He made sure all of that was taken care of. And he paid for all that. He took me to the dentist. Took me to the eye doctor, because once, he saw me outside, doing my thing, and he said, "I saw you, the police rolled right up on you and you was squinting. You didn't see them."

I started laughing. I said, "Nuh-uh."

"Yeah, you did. I saw you. That's how come they rolled right up on you and you went to jail." So we went to the eye doctor, and sure enough, I needed glasses. They had put those drops in my eyes, so when I went outside, I couldn't see. But Coolie guided me home.

Not too much longer after that, my tonsils were inflamed. I had had tonsillitis almost my whole life, and he took me to the doctor for that. I mean, he just literally took care of me. That was why I fell in love with Coolie. And Coolie fell in love with me. We were Mr. and Mrs. Coolie, and we were happy. We were happy like that for years, five, six years. We went to the movies. He took me to the museums. He took me to the other side of town to the best restaurants. We went to the park. We went grocery shopping together. We went places together, and people looked at us and asked us if we were brother and sister, cause, you know how when you with somebody, you sort of start to look alike? "Y'all look like y'all together."

Coolie could tell me anything. We sat up at night and talked way into the morning. I used to ask him questions. "How it feel to kill somebody?"

He looked at me and said, "It's a feeling you never wanna have. Lotta people talk about ain't nothing to take a life, but that ain't true." A lotta times he had nightmares, and he'd grit his teeth real hard at night. There was turmoil inside there. He had a lotta dead bodies on him.

Coolie had a jean jumpsuit and a cap and some shoes he put on when he was going to go put in some work. That's what he called it: putting in work.

Like, once, when I was working the stroll, this guy walked up on me and beat me up. I didn't even know him. He just felt like it because he saw me as one of the girls out there. I went home crying and told Coolie, "He beat me up. I don't know him and he just put his hands on me."

"Okay, okay. Calm down," Coolie said. He calmed me down from crying. Later on that night, he put on that jumpsuit. I never saw that dude again. I can't tell you if anything happened because Coolie told me this: "The less you know, the less you can tell. This ain't something you need to know. I wouldn't put that on you for nothing. For you to know. Why you keep asking me?"

"Cause I, like, got, you know . . . I can ask, right? We in love." But I understood. By the end, Coolie and I had this relationship that was peas and carrots, fingers and a hand. You couldn't get around it. Jackie came in and looked at all this that was me and him, our relationship between each other, and was like, "Well, damn." He had messed around and fallen in love with me.

+ + +

It was real, but I was too young to take on the responsibility this man was trying to put on me. I couldn't be in a relationship and be in the game. Settle down? Be a wife? I hadn't thought about none of that. Kidnappings, having babies was still following me around, eating me up. I didn't know. I knew I just couldn't do it right. Live the right way. Several times, I had something right in my hands that could have made me end up really well off, but I couldn't maintain my own self to do it. I couldn't look that far ahead in life.

+ + +

Coolie used to tell me, "Don't think people always like you. Sometimes folks want to know if they can get to me through you. See, if they can get to you, they can get to me."

"Okay."

Sometimes I think I loved Coolie so much because when he was telling me one thing, he was actually telling me another thing. Coolie had told me that "sometimes folks want to know if they can get to me through you," but what he was also saying was: This Tommy Knox business has got to stop. All that coat shooting and Jackie nodding. I was living with Coolie, but I would stop by the old building to check in on Jackie. Sometimes Tommy would be there. He was telling me to come back. And when I said no, he'd smack me in the head or pop me in the mouth. Coolie was like, alright, I'm gone go talk to him. I was more nervous than he was. He wasn't ever nervous, cause he was cool.

We rode around the corner, and Knox was outside his car. Great timing. Coolie went over. Knox saw him coming and backed up a little bit. "Yo, I understand, man. You know the funky bitch, that bitch. She a bitch, man."

From the car I noticed that even though Coolie was shorter than

Tommy Knox, Coolie was the bigger man. "Hey, man, we ain't got to go through all that name-calling."

"Well, can I say something to her?"

"You can say what you want to say. But you can't fool with her from now on."

"I understand, man."

Tommy came over to the car and leaned in. He whispered, "Bitch, get out the car."

I didn't move. "I ain't gone be with you no more, Tommy Knox." I thought he was going to hit me in the mouth, but with Coolie standing nearby, he just looked real ugly and backed up.

Coolie got in the car. As we rolled away, the song came on that was out by Barry White's girlfriend, "I Belong to You"!

Coolie looked at me and turned the song up. "You hear that, baby?"

"Yeah!" I was all excited. I wasn't gonna get beat up by Knox. It was like we were riding off into the sunset. Me and Coolie.

I've never been ashamed of my past because for some reason I always knew that my past was not my fault. I always knew that the circumstances that I was given were not me. I knew there was always a better life for me. There was something ahead of me. And what I was going through was a struggle, and things that were happening to me were NOT Brenda, but they were Breezy. And that Breezy would take me through it.

My grandmother Ma'Dea raised me. She had a beautiful laugh. It was strong and full of life, it also made you want to laugh, too. Everybody knew if Ma'Dea hit you, you were going to get knocked out. So didn't nobody mess with her.

This is the only picture I have of my mother, Ernestine. She was beautiful. I wish I could have known her but she died at sixteen years old. I was six months old.

Around 1973, I started slipping between family and the game. I started to get close to my dad, but over at his house, babies were crying, kids were going to school. That was square life.

As a little girl, I always wanted to be beautiful. I grew up and I wanted to be all the Supremes, because I had a song in my heart. I still got that song in my heart.

By the time I was sixteen, I had both my girls. Peaches (left) was a quiet spirit and from an early age could see my spirit. Prune (right) loved me unconditionally and was protective of me.

I loved, *adored* my uncles, especially Joe (center). I was always talking to him, all day, every day, and he never told me to cut it out. I just followed him around and he let me.

Brothers were wearing the Ivy League look and were sharp as hell. My uncle Lee was one of them.

This was my wife-in-law, Elsie. Elsie was my Caucasian gold card. She got me into upscale hotels and elite clubs. In those times, around 1976, a Black girl alone couldn't gain entry into such places.

At the Players Ball. I was so excited to be going at the time, though, looking back, it was the grimiest, most stupid bullshit. My pimp Sonny had broken my arm a few weeks earlier, so I put sequins over the cast. Because even with a broken arm my goal was to be cute.

When tricks get caught with us, the police don't dare take them to jail, they take us to jail. Cause we're "the problem." Black women are the PROBLEM. Not this white guy from Skokie or Wilmette, or wherever.

COOK COUNTY
SHERIFF'S POLICE DEPT.

0·7·3·6·7·5·1·0·1·1·'94

COOK COUNTY
SHERIFF'S POLICE DEPT.

0·7·3·6·7·5·1·0·1·1·'94

In California, what really saved my life was rolling with the Do-Low Crew. They were my family. I still see California Stephanie (left) and Jazzy (right).

I met Stephanie Daniels-Wilson when I was in treatment in 1997 and my face was all messed up. She treated me like she already knew me. She quickly became my ride or die, my friend for life. A lot of times, when I tell my story, people don't believe it because so much happened. Stephanie believed me.

Stephanie and I started the Dreamcatcher Foundation because we wanted to help girls who were caught out there the way I was. *Dreamcatcher*, the documentary about me and the work we do, won a Sundance Award in 2015.

Here is when I decided Keith, who I married in 2005, was a keeper: I got sick and it was below zero outside. He didn't have a car but he walked to my house to bring me comfort food and medicine.

Jeremy was my little stinker. He was five years old when we adopted him.

When I think about it, God gave me three angels: Bree (left), Peaches (center), and Prune (right). In spite of my flaws, they were praying and rooting for me to come back to myself. For me to come back to love.

Surrounded by my loving family. It took so many arms reaching out to me to get me to this point. There are so many different ways women show their resilience. We can overcome things in life, such as molestation and sexual assault, that we too often keep inside. But even through the pain we still give love, we still nurture, we still provide. We stand STRONG. And we keep reaching out to uplift one another. That's a real woman. We persevere.

Chapter 9

Love in the Game

I got with Coolie, but he wasn't my pimp. He was just a brother in
the game. Didn't nobody know I was giving my money to Coolie,
because he didn't pull all that pimp nonsense. He was made, not
a pimp. He knew my thing was prostitution, but in our relationship
there was no shame in me being a prostitute. Prostitution was just
another kind of hustle, one he'd prefer me not be in on, but at the
end of the day, you got to do what you got to do. We got to get
money—that's the bottom line. We both understood you got to get
money. You can't leave your house every day and come back with
no money. It didn't stop him from loving me or feeling close to me.
It was a job. Still. Coolie wanted me to have different things to fall
back on. Nobody ever had just one trade. That was Coolie's thing.
He spent a lot of time picking my brain, trying to find out if I had it
in me to do other things. He used to tell me the game was so much
bigger than just prostitution.

He didn't want to be in the drug game. It was too dangerous, he said. But he knew all the other games that girls could get into. In his opinion, prostitution wasn't the only way for a girl to make money. He didn't look down on it, but I could do other things. As long as I got money, he was happy. He asked me did I know how to be a booster. He hooked me up with some major players who were confidence women and knew how to run a con game.

There was another game called creeping. Before hotels started using the cards to get into the rooms, there were keys. Mainly we would do Holiday Inns or the kind of hotels where businessmen were. We would pick the locks quietly while people were sleeping inside. Then we would crawl in the rooms, steal their briefcases and wallets. That was a whole profession, and we were called creepers.

Coolie put me with girls who were thieves; I learned how to steal. He would rather me be a thief, so I didn't have to use my body so much and deal with so many guys. For him, that was just a more dangerous lifestyle. So I became a good thief. There were times where I could go and actually peep out different places and tell Coolie about it. Sometimes I came home with no money. I tried and it didn't work out. He would ask me, "How did it go? What did you see?" He made me practice at home. We would lay in bed, and he would let me pick his pocket. "Oh, you so slow." We would play around the house, and I would try to pick his pocket without him knowing. I became very good at it. "You got my money, don't you?"

"Yup. I got it."

"That was good. That was a good one. I didn't feel it when you got it." I learned to walk up to a guy who was intoxicated at the bar and pick his pocket. I was really good if I was in a car with a guy. Coolie was a brother who knew how to work a scenario: like, one time, I took a pimp's money and his jewelry. We had smoked a joint and we drank some Dom Perignon. I took care of the business and he fell out. I took his money while he was asleep. But. There I was with his money and his jewelry. Nice stuff. Diamonds, gold chains. So what was I going to do? I called Coolie, and he said, "Get a cab. Right now." I got a cab to his house, got some cold jewelry, and I never heard anything else about it. Not because I got a break or I got lucky and didn't bump into the wrong people. It's just that when the pimp woke up, he thought, "Man, I just messed with Coolie's girl." That alone made a lot of nonsense disappear. Coolie used to tell me, "You got to learn who is out there." I was just out there, young and a cutie pie. Seventeen years old. I was infatuated with anything that made me look good and feel good. I *wanted* something good.

Coolie was the first brother who could do that for me. Before, I had met assholes who only thought about using me for their benefit. Nobody before Coolie had thought there could be benefits all around. When I was young, I would walk down Madison Street and cause pure collisions. And I was gassing myself with it. I was having a ball. "Oh, look at that." The men I started attracting didn't know what to do with me.

Let me show you what I mean. I had been with Coolie for almost a year when I figured out I made more money going out to Rush Street at lunch and meeting a guy by chance than I did on the streets. Rush Street is where all the money is. I was at this place called Magic Pan and I was eating crepes. I was down there with a stewardess girl who was my friend, and I was down there just kicking it. This white guy kept passing by our table, and he kept winking. Handsome white guy. I went into the bathroom, and when I looked up, he was coming into the bathroom with me. He came in right behind me. He said, "Girl, you fine as hell."

I started laughing. "Thank you."

He said, "You want some blow?"

"Maybe a little bit." You know, back in the day, dudes had coke on 'em all the time. It was polite business to do a little coke with them. Being out there was the first time I really did cocaine. And I wished I had never tried it, because I liked it. It didn't make me sick. All that other stuff, the heroin and syrup, made me sick. So I didn't ever do them more than once. But cocaine? I liked. We were in the bathroom, and he took the coke spoon out.

"Here have some," so I took a little toot. "So are you here with your friend?"

"Yeah, that's Ducky." Her real name was Vivian, but we all called her Ducky and Ducky was a Pan Am ho. Spoke five languages. Fluently. She flew all over the world on Pan Am. That was when there was money in the sky, baby. She had an apartment in Paris, and she had an apartment in New York. She had a house in Chicago. She was a well-kept bitch. Nice little tight body. Educated. She took me to see people. Entertainers, baseball players, folks like that. Ducky took me to my first millionaire party. There was this diplomat from Lagos, Nigeria, throwing the party. We stayed in the Waldorf Astoria, kicking it. Frank Sinatra was up there staying on a whole floor. I kept punching the elevator to Frank's floor, and his bodyguard kept punching me back down, "Sorry, can't let you in." I'm like, "Tell Frank I said hi." That guard was cracking up. He thought I was so cute.

Ducky and me, we were kicking it so hard, I got ten thousand dollars off that Nigerian diplomat. But he was crude, a chauvinist type, arrogant son of a bitch. He had a big Johnson, but he didn't know what to do with it, and if he didn't watch out, he could end up messing a girl up. I had to *whoa, whoa* him. He was having sex with me like he was angry at me. You know dudes sometimes want to have sex with you to see if they can hurt you? Talking about, "I'm gone tear this pussy up." Then they end up messing up your coot. I had enough sense not to let some dude ride me like that. I was like, "Whoa. You too rough."

He was getting frustrated, but I still needed this money. So I pulled a slip on him. I said, "Come on, let's do it doggy style."

"Huh. How you do that?" So, I showed him how to do it doggy style. I can control that junk better doggy style. When they get me from the back, I can control how much he put into me. I direct my muscles and everything to keep him in place. First of all, when he goes in from the back, he has to go through booty and thigh, and that's a lot before he can get to my vagina. I can control some of the shaft length I have to take. I had learned to control tricks from hurting me. Some of these assholes wanted to throw my legs up that away. I'd have female troubles for two weeks, hurting. So I learned what to do.

You have to know I didn't go to that party as a prostitute. I went there as Ducky's friend, and they thought I was a daycare teacher. They wanted to give me money because I told them I needed a car to get to work. I was living with Coolie, but I was in places all over Chicago, meeting all kinds of tricks. Doing all sorts of things.

Downers weren't my thing. Alcohol didn't work with me. I didn't like the drunk feeling. The buzz is okay, but being very drunk? No. I couldn't be sloppy. But coke? Yes, please. I think I took to cocaine so well because I had been taking the diet pills. There was a time when you could take diet pills like M&M's. Doctors gave prescriptions for diet pills like candy. I mean, everybody was focused on the downers and heroin, but any doctor would give you diet pills. First I took them because they kept me up, and then they cut my appetite and I needed to stay beautiful and slim. I lived in two different worlds. In the Black community, the guys liked women who had a big booty, little waist, all that was popping in the neighborhood. But when I got around white people? I had to be slim. I could have my curves, but I had to be tight. White boys used to be intimated with too much booty. You needed just enough. So I had to bring it down to compete. I had it just right. Not too much, not scary. Just a nice young ass. *Pow-dow.* At one time, I got my waist down to twenty-two. Everything was tight. So when I tried that cocaine, it kind of coincided with what I was doing with the diet pills. It gave me a euphoria, and when I did it, it made me think I knew everything. When I snorted a line of coke, all of a sudden I got brilliant. "Well, you know the Dow Jones average . . ." I talked my ass off. I was making my tricks laugh with all this outrageous conversation I threw at them.

Like the guy who I met at the crepe place, the white guy. He was in my life for many, many years.

His name was Leonard Weinstein. Lenny had a vision. Bucktown,

West Loop, all that area, he started putting money in houses down there years ago, in the seventies. He kept telling me, one day, this all be worth a lotta money. He was going to work, and you could see all the potential in the real estate he invested in. He had a vision—and he had cocaine and a whole lotta money. I could go to his house and get cocaine and money from him when I went to his house. I went to his house to get rejuvenated, and everything was high-end. When I came back to Chicago many years later, all that area was way up there, so I know he got his money's worth. If drugs didn't take him out, he got his money. He made money, and then he would have the urge to do drugs, and he would call me. There was a white middle-age woman who he was with from time to time. He brought me and her in the office, and he talked her into having a threesome with me. He gave me some dope I never had before to get high on, so I was sitting up there stupid. He was the only trick I used to get stupid with, because he always made sure I got home and I got my money and everything I wanted from him. I remember one time he gave me some kind of drug, and we all sitting at the table slumped over, mouths open, looking at each other, talking about, "I love you."

"I love you, too."

"You're great!!" We were sitting at the best table at this high-end restaurant bar, and we were all falling into each other. "I love you!" I couldn't go to the bathroom by myself. "Take me to the bathroom, I gotta pee."

"Okay, okay."

When I went home, it took the whole next day to get off that stuff. I don't know what he gave me, but damn it, it had me high, paralyzed, and in love.

Of course, he had some freak in him. Lenny liked some weird shit, but it feels unfair to get into it here, because he was important to me, and he was a kind man. And brilliant, and maybe his brilliance drove him to a level of craziness. I don't know. I do know that no one was getting hurt.

Most of the time I was high with Lenny, and because he was so good to me, I was always kinda down with what he was doing. Yes, the weird part was weird. But most of the time, I was laughing my ass off, shouting, "We're all in love!" Whatever we were doing, I was in love with. It was some seventies nonsense; everybody in love. But at the end, before everything was shut down, before the last person left, it was my job to get Lenny completely off the way he wanted to. That was what he was really paying me for. And the man paid me a lotta money.

So I was happy. I was living with Coolie. The kids were with Ma'Dea. I went and visited my girls every weekend. Peaches was a beautiful little girl. Prune just made me smile for no reason. Coolie went over to my grandmother's house and met my babies and my grandmomma. Coolie told her, anything she needed, she would have. "These babies ain't gone be over here without nothing."

I worked or went out, but Coolie went out and hustled, too. We both would put the money we made in the top drawer in a dresser in the bedroom. If I needed grocery money, I took it out of the drawer. If Coolie needed the rent money, he took it out of the drawer. In the game, it was like we were a married couple. He went over my grandmother's house and gave them money, went grocery shopping for her. He had a daughter named Tonya. Coolie would take out Tonya, Prune, and Peaches for the day. I looked up, and Coolie had taken them to Six Flags Great America and come back. He was a good-ass person.

We were good people in a bad situation, but we weren't bad people. We had great intentions, and we were trying to sustain a relationship, a romance, a lifestyle, a home. Coolie brought me stability. He taught me how to take a bath. My idea of taking a bath was run the water, hop in, soap up, splash the water around, then get out. Coolie said, "You not taking a bath right."

"What do you mean?"

"Baby. You get in the tub and you get yourself wet. You need two towels. One for your face and one for your body. You take your body towel and soap it up real good. Then *stand* up in the tub and scrub your body all over. And then turn on the shower and rinse yourself off real good." Otherwise, I would be sitting in dirty water. I came from the slums. We didn't have showers when I was growing up. We had tubs and a sink. He brought colognes into my life. He used to go downtown to Marshall Field's and pick me out nice colognes. Or take me down there to get a makeover. He sent me to the beauty shop. He told me I shouldn't just do wigs. "Go get your real hair done." He called the boosters over. At that time, if you were in the game, you didn't go to stores to shop unless you went and had an outfit tailor-made. If you wanted clothes off the rack, you called professional thieves who we called boosters. They came over your place and brought all of your clothes to you in your size. Coolie bought everything they had for me. Whatever they had in my size was mine. He bought by the bulk. "Give me everything you got for her in her size."

Sometimes I didn't even know if I liked the dress or not. But it was in my closet. I had outfits that were so expensive, I hadn't realized it until later on. I'd walked by Barneys and be like, "Damn, I got that on a hanger." I had alligator shoes. Coolie kept me pretty. And that was when my body was at its peak. I was still making the cars run off the road.

Coolie and I were together for seven years. But then the relationship started getting rocky. I used to run away from Coolie sometimes. I didn't know why. Or maybe I did. I was young, and Coolie wasn't the only guy who liked me. I was still that person who wanted to be loved by everybody. And there were a bunch of guys trying to get me to be their girl. There were other places that sounded so interesting to me. I always had my kids and I had to make a decision when it came to them, but running away let me forget about it for a while. I let myself think I was running to some get-rich-quick scheme, and I would drop off a heap of money. If that worked out, that would change the game. Right? If I ran away and found a pile of gold, I could be a better mom or stay at home with them. If I ran away and I found the end of the rainbow, maybe I could have a baby by Coolie and not have to work the streets. But that never worked out. I would always come right back home, but I ran away to places where I had no business being. Sometimes I got myself in a situation and I was scared to go home. I would get with a guy, just partying with them and kicking it, and then the guy would want to be my man. They'd want to talk it out with Coolie. He can't do that. He'd get us both killed. I liked the party favors. But I liked home back with Coolie, too. I'd meet new people and they'd be interesting, but more than once I stayed past my expiration date.

Coolie did his own thing sometimes, too. Made me angry. Everybody knew we were together, but both of us had relationships outside. But the rule was: don't bring nobody home. Like one time I was out of town working, and I came home and he had this young girl in bed with him. He knew I was on my way home. And to top it off, this was a girl he went to school with. She was a square. She wasn't even from the streets. He wanted me to see it.

Nobody was a saint. He was drifting and so was I. But I think I destroyed it more than anything because I was young and impressionable. There was a whole world out there. Sometimes I got locked up and went to jail, and I met hos who said they worked up in New York and there was a lotta money there. They went to Florida and there was money there, too. I started thinking to myself, why am I just working in Chicago? Because I was actually running out of Chicago space to work. When I say I ran out of Chicago space to work, I mean I could go from one side of the city to the other and get paid, but eventually, working on a regular basis, I got to be known as a prostitute. When I came up on a scene, the police were like, "Go home or go to jail." And I had to challenge them because I hadn't made money yet. Back then I kept bond money on me. That way, if I went to jail before the night was over, I bailed myself right back out and went back to work.

But I wanted to get on the highway, too. I wanted to get on the road and make money, maybe rob up on some big money, then come back home and chill. I wanted to explore other cities I had heard about. I was infatuated by the world. I wanted to go and see what it was all about.

So I stole a credit card from a trick, and I went to New York. Caught an airplane, got me a room at the Sheraton on Lexington Avenue, and had plans to stay because I just wanted to see what New York, New York, was like. As soon as I got there, I called Coolie and cussed him out. "Screw you and your socks. I don't care about you and your toes, my friend. Yeah. I'm in New York, so take that. You can't do nothing about it." I was in New York and he was in Chicago, so I was saying things I wouldn't normally say. I was just giving it to him. "You ain't shit, my love. Screw you in your nose. You can't do nothing about it." I was talking slick shit.

All Coolie kept saying is, "Yeah. Yeah? Yeah. Gone talk that shit, girl."

And I was like, "Yeah! You think I'm playing. I'm gone find me somebody else. We gone set it off. 'Round the world."

I hung up the phone and stepped out into the city. New York was sweet as hell to me. Everybody says New Yorkers are standoffish and mean, but that ain't true. Everybody's about welcome over there. I went to Studio 54. Hung out for two days with Boz Scaggs and all his boys. They treated me like a kid sister. I went to a place called Leviticus and danced all night with Joe Frazier. The guys I met were superfine. New York had so many nationalities, the melting pot there was amazing. In Chicago, we are kind of Irish, Italian, Black, Hispanic, Puerto Rican, Polish people. You go to New York and you have Hungarian, Gypsies, people from places you never heard the goddamned name of. A lot of Dominicans looked Black, but they weren't. Fine-ass men named Jesús, and they look like Jesus, cause they so beautiful. Men with pretty eyes and long hair and pockets full of ounces of cocaine.

Sometimes they pulled out so much cocaine I got scared. "Wait a minute. I know we going to jail. You be the FBI or something? Something is going off here and I can't stand it. Why is everybody got everything?" New York had after-hour sets that never closed. We had after-hour sets in Chicago, but not posted up like this, where they were social clubs and I could just walk in there any time of day and just get any goddamned thing I wanted. That was what New York was doing to me. I was from Chicago; my eyes were popped out. About a week into being there, I was the social butterfly of the whole set. I went up to Harlem, I was out everywhere. I done found a dude. I mean, he was square, but he took me to all the places to impress me. I was meeting everybody. I had been in New York for about three weeks and I was having a ball. So one night I came back to my hotel and who was sitting in the lobby? Coolie! You could have knocked me over with a feather. I was done, cook me.

He walked up to me. "Just keep on walking; let's go up to your room." I didn't say anything. I had my mouth open, but nothing came out. Yup. I mean, he just came to take me home. "You had a lot to say, didn't ya?" I was thinking to myself, *Yes, I did, and as soon as I have the chance, I'm gone have a lot more to say.* On the ride up the elevator, I kept thinking—what was he gone do, what he gone do? But he smoothed me out, and we stayed up in the room for two more days, just having insane sex.

"I missed you, Daddy."

We went back to Chicago. But he now knew I wanted to travel. He got it. He told me, "Go work your way to work."

"Work my way to work?"

"Yeah, work your way to work, then come back home." He said, "You know how to do whatever you want to do."

At first, I got angry. Work my way to work? But then the concept made sense. If I wanted to go to New York, then I needed to work my way to New York. Hadn't he taught me how to steal wallets? What was keeping me from stealing a credit card and going straight to the airport? At that time, it was easy to hop on a plane. You could be Mrs. Applebottom. Nobody was checking. And then once I was wherever I wanted to be, what was stopping me from snatching another card and getting back home? It's all about the hustle. I was thinking traveling was this big thing I had to do, but Coolie told me it was simple. It's all about work. I could add more money to the drawer; I could make a good life somewhere with Peaches and Prune. And I could see the world.

That's how I ended up in places. Plane, train, kite, bike, any kind of way I could get there, I would get there. Wherever the wind blew was cool with me. And one place could lead to another. Like, I was downtown Chicago, working on Rush Street. I crossed the street to the Marriott right there, one block from Michigan. Beautiful Marriott. There was a big superbus sitting up in front of it. Inside were the Harlem Globetrotters. I knocked on the door of the bus. "Hey!"

The bus driver opened it and said, "It's a pretty girl out here!"

I was like, "Where are the Harlem Globetrotters?"

From the inside I heard, "Here we are, baby." I saw Curly and that was it. I started kissing on him and hugging him. He was very handsome, with the biggest smile. We started talking right in front of the bus. He was hugging me back, and he invited me up to his room.

"Sure." I sat down, and I had these big sunglasses on because Coolie had hit me in the eye. I had done the best I could covering up with makeup, but I still needed the sunglasses to hide the bruise.

Curly said, "Relax. You can take your sunglasses off."

"I'm cool."

"You can take your glasses off." He came over to me and gently slid them off my face. "Wow," he said, kneeling down in front of me. "Who did that to you? When I see a woman's face like that, I get upset by it. I got something for a guy who treats a woman like that. I hate men who do women like that." I started to cry. "Don't cry. Just relax. Women shouldn't be treated like that." He got up and went to

the bathroom to run me a bath. I think he was trying to cheer me up.
It worked. We talked for a long time. Late into the night. He ordered
room service. He even listened to me talk about Coolie. I could feel
that he felt kind of bad that I had to go through it. He made me feel
so good. I stayed the night. It made me feel important. It wasn't so
much that he was a Harlem Globetrotter; he was a guy who was so
cool and understanding. It was like I had stepped out of one world
and stepped into another. I had stepped out of my chaotic lifestyle and
stepped into a moment a peace. And I stayed for it.

Every time we met, it was always the same. We always had a great
time together. He was a good person and so beautiful. We became
friends. We laughed together a lot. I had been treated like a queen
before, but Curly was a gentleman. He didn't care about the lady of
the night in me. He was like, "I just feel like women should be treated
properly." He put me in his bathtub, bathed me, pampered me. He was
very old-school. I mean, I got my money, but he was just a honeybee.

He told me, "If I'm ever anywhere, this is the name I use and
these are the hotels where I stay at. So if you hear that the Globetrotters are in New York or California, here's the alias that I use." I met
up with Curly all over the country. We had a real nice relationship.

✦ ✦ ✦

Those are the kinds of opportunities I ran into. Back in the day, it
was easy to get to celebrities. It was all about being in the right place
at the right time. About what you know and who you know. Like
when I had my huge twenty-first birthday, a little while before I met
Curly. Finally, I was twenty-one. I was grown. It was a big deal to
me. We had the party at one of Coolie's friends' lounges, and all the
players came—Bishop Wine, Big Al, Schooldolie—all the big guys
in Chicago came, and the guys from out of town came to this super
after-hours party.

Even though I didn't realize it, I was outgrowing my relationship
with Coolie.

I was still Mrs. Coolie, but some people were laughing at me.

Coolie was stepping out on me and not making a secret about it. I didn't know that then, but later on I figured it out. There was this girl named Joyce, and when I was gone, Coolie was always over her house. And when I was home, I was getting high. Coolie was also having his way with her sister. He got Joyce's sister pregnant. With twins. I found out about it and confronted him. He hit me in my eye that day. Just like any man. He had never done that before.

Things just started to get really weird around us and our relationship. Some of his friends were coming at me. I didn't think about it at the time, but some of them were doing that because they knew more of what was going on with Coolie than I did. Around the neighborhood, it used to be, "Don't mess with that girl. That's Coolie's woman. He'll mess your ass up about that girl." But that didn't happen anymore, so things were probably happening that I didn't know about. Our business got out on the street. He was hooking up with squares. Maybe he was talking to people. I don't know. Maybe people were telling him things that I was doing. I was hanging out with drug dealers, hanging out with pimps. Things started to shake.

Then he started to ask me to bring other girls to him. And I was doing it to please him, but he was trying to replace me. We were just falling apart. I got this dude, Ricky, Pretty Ricky, out of spite. He was light-skinned and was about six-two. We used to call him Pretty Ricky because he used to wear "man makeup." Ricky was a real punk. Coolie called him one day and told him to come over there so he could talk to him like a man. I told Ricky, "You going over there? And you gone take me with you?" I didn't want to go. This was a trap. Coolie wanted us to meet at his friend Art's place. And Art's ex-police. When I walked in there and saw Coolie and Art and Connie, who was this really tall pistol-toting bitch who would shoot anything, I knew exactly what was happening. We were about to get our ass whooped. Coolie hit me first, and then he pulled a pistol on Ricky and said, "Where that money she gives you?" This stupid asshole had the nerve to have the money on him. Coolie took the money, robbed him, beat me up, and put both of us out. But I had hurt Coolie. So I hid out on the North Side, and Ricky got me a little apartment. I was really trying not to run into Coolie. But Coolie ran into Ricky again, and Coolie beat him up at a crap game.

I figured it wouldn't be long before Ricky ran away from me. I thought, *He gone get enough,* cause everybody was intimidated by Coolie. Very few men were on his level.

I was looking for help and bumped into Boony Black. This guy was a big name in Chicago. Coolie had said that I couldn't have another man in Chicago, so just to show Coolie he couldn't boss me around, I started running with this gangster named Boony Black. Boony Black was a killer. He wasn't intimidated by Coolie. In fact, he might have been a little more dangerous. I'm glad that it never came to that, to see who could be the most dangerous about me. I don't know what would have happened then. Boony Black liked me, but just as a person. He didn't want to be with me, he was just a good guy. But I was under Coolie's brand, and Coolie made it clear that I couldn't get with nobody in Chicago. I had no choice but to travel.

It took me a while to stop talking about Coolie, to stop thinking about him. I didn't even know I was doing it until one guy said, "Man. Please don't say nothing about that man no more. You talk about Coolie all the time."

I was still stuck there, but once I got on the road, it felt like a whole new world for me. I was meeting new people. I came back to New York for a year. For a minute in New York I didn't prostitute. I was kind of like with this dude, that dude. And I bartended. Ran into a lot of celebrities. Had a relationship with a woman, this girl named Annie. I was with her for a little bit. I never knew if anybody was gay or straight. I never had a choice to pick what I wanted to do. That was taken. Most of the things I did was survival.

I left New York and went straight to Philly. Philly to New Jersey. Ohio, Pittsburgh. I hit all the East Coast spots. And all during that time I had a safe space up in Canada. Sault Ste. Marie, Canada. It was right on the border of Michigan, but it was Canadians who came to the whorehouse. It was Canadian money we made. This was my safe place because it was in God's country. It wasn't a legal whorehouse, but you could go up there and hide from the police for years. The girl who ran the place, her man used to gamble with Coolie, and he was the one who told me about it. He told me if I ever needed to lay low, I should come up there. His name was MD. Serious white folks who had never did anything lived up there in this little small town. The whorehouse was part of the town culture. And they knew, if you were a Black girl, you were coming up to the whorehouse. I didn't even have to tell the cab where to take me; he knew. Laughing all the way.

They set it up in this town that we had to go and see the doctor every two weeks. I mean prostitution is prostitution, but everybody needed to be safe. That was mandated. You went to the doctor and got checked for STDs, got your blood work, got your diet pills.

I sent back as much money as I could to Ma'Dea and the girls. When I was with Coolie, I would see the girls every weekend, but when I was traveling, seeing them often became a struggle.

Once, I had to deal with these crooked-ass cops; they were selling drugs. And they were a part of a drug ring called Market 10. Big scandal. This one time, they came up to our house on Ohio when I had just got out the bathtub and I had my bath towel wrapped all around me. I glanced out the window, and I saw a cop car outside our place. I went to the back, and I saw them sliding up. They seriously thought they sneaking. They all got guns. It was summertime, so our back door was cracked open, but Coolie had bars on the doors and had everything locked down. I looked at them and said, "What?"

"Open up the door."

I said, "I can't."

"Why?"

"I don't have the key."

"Open the door, smartass."

"No. You got a warrant?"

"Naw."

"Well, then, break that door down, then. Do what you got to do."

I was always told by Coolie, don't let the police in, let them break in. I walked away from the back door and put my clothes on. It took them a minute to take the bars off the doors. I was dressed, and I called Coolie and told him, "The police at the house. I'm going to call you back." Coolie had guns everywhere. They were pulling out these guns. So they were going to take me to jail. But I wasn't worried. First of all, my name was not on the lease. Second of all, screw them. They asked me questions, and I said I had no idea what they were talking about. "I'm a prostitute. The only thing I'm doing bad is right here. See this?" I pointed at my honeypot. "That's my pistol."

So they came out. "Ah, ah. This gun shot a state trooper. In Indiana. It's a hot gun!"

I said, "Okay. Well. Do I look like I go on capers and shoot folks? I mean, really, come on now." So they were like, she ain't gone give us nothing. And they were right about that. "Can y'all please give me a bond on whatever you trying to give me? Cause ain't none of this stuff mine. This not my house."

Finally, after they did every intimidating thing they could do to me, the sergeant walked up and said, "Her bond is posted. You got to let her go."

Even though this was the end of the relationship, I still felt Coolie had raised me right. Don't ever say nothing. If y'all gone pull guns on me, so what? I was willing to go the whole roll. I'd never tell on Coolie. He was my man.

Part IV

Running

Chapter 10

Chi Town's Finest

I was working my way to work, and I was situating. Ma'Dea was doing okay. She knew I was out there. She accepted it. It wasn't like she liked it, but it was something she felt she couldn't do anything about. Her baby was pretty much out there. And she damn sure was going to hold on to her great-grandbabies. I remember once, I had been out there for two nights, partying. I was still with Coolie then, but I didn't want to go home to him, because, I don't know, I had been out there kicking it with a dude. So I went over to Ma'Dea's to lay down. I'm dead tired. But early, early in the morning she said, "Get up."

"Get up?"

"You can't be here when the girls wake up." I was upset with her because she was putting me out, but I also remember how my babies looked at me every time I left. *Is Momma gone stay or is she gone go?* My babies were lost, I could see it in their eyes. I was lost, too. My little girls were thinking, *I want Mommy to stay but she gone go.*

Prune, my eldest, was four and really feeling the pain. And Peaches was taking care of Prune, even though she was the baby. Prune would just lose it when I left. I never knew when I was coming back.

Coolie would drop off money to Ma'Dea, but he was in and out and nothing was steady. I wasn't able to control any of my situations. That was how it was with us. I kept hoping that one of these days, I was going to be a momma who knew when she was coming and going. But how could I be a better momma and stay in the game? I needed peace and quiet to figure that out. So I ran off to Canada.

One day, Coolie called me. Madame Lisa got the message. She came to me, "He called for you and wants you to come down."

"You know why he wants me?"

"I don't know. Maybe because you ain't making the money fast enough."

"Maybe. It could be anything, right?" I packed and left straight for the airport. I couldn't figure it out, but I didn't think I was going to get the news I got.

It was morning when I got to Coolie's. He had been drinking, and he looked at me and said, "Ma'Dea dead." That wasn't the best way he could have said it, but I think he didn't know how to give me that news. My grandmother was gone. My girls, who were just five and six years old, had found her on the floor of the dining room. There was a trail of shit from the bathroom to where she had fallen.

When my aunt called, my girls picked up the phone.

"Where Ma'Dea at?"

"Ma'Dea dead! Ma'Dea!" they shouted.

"Quit playing, put your granny on the phone."

"Ma'Dea!" My grandmother was a pillar of strength. She was in her late fifties, tops. I lost it.

There was a funeral.

After Ma'Dea died, everything changed. Everybody just assumed I was going to take care of my kids. But at twenty-one, I needed help, but I didn't know how to say that. I wanted somebody to say, "Let me help you." I brought the kids home, into the life that Coolie and I had. He started staying away from the house more. And I didn't want him to stay away. But he did. It was a different life now.

The girls spent a lot of time over my dad's house. I was always dropping them off so I could go to work. But sometimes I wouldn't go to work because I would look in their eyes and see they needed me to be there. But even when I was there, I was screwed up. I was torn up inside. It was too much. All that was too big for a little girl like me. It was a lot of big stuff going on. I was twenty-one, but I wasn't twenty-one, you know what I mean?

I loved my daughters, but I just didn't know how to deal with the responsibility of two children. I look at it now, and I see I could have gotten on welfare, on public aid. I could have gotten my rent and everything, because they were doing that then. I could have gotten food stamps. I probably could have gotten some good-ass job, because they were giving jobs to single moms. Some of them have even retired from them jobs they had up there in City Hall. All those good little clerk jobs. I could have done something like that. But I was enmeshed in street life.

I knew people who had kids in the street life, and I had always thought, *That isn't gone be me.* But this was a rollback that I wasn't prepared for at all. I was not prepared to be a mom, so I half-assed raised my own kids. Life was trying to make me ready, and I wasn't ready. I was making some bad mistakes with my kids because I was grieving. I didn't realize I was grieving like I was. My grandmother was dead and buried.

Nowadays, Peaches and Prune go and visit her, but I don't. I visit her in my own way. I talk to her from time to time in my mind. I look in the mirror, and I see her in my face. Sometimes I hear her say shit she definitely used to say. It took years and years, but I finally understand her. She was a woman who was abused, too. And because of that, she became an abuser. I understand her being frustrated with me; I understand how life frustrated her. She was a woman who worked hard as hell all her life and all she had to show for it was the bare minimum. She was a woman who made lemonade out of lemons. That's what she did. She was an excellent homemaker. We would go into these hole-in-the-wall shit apartments and Ma'Dea would turn it into a home. But that's what I know now. Back then, I was clueless.

My girls started going back and forth from my house to my daddy's. I went on the road. There was a hardness between me and Coolie. I started snorting cocaine a lot. That became my downfall. I was running.

I was getting cocaine from everywhere. This was the party scene now. It was disco and cocaine. I had customers who were on the stock market; they always kept cocaine and marijuana. White people were having so much cocaine, and I was dating customers from the street who always had these party favors. They gave me cocaine along with giving me money. They would give me money and then lay out these lines of cocaine. Folks were wearing the gold coke spoons around their necks with the shirts all open and the disco suits. That was what was going on. Everybody wanted a bunch of pretty girls on their arm and their little buddy cocaine in their pockets. "We'll go here and do that and toot to the highest and have some fun." Nobody was saying, let's go home and be responsible. I used to be that person who went to work and came back home. Real responsible shit. The only way I didn't come back home was if I was in jail, and if I was in jail, well, eventually I'd get out, cause at a certain time they just released you.

But the cocaine changed all that. With cocaine, there was a euphoria, but when you came down, you crashed, and when I crashed, I couldn't deal with kids. So I was neglecting my kids, and they were being left with everybody, and they were everybody else's responsibility. It's a blessing they are still intact, because I lived a life where my kids could have been my collateral damage. I'm so glad that God and my momma up there were looking out for me.

I did some dumb shit. If there was dumb shit to do, I would do it. I would get myself into a fix, and my brothers would come and rescue me. I would call them and say, "This guy got me and won't let me go blah, blah, blah."

"Where you at? Just tell us where you at."

One time, I had told this guy I would deal his drugs and I would give him his money later. When it was time to pay the piper, I didn't have the money and I was sitting up there looking stupid. The dealer sitting up there talking about how he gone mess me up. I told him, just let me make a phone call. I told him I was calling for some money, but I was calling my brothers.

A little later, my brothers knocked on the door, and the dealer was like, "Yo, who at the door?" There were some words and then there was a kick in the door, and my brother had the sawed-off shotgun and put everybody on the floor.

My brother told the dealer, "You just let her go." My brother Terry, who is in jail in California, wanted to put everybody down, and my other brother was like, "Naw, man, we didn't come here for all that." But that was what type of guy my brother Terry was. Terry took some convincing. "Man, let's kill these niggas. *Come on.*"

My other brother was like, "Man, we didn't come to kill these niggas, we just came to get our sister."

I drifted. I had this white guy, this trick Jack, who wanted to marry me. Had I been a little bit more mature, that woulda been a good way to get my kids back, have a nice home, and lay back and be taken care of. Instead, I didn't have time for Jack. I let Coolie's other girl date him. I left Chicago, and she ended up marrying that dude, and he sent her to nursing school, and when he died, he left her all his money. But that wasn't mine; that wasn't me. Guys would want to make a ho into a housewife, but I wasn't ready. And when my ho friends got married to these tricks, they wouldn't talk to me anymore. I thought to myself, *Bitch, if it wasn't for me, you wouldn't be where you at. Look at you with your stanking ass. You keep him.*

Jack was crazy about me. Jack married her because I didn't have enough sense to keep him. All the pain, all the molestation, all the beatings that had come to me way too early in my life, I was just a ball of confusion walking around. To look at me, you would think I had it all together. But my life was so jumbled and chaotic and crazy,

I couldn't make a clear choice if my life depended on it because nothing was clear. All I was thinking about was running. Running from Chicago. Running from Coolie. Running from the responsibilities of my kids. Running. Running from Ma'Dea's death. Running. Not thinking of the collateral damage I left behind. The conditions that my kids were living in. I was running from my life. Let's face it, whatever Ma'Dea was, she was a crutch for me. She had my back; she had my slack. She wasn't going to allow me to drag my babies around from pillar to post. Now that she was gone, that was exactly what I did to them. Some days it would hurt me to know that she was right about me. She used to say, "Girl, if I wasn't here, you would drag these babies around from pillar to post, Brenda Jean."

"Naw, I wouldn't." But she knew that I would.

That's when my cocaine started getting out of control. Before that, I could take it or leave it. Now getting high was the thing I wanted to do best, as opposed to being a good ho, a good lady. I was just another bitch out here. My kids were around me, but I didn't hear them. I would see them, but I was disconnected. I tried to transition away from Coolie, I tried to transition away from Ma'Dea's death. But I just couldn't. Every time I looked at my babies, I saw pain. What am I supposed to do with these kids? I couldn't bring them back over with me and Coolie. They were an interruption into his lifestyle, too. Driving a Cadillac, he was getting a lot of attention from girls. They all knew about me, and I still had my position, but I was losing it. I knew the slip was coming.

Even now, all these years later, I can find myself scratching at some old pain that won't leave me alone. I'll ask my daughters about it, but their memories are so different from mine. "I don't remember nothing special. I just thought Coolie was your boyfriend. He had a daughter that he used to bring over. I would cry really hard when you would leave and Peaches would calm me down." (Coolie had a daughter, but her momma was a dope fiend, so he had his baby over at his sister's house.)

I can't help it; I scratch at another memory. "I liked being over

Uncle Jethro's house because they treated us like their kids." My babies. My sweet babies, is that all you can conjure up from that time? "Coolie never said much. Laid-back." And? "You used to have clients come to the house. Sometimes you would leave town. I remember my grandfather came and got us one time. I don't remember much. I don't remember talking to Coolie."

When I step back and think about it, I realize God blessed my two girls and let them only remember what was harmless in their childhood, that their adult lives wouldn't have anything awful snatching them out of their dreams. "A lotta stuff I blocked out, Momma. I blocked my feelings out." I listen to my babies, and think there is a God and He loves me and mine. He knew only His love and grace could help my girls put head to pillow and sleep through the night.

Even when I try to give myself comfort with all of that, when I talk to them, it is hard to hear because I wanted to be a good person. I wanted to be a good mother but I didn't know how. I was supposed to protect these two kids, but because of the life I was leading, they needed to look after each other. And they did. They are as close today as they were when they were little kids, and Peaches will tell you that. Peaches will tell you, "I never fought. I never had a fight cause my sister fought for me." Prune did all the fighting. If you wanted to mess with Peaches, you had to go through Prune. Even when I came back into their lives, if Prune thought I was stepping out, she would tell me off. She was protecting Peaches because they didn't know if I was going to stay or go or what motivated me to come back into their lives.

They are like two big sisters to each other. My granddaughter Mimi has two mothers; she doesn't have a mother and an aunt. That's the way they take care of their kids, that's the way they take care of each other, and that's a blessing. I have a picture of them holding on to each other, and you can see everything in that picture. Prune is the taller one, and she's looking down at her sister, and you can almost hear the expression on her face: "I got you." Their arms are on each other waists, but Peaches's eyes tell the whole story. "No, I'm gone take care of you." Kids shouldn't have to go through that.

It didn't help matters that my relationship with Coolie was falling apart. Coolie left me. I didn't leave Coolie. Coolie went and got another partner somewhere. Like I said, he had other interests. I was very hurt by it all. He was still dealing with me, but like I was an option and not a priority. I was his girl in name only. Everybody thought I was Coolie's girl, but he was gone by then. He was a selfish son of bitch by the end. I had brought him up, when he had two, three dollars in his pocket, and now he had a Cadillac. Bitches were all up in his face, and somebody had given him an opportunity to sell a lotta dope, so he had a lotta dope. Our relationship kept falling.

I left town to work, and when I came back, the apartment was gone and Coolie had given away all the furniture we had bought together. That's when I really started running.

I was able to get an apartment in Rick Miller's building. Rick Miller was a big drug dealer at that time. He was ex-police. He was selling a lotta drugs, and he had this building over there on Washington and Central, and I was the kind of girl Rick wanted to rent an apartment to. Pretty and young. I started going back and forth from Chicago to New York. Sometimes my kids were over at Rick Miller's building and sometimes they were over at my dad's. Sometimes I would just pick up and hop on a plane or a bus. And not just to New York. I traveled to Charleston, West Virginia, to a place where this guy named Wilson, Black guy, had these truck stops and whorehouses. I heard there was a lotta money there, so I went, and I made a nice amount of money, but I kept on running. I ran back to Chicago just to show Coolie I could.

That was the kind of dangerous game I was playing. I was just trying to survive one day at a time, trying to keep my head above water. Trying to outthink these fools, trying to stay one step ahead. Everywhere I went, I left collateral damage behind me. I just kept moving. Everybody was saying about me, "Yep. There go Brenda, I heard she done fucked up stuff again." And I felt it. Every time I left another place, it was because I had suffered a major failure and I had to get outta there or I had to leave in the middle of the night. I would choose a pimp and act as if I was going to stick there with them—getting high, having sex, being introduced to their street games—but even though I hadn't left yet, I was already out the door. I was burning bridges and damaging myself. It was a critical time. Good damn thing I moved on or snuck out in the middle of the night, cause if I hadn't, someone was going to really, really hurt me. I was playing games and just doing shit that could get a girl hurt, cause I was hurt. I was hurting.

Sometimes I would find somebody I liked. I had gone to Ohio to work, and I met this new guy, Ricky, who picked me up there and took me to Philly to work. I have his name tattooed on my butt. He was a real charismatic young boy, wore business suits even though he was a pimp. I became one of his ladies.

I remember being in Philly; this was around 1979, '80. I was working at the bar on North Tenth and Race. It was like a tavern, with barstools all around in a circle. It was a real dump, but I was making great money. We worked during the daytime, in the afternoon. We waited for the customers to come in. They knew that whatever girl you sat with was the girl you could buy. Girls couldn't leave the bar till the guy bought them a drink, and all the drinks cost ten bucks—if it was water or juice, it was ten bucks. That was all the bar asked for: ten dollars for a drink. Then hos took the trick, and we got all the money. I could get two, three hundred dollars per guy.

I would always take my tricks to my hotel over across the river in Camden because it was harder to get a hotel in the city. Camden was off the turnpike, and the city was broke and run-down, and that was the nicest hotel over there back then. It was right by one those silver diners. It had the worst food, raggedy-ass food, but they were open twenty-four hours.

I remember I had five, six thousand dollars holed up in my room. I was working and saving my money, sending the rest to my girls. But I was so lonely. New Year's Eve, I got through working and I came back to my hotel room because, you know, girls didn't work right up until midnight on New Year's Eve, because things get too rowdy, people get too drunk on New Year's Eve. They shoot on New Year's Eve!

I had a bottle of champagne, but I didn't have shit to do, so I went down to the desk. The desk guy knew me and I told him, "Well, we might as well toast it."

"Alright, well, look at that! That's some real champagne."

"Yeah, it is. Let's drink it up." He had this little TV and we toasted the New Year. We just kicking it and talking. But then he got real busy, and I said, "You want me to help you?"

"You can, if you want to."

The folks were coming in and were renting the rooms. Coming and having sex, and coming back out, so he was renting the rooms hourly. I would run up, tidy up the room, throw a new pillowcase on, run back down, and tell the desk man, "Now that's ready for another motherfucker." And that's how I spent one New Year's—kicking it with an old, bald-headed white man because I didn't want to be in my room by myself. I was so lonely.

At least when Ricky was in town, I didn't feel by myself. He was so tender. He was different. He made me feel good. He was giving of himself, not like the normal dudes who want to be ice-cold, and "bitch, this," "bitch, that." We were never like that.

Ricky had another lady who had been with him. All three of us used to have sex together, cause, you know, it felt good. But that was so unhealthy. I was covering up all the pain with the physical shit. With the money, with the sex, with the laughter and the instant shit that happens with you involved with those types of things. I was numb across the board. I was a zombie; the only thing I was good for was eating up the living.

+ + +

When I was with Ricky, I felt good. But he would leave me for two, three weeks at a time because I was supposed to be working. But that meant I was left to my own devices, and I was very lonely. I was a very good ho; I would do my work. I would get my money, put it up, come to my room, get me a little something to eat, sit up, and watch TV. And I would cry. I was grieving Ma'Dea; I was grieving Coolie. I really loved Coolie, and Coolie had quit me.

At that time, I contracted hep C. I was working at a massage parlor on Broad Street in Philadelphia. This guy named Bart was the manager. Bart shot up methamphetamines. I had never had that shit, and I remember the first time I ever did, I drank it. You could snort it; you could drink it; you could shoot it. I drank it in a soda, and it kept me hyped for like three days. I was like *zoom, zoom, zoom, zoom*. Which was okay by me because I could work at the massage parlor all night. Stayed up and got this money.

Bart saw that I didn't have a man—Ricky was out of town all the time—and I was free and loose and was game for anything. "Come with us," he told me.

Bart had a woman who looked like the walking dead. Everybody said, "She used to be beautiful." But she had been doing these methamphetamines with him and had turned into a creature feature. It didn't register with me that if I did that shit, that could be me one day. We went over there to his nice little apartment in a high-rise. Nice for a dope fiend. We sat in the middle of the floor. They were shooting up. So I stuck my arm out. Just that easy, just that quick. To look back on it, I didn't know shit about shooting. I used after both of them had used. You feel what I'm saying? They told me it was fine. "Oh, you just do it like this and like that. And then you just clean it up like this." Later on in my life, I found out about dirty needles. See, education wasn't out there like that. I let this dude stick me with a dirty needle. A hot needle, an on-fire needle. Needle was flaming, tower inferno. There were probably a hundred people who had used that needle before me, and I was sitting there with my arm stuck out. But I was in pain, and all I wanted was for the pain to go away. Of course, all I was good at was putting more on top of it.

Chapter 11

The Tricks of the Trade

After working the hotels, the bars, the streets, the brothels, the escort services, and the strip clubs, I noticed there was certain types of tricks. And I got them down to like six or so. There's the average drive-around-on-the-street trick, and that's one category. He has three or four subcategories of him, the street trick. There is the trick who rides around looking for girls for hours, maybe two, three hours, from destination to destination, from one area of prostitution to another, until he finds what he wants, and once he sees what he wants to pick up, he's got to play a game with her of riding around the block, unless he's already dated her and he knows her. He's doing that because he wants to make sure she's not a cop or he's trying to get a safe moment when he thinks she can jump in the car without anyone seeing her. And guess what? We play the game with him. We don't want nobody to see us either.

Then there's the second street trick, who becomes like the boyfriend, who puts you up, and you start to say, "He's my regular." We know on a Wednesday or a Thursday what time he's going to come around. It's like clockwork, it's unbelievable. You can depend on him more than you can depend on your own damn man. He's gonna show up.

And then there's the dangerous street trick who picks up girls to have sex with them and then wants to take his money back or beat the girl up. Whatever anger is on his back, he takes it out on you. Those are the dangerous ones. Those are the ones who come out for blood, and we try not to get in the car with them. We warn each other about those guys. Usually, when a girl gets hurt like that and she lives through it, even if she won't tell the police, she'll tell the other girls. "He was in a green Chevy; this is what he looked like. Look out for him; don't get in a car like that." If he's white or he's Black or he's Mexican, we are going to hear from the girls. I don't care what's going on out in the streets, we don't want another sister getting hurt.

Those are the street tricks.

Then there is a category on the escort side, from the strip club side, the type of trick who spends more money. They come in respectable and like gentlemen, trying to make jokes. Like I care. Trying to make light conversation and trying to be funny, but you don't care. You don't like him. In your heart, you're like, *You make me sick because I have to laugh with you and I don't want to.* But you have to be charming and shit like that.

Then there's that sugar-daddy trick who comes to see you, or you catch a taxi to go see him, and this man spends the night and you have to listen to his rhetoric. I mean, they are paying for it, but you have to listen to that shit *all night.* You usually dislike him the most, because it's not a quick wham-bam. I'm suffering listening to this bullshit all night, and I hate him right now, and I can't do anything about it because maybe he's given me half my money and I get the rest of it when I get ready to leave. If girls could get their money upfront, there would be a lot of tricks in trouble. We keep those tricks because when nothing is going on outside or there's a crisis, that's the trick you can call and who will drop off money to you without the sex. It's like a down payment on a pussy. And you hate that because you know when he calls you again, you've got to pay up.

Some tricks actually think you like them. They want you to tell them what great lovers they are, how good the sex was, and you have to sit there lying your ass off. You really want them to shut up and get out your face, but this is a part of your job and he thinks he is doing you a favor. I used to think to myself, *Is he really serious?* I'm on my knees and the whole thing is making me want to throw up.

Then there is the superior trick who talked to you like you are shit from the beginning. They stay on that flow, but they come and see you often, and they pay you very well. So you accept the grandiose look on their faces. Those types of tricks will look at you and say, "Get out. Leave. I'm done." And the same time, you are thinking to yourself, *He ain't shit either.* Most of them play a role with you and it gets deep. They get into the role until the orgasm is over, and then they turn into another person. You've got to be careful. See, because everything he did with you came from lust, he did everything to get taken care of, and once he releases himself, I promise you, he turns into a whole other person. Reality sets back in. Now, one or two things can happen. He might want his money back; he might want to hurt you because he feels so guilty about it. But at the end he's not the same nice person. Now I'm a disease that he needs to get away from. He's looking at you that way and you feel it. It gets uncomfortable. That's why girls are always on their p's and q's and try to get away from a trick as soon as it's over. Not that they are so scary, but things can turn into something very wrong in a matter of seconds.

I learned how to act tough and sexy at the same time, and I developed a sense of humor. When I was with a trick, I'm trying to make them laugh through this. I do something nutty or quirky. If he's still looking at me with blank eyes and he's not responding, then I know this might not end well and I know I might have to fight my way out of this. So I'm ready. If we are in a hotel room, I'm on the side next to the door. I'm going to stay next to the lamp because I might have to pick it up and crash this trick in the head. I'm going to stay next to something I can grab. I remember one time, I hit this dude with this big-ass ashtray. That was all I could get to protect myself. It's not just a sex thing, it's a live-or-die thing. You can die out there just as easily as you can go out there and get your money. You get into the wrong car and that's the last car. You check into the wrong hotel and you don't check out.

Most of the time, girls are trying to figure out, *Who am I getting into the car with today? Who am I walking into the room with now?* Knowing that can save your life. If you can't figure that out, you can get punched in the face, strangled, or murdered. And after a while, if you go through that stuff enough, you take a little swig of a drink or a pill or a joint to give yourself some courage. You take a little bit of this or that to throw off the heebie-jeebies. I've had tricks who have offered me extra money to do stuff I don't do. "Oh, come on, you girls do everything." And before I know it, I'm being forced to do something I didn't want to do. Or he's penetrating me anally or whatever without my permission. He thinks that's fine because he's going to throw you an extra hundred. He'll throw money at you and walk away without feeling any responsibility. "I paid her, so I get what I want." And I'm feeling like garbage on the floor. You know you can't fight back because if you fight, that will make it worse. I remember once being anally raped by three Black guys; they were trying to hold me still in the car and I kicked the windshield out. I didn't know at that time how hard it was to kick a windshield out of a car. I was just trying to get away from the brutal rape they were putting on me.

+ + +

I've been caught a time or two with a customer and his wife catches us. She figured he was having an affair, and that can be dangerous because jealousy can have an ugly head. I learned something from another girl. She said, "Girl, when one of them married bitches roll up on you and you with her man, let her know right quick, 'I'm a prostitute; he paid me to do this. This ain't personal.'" And I learned to say that right away. "Wait a minute, ma'am. He paid me. I'm a prostitute. This ain't no affair; this ain't personal. Ain't none of that happening." Most women when they hear that, they look at you. "You a prostitute?" And they'll look at him and say something messed up about you. "You with this ho? You with this bitch?" Trust me, those ladies give you a pass. I've had some women turn to me and say, "Okay, sweetie, did he pay you?"

"Yes, ma'am. Yes, he did." And then I say, "I ain't in this," and I walk away. That was some marriage shit; I'm a ho. Women are afraid of their men being intimately involved with another woman. I'm sure because I was just a prostitute, they went home and she forgave him. When you are out there and you are working with these types of guys, there's one thing you should never forget: he's a trick, and at the end of this thing, he's going his way and you are going your way.

Folks tell me, ain't all that happen to you. But I'm sorry, it did. I wish it hadn't. I wish to God I was lying my head off.

Chapter 12

Keep It Moving

I left Philly. I thought I would go to Canada, get my thoughts and shit together there. I didn't make it, though. I got turned around and made it to New York.

I thought I was fast, but New York was faster. I was just in the atmosphere of what was going on. I hung out with Black entertainers, too, especially at that club, Leviticus. I was a social butterfly, and after we hit the clubs, we would move on to the social clubs, there in Queens, and cocaine at the bars. I met interesting people. Arthur Prysock: "Here's to good friends, we onto something special." He was a jazz singer and a good person. We weren't having sex or nothing like that. He just wanted girls around. I used to hang out in this place called the Tennis Club, up in Queens, and that was where I saw Johnny Mathis. I found out he was gay. He was totally not interested in my ass. I had on this nice little tight spaghetti-strap dress, no panties on, he didn't even turn his head at me. I remember meeting Diana Ross in this upscale beauty parlor; it was that year she was doing *The*

Wiz. Everybody always talked about how much of a diva she was, but actually she was very refreshing, very nice. I was sitting up there, staring at her with my mouth open. I mean: Diana Ross.

And I had this guy named Hymie. I had met Hymie's ass on my first lone stay in New York when Coolie had first come and got me. Hymie had taken me out to dinner and shit like that. So when I came back to New York, I looked Hymie up. Hymie was my enabler, my go-to man. He made everything right if it was going wrong. He was an older guy, black as the ace of spades, and he really liked me. Just a regular middle-aged Black man. I was a good piece of ass for him, and I think it might have been a little bit more than that, because once when I went to jail in Jersey, he came and got my ass out of jail. Hymie had been in Vietnam. He used to talk about that all the time. That was where he got his name, Hymie, because his real name was James, but they called him Hymie when he was in Germany. Hymie is "James" in German—actually, I don't know if that was true, but that was what he told me.

Hymie thought I was interesting, and so did his middle-aged friends. I would hang out with all those little pot-gut guys. Hung out, had dinner. Made it with them, too. I was living with a friend of Hymie's. When Hymie introduced us, Annie liked me right off and wanted to have a threesome with us. So Annie came over to Hymie's, but Hymie had to go, and by the time he had got back, me and Annie had already had our little twosome. We had already got our little freak on, so she said, "Why don't you come stay with me?" So I started staying with Annie. And that was my life in New York. I was sneaking in a little money here and there, but basically, in New York I was taken care of by people. I would just meet interesting people, and they would take care of me. But as much as I loved being taken care of and looking at everything fresh in New York, I guess I wasn't done with running away.

We have the internet now, but back then we had word of mouth. We girls would sit up and talk about places we had been, people we worked for, and a girl might say, "You would do well at so-and-so."

Some places liked light-skinned Black girls, some places liked curvy girls, and if you met a girl who met the criteria, you passed it along.

"Oh, really? You think so? Give me the number."

And they would say, "Tell her red-haired Karen sent you." And these madams trusted the red-haired Karen enough to know she was sending somebody she could work with. That's how I found my way to Miami and went to work for a Cuban lady. I never met her; she was just a voice on a telephone. She was basically with Mob Patrol, not Italian, but Cuban, and she had whorehouses. You could get a booking with her, and all you had to do was take care of the business. But I messed that up. She sent her man over to get her money, but I didn't have it. So they wound up putting me out. Her man was supposed to take me somewhere, rough me up, and drop me off. He didn't rough me up, though, he just dropped me off, which was a blessing. That was how I knew my angels looked out for me. He looked at me and said, "You just a dumb kid; get on outta here."

"Thank you. I learn my lesson."

I was standing on the corner with my suitcase, crying. I didn't know what I was going to do. I was in this rough section of town because that was where he dropped me off. I guess he figured I'd probably get roughed up in this neighborhood, and if I didn't, I was just lucky. Then this guy pulled over, and I hopped in his car.

"Where you want to go?"

"I don't know." I started crying and told him my boyfriend beat me up and took off with everything I had. I mean, I couldn't tell him I just got kicked out of a ho house.

He was shaking his head. "This just so sad." So he drove me to his house and told me, "You can make some phone calls." I'm a prostitute; I was thinking, okay, I'm in and he probably wants some sex and stuff like that. But you know what? He never ever asked me to do anything. He was just a good person. He had a room; it was little bigger than a walk-in closet. There was a little toilet, with a curtain over the toilet, and then a sink and a table with a hot plate on it, the bed, and a chair. That was it. Hot as a firecracker in that room, so we had to keep the door open. He was living humbly. He gave me the bed, and he slept on the floor. He told me he was from Cuba. He was a dishwasher, and he had left two daughters in Cuba. He hoped that somebody would show his daughters the love and help he was showing me, if they found themselves in my situation. I stayed there almost a week.

Somebody gave me Miz Nellie's number to call. I should have called her from the beginning. She was set up in Natchez, Mississippi. For almost fifty years, Miz Nellie Jackson, who was a Black lady, ran her brothel. White men only. I stayed there for a while, cause I had nowhere else to go. I was there for about a month, a long time for me. Normal hos stay for about two weeks at these places, but Miz Nellie liked my little young ass. I turned twenty-five years old at Nellie's. They say your brain becomes fully developed at twenty-five. I beg to differ. I didn't have a damn bit of sense. I think Miz Nellie thought the same. Most times she looked at me with a *this little child* expression. You know, I think about it now, and these people who I bumped into and dealt with, they were just shaking their heads at me and the situations I got myself into. And I guess I was fun, too. I was bubbly, and people took a real liking to me. I used to watch Miz Nellie's poodles. She had all these white poodles, and she had one black poodle, and she called that one her nigger and named him Pepper. Pepper was the only one who used to go outside and hang out in the neighborhood. He had a special door he would use to come into the house. All the rest of the puppies slept with Miz Nellie, but Pepper slept with me. I washed all her dogs.

Miz Nellie used to have guys who cooked for us. They worked on the oil rigs, but when it was off season, they would go to Nellie Jackson's and cook for us. She had a back house, and they could stay there if they wanted to and then cook for the hos. And man, could they cook. That was some excellent food. Them guys used to have fresh-baked rolls and biscuits and shit, like they were in a bakery or something. Really good-ass food.

But at the end of the month, I was ready to get moving, so I went to Johnson City, Tennessee. A girlfriend of mine had told me all about it. Her name was Angel. And if Angel told you the bookings were good, they were good. Johnson City is a tri-city area; Kingsport and Bristol are the other two towns right next to it. Three railways came through there, right into downtown, and they had two airports, too. That was how the hotel managed to have the kind of business they had. People came through. Salesmen, all kind of guys who, when they stayed at the hotel, if they wanted some action, they could get it. I was working for myself; I didn't have a pimp then. My "pimp" was the bellman. Angel was the bellman's girlfriend, and she gave me some of my clients. She handled all the bookings. They got 40 percent of my money.

The bellman had a friend who he introduced me to. He had a liquor store in town. He liked me. So when I got through with my bookings, I stayed with him. But he was cranky. After a month or two, I needed to get away from his cranky ass, so I called my girlfriend Candy. She was down in New Orleans, and she was telling me how good the money was there. She was making money hand over fist. She had an apartment. It's popping down here, she told me. The cranky dude got me a ticket. He thought I was just going down there to work and then I would come home to him. I mean, I can't believe that fool thought I was coming back. He was *cranky*. Besides, I was thinking to myself that New Orleans was my chance to get my act together, get myself a straight job or something, make some money. I had been wandering around all over, getting into this, getting into that, trying to run away from all this grief that sat on top of me. I was still grieving Coolie and Ma'Dea. I needed to put all that down. New Orleans felt like the right place to get that all done.

Chapter 13

The Unforgivable Things We Do

Candy had an apartment already set up in New Orleans, and I moved in with her, and she was working in a strip club on Bourbon Street, and I got a job there, too. Candy was a good stabilizer for me, and I was doing well with the money. I had been in New Orleans for almost a year when I made a big decision. I went and got the kids again.

For a minute, I thought it would work. I had gotten a job at the Superdome. They were building it, and all I had to do was watch a certain area all night. I damn near slept through most of my shift. I worked for the security company and then I would go strip. I'd ho on the weekend.

I got a little friend named Ed. He was a friend/little bit boyfriend, and thank God he was a good person, because I left my kids with him. I was opening my kids up to too much. All kinds of stuff could have happened to them. He didn't do nothing to them. Later on, my girls told me, "We used to run Ed. He would do anything we asked him to do, Momma." He was a great guy. Thank God. Thank God.

I met a guy from California named Crockett. I met him at the strip club. I liked working at the club. The whole thing made me feel like an entertainer instead of a ho. It's all about the lap dances and the champagne room. I could make enough money at the strip club that I didn't have to turn a trick unless I really wanted to. Crockett was giving me fifties and hundreds across the floor and impressing me with his big talk. Middle-aged guy. He looked really legit; he had this nice jewelry. He was this dude with game. Crockett had been coming down to New Orleans for maybe about six months. He was coming to town to get water, PCP, and they were transporting it back in a van. They wanted to use me as a mule, but I didn't know that. They wanted me as a front to be in the van with two guys. I thought it would be so easy. Get a bunch of money, enough to move into a bigger apartment. I risked so much, but I was in love with that fast money.

On the way to California, Crockett got the idea he could get money out of me, too. So when he took me out there, he had a friend in Laurel Canyon, in LA, who happened to be a nice girl. That was where he took me, to stash me for a couple days until he could figure out what to do with me. See, Crockett had drugs in that van, and he had to deal with that situation. I was just another life to play with.

I had left my kids in New Orleans with these two girls I had let stay with me. They were strippers, and they had nowhere else to go. They were going to watch my kids for a couple of days, and then I was going to come back. But I didn't. Then some guys came by looking for me, wanted to do something to me. See, I had messed around with another dope dealer. He had given me some shit to sell—like two pounds of weed, cocaine, and shit. I sold that shit and moved, moved with the money. And he had found my apartment. Those two girls said, we need to get these girls up out of here.

I was a mess. A hot mess.

Once, I went to a clairvoyant, and she told me my mother was watching over me, because she could better help me from the other side than she could on this. I totally believed her. This wasn't the first time people had been out there looking for me. I had some serious angels watching over my ass and my babies. The dudes came over there and were like, "What—she didn't take her kids?" Those two girls living with me in New Orleans? Thank God those girls got my kids out of there and got them to safety. They saw that something wasn't right, and they called my auntie the next day.

So I was in California, and I was stupid and embarrassed. I couldn't get back to my kids, and I was calling and not getting any answers. I was panicking. I was praying. I was doing all this shit when something said, *Call Aunt Josie.* I called her and there my kids were.

Aunt Josie lit into my ass like white on rice. "You ain't no good, Brenda Jean. You left your kids, these babies, these angels. Nine and ten years old, and you left them, Brenda. I'm so glad that the girls remembered my number to call me."

She was telling me what happened, and I had no defense. All I could do was listen to her telling me what a loser and failure I was. Things could have worked out in a way that I could have never seen my kids again. Somebody could have come by and snatched my kids up. I know what the world is full of. How could I have done that? I was listening to her, and the last thing she said to me was, "You need to stay out they life, Brenda Jean. Stay out they damn life. Stay out. Until you ready to be a mother, stay out. Because every time you come into they life, you leave again and you hurt them again." She was right. She was damn right. Who was I to keep hurting them babies like that? I knew how my daughters used to look at me when I walked out the door. And I carried those looks. I carried all of that with me when I went back out on the streets. After I talked to her, I knew that they were safe, and I said to myself, "I don't deserve those kids. I need to leave and allow them to be happy." I could remember how happy I was in Evanston. I wanted that for them. I thought about how much better off they were without me being in the picture. Prune was ten; Peaches was nine. Leaving them was the best thing for everybody.

So I began my life as a California girl.

Chapter 14

Famous in California

The first thing that girl in Laurel Canyon told me about California was to watch out for STDs. "They share diseases here like candy. You gotta be careful and know who you messing with." Not too long after that, AIDS started popping up. This was in 1982. I was stripping at this place called Charlie's, a bikini bar on Crenshaw and Florence. Crockett got me the job, and I would see him every now and again; he'd come and get me from the Laurel Canyon house, and then he'd have me sitting in his luxury van for three, four hours while he was in a card club. Crockett was a heavy gambler.

Working at Charlie's helped me get my independence from Crockett. I met a bunch of guys and girls, and I just didn't need him anymore. I sort of hit it off with one girl in particular—SeQuita. I told her how I was living in hotel rooms when I wasn't up in Laurel Canyon.

"Damn, that must be killing you."

"Yeah, it's killing my money."

SeQuita offered to let me come stay at her place. So I packed up nothing and went and stayed on her couch. At the lounge, I was dapping and snorting here and there, take a little tip here, but I was still all about trying to stay cute. But I was headed to ugly, because I was on a mission to destroy myself because of what I had done to my kids. That was all weighing on me heavily.

I got involved with this dangerous drug dealer, Big Alden. Alden used to come to Charlie's to sell the girls drugs. I walked to the back office, and because I was a little ho and Alden reminded me of players I used to date, I asked Charlie, jokingly, "Who's that nigga right there? Cause he look like a player." The next time he came in, she introduced us. He was a sugar daddy. He took me places that I couldn't believe and did things with me. Once, he took me to the mountains, to these caves where there were jacuzzis. We did a lot of wining and dining and had way-out sex.

In some ways, he was the sweetest guy in the world. But he was a drug dealer; he was controlling. He was the type of brother you can't leave. SeQuita thought it would be funny if she told a lie on me. She told Alden I had sex with this other guy. I didn't know she had told him that. SeQuita and I had come home from work, and we had gotten a little high. I went in the living room and made my little place on the couch. She went into the room and closed the door. I was sleeping on her sofa, windows cracked; it was night. It's a first-floor apartment, and in California most of the apartments have metal bars on the doors and the windows. I'm sleeping right by the window; it's summertime, the window is up. I heard this motorcycle and then I heard gunshots, *pow pow pow pow*. I'm so startled, I rolled off the couch and fell on the floor. This bitch SeQuita is as quiet as a mouse; she didn't even come out of her bedroom. She *knew* that was Alden out there shooting up the place just to mess with me, intimidate me. That was the type of shit that was going on.

I went out with Alden one night, and he took me over to his friend Paul's house, and Alden pulled a gun on me and tried to make me tell him I had sex with some other dude. But I never had sex with the dude. We broke up after that. It was for the best. I was a hustler; I was a ho. I couldn't work like I wanted to because Alden was so jealous. I didn't understand. I was a dancer. I had to get money. How did he think I got my money?

That was the end of Alden. Too bad it wasn't the end of SeQuita and her shenanigans.

+ + +

One day, SeQuita came in from work and went to her bedroom where she had her little table and shit and started getting high. She took out this little black bag with some clear tubes inside. She also had a glass bottle full of grain alcohol. Then she put a glass mirror flat on top of the table. She sprinkled the rock on the glass. I didn't know why yet, but she made a line of the white rocks and chopped them up, fed them into the pipe, then she pulled out this long wire, like a knitting needle but skinnier, and told me to dip it into the grain alcohol. She showed me how to hold it and how to hit it. Oh my God, it was a euphoria. Getting high picked me up; I felt like I was up on top of the world. I could have a conversation about anything. My girls, my problems were very far away. Brenda would leave and a new me would appear. I think to this day that my nickname that stuck, Breezy, developed out of crack. She was my more confident self, my controlled self, my powerful self that could knock everything down. My more criminal self would come up from smoking crack and it would make me so creative. The crack would create a situation and drinking Cisco wine would validate it.

I looked at her and said, "Give me some of that." We finished that off and I said, "You ain't got no more?"

"Naw. That was it. You want to get some more?"

"Yeah."

A couple of months later, I hooked up with this little cutie pie. Lamar and I were kicking it, but wouldn't you know it, SeQuita told my new man that she heard I was having sex with somebody else. She put this sympathy act on, and then *they* started going out. And she got pregnant behind it. I didn't know all this shit was going on around me. All I knew was, suddenly SeQuita told me I needed to go and find my own place.

That was fine. I needed to get away from SeQuita. I had lived on her couch for about six, seven months, and it was time to move on. She had too many trifling ways. She had this uncle who used to be the road manager for Ray Charles. Sam was his name. When he came over, they would go lock up in the room to get high together. Weird. And she always wanted to manage how everybody got high. One time, we were getting high together, and in the middle of it, she started putting up all my shit. Had she lost her mind? That was my money and my dope. I ended up going across the street and getting high with the gas station guy. I had started spending time with Dennis Edwards, who was one of the front men for the Temptations. Dennis and I were really good friends. We did not have sex, but we did get high together, because now I was starting to get high. Okay? I had moved beyond recreational use. I wasn't going out spending my money on getting high, but when an opportunity came my way (and there were a lotta opportunities to get high!), I was there.

The problem was SeQuita. When I wanted to get high, I was still going over her place to do it, and she just wanted to run everyone and everything. Dennis, his bass player, and I were over SeQuita's house, and she would always try to create these situations where I was bringing over people who have drugs and money, and she would try to put me out the situation. Finally, Dennis said to me, "Who is she? The high organizer?"

And a little after that, I left SeQuita's for good. The girl was just too bossy.

When people get high on drugs, they go through two or three personalities before getting high is over. I wasn't into the high like that—not yet. I wasn't as deep into smoking that cocaine as other people were, but I was getting there. I didn't understand its power. I was trying to do two things at once. I wanted to have a straight life and then have my drug life on the side. I was dancing at a club out in

South Central when I met an electrician named Charles who became my boyfriend. He was a good, decent guy, but I was starting to be more about the drugs than about the dancing. Charles had to let me go because I was toxic to the way he was living, and I understood. I was in a spiral. I'd wake up one morning in one part of the hood, then spend the day roaming, bumping into drug dealers or other girls. I was working at another strip club in Gardena and sleeping with the manager. But I wasn't going to stay with him long because I was too wild. I bumped into this big Mexican drug dealer named Albert; he used to give me a lot of drugs, give me a lot of money. But before I knew it, I needed more money for more drugs, so I started hitting the streets. I knew how to do that. I would go to the strip club and then go in the streets afterwards. I wore leather, this real dominatrix stuff, but sexy. And I started hanging off Figueroa, in South Central. It was so easy to get so much money over there. I didn't know why these hos weren't out there getting money. I would see girls out there, but they were always acting like they weren't working. I'm from Chicago—we get paper. I watched these girls "working." They were strawberries. Strawberries are girls who have sex for drugs. I had never heard of that until I came to California. That was what it was all about at that time. Crack was popping. Crack was there. The young dealers were walking up and down the sidewalk. "You need something, young momma?" And of course, I did need it. But I also needed somewhere to smoke that. The dealers would point out a house, and for a little fee they let you inside. As long as you got drugs, people would be nice to you and you could stay as long as you like. But as soon as you done, they kicked you out.

Everybody was hanging out at the drug houses. And there were all kinds of drug houses out there. Sometimes the people living there would let the drug dealer set up in the front of the house if the dealer paid the rent. And then the people would live in the back of the house and we weren't allowed to go back there. Sometimes these drug house would just be empty. Nobody lived there. It was just a bunch of squatters. Nothing was inside but a couple of couches and some bare mattresses in the bedrooms. You could hear the rats running around. Buddy's drug house had a lot of roaches. We would laugh and say Buddy's roaches were high, because when you turned on the light, the roaches wouldn't run away. I'd go to get my stuff, and I'd see some neighborhood girls sitting on the porch steps, and I would come back, and they would *still* be sitting there. I was wondering: Do they live there? But I found out what they were doing. They were waiting for some dude to come through, they'd give the dude some head, and then he would go and get the girls some crack. That kind of transaction was not for me.

You know what's funny? Those girls looked down on me because I was a prostitute. But I was looking at them just as crazy. Women have different mentalities. They can act like hos, but they won't admit it. What's the difference between me turning tricks and getting money, and them sucking wang for rock? Undercover shit. I was more flamboyant; I was out there. I was from Chicago. But everything was different when I got to California. I had to learn how California was. I knew they spent a lot of time sucking a lotta wang for a hit. And I was like, wait: you can go and get your *own* money, sit down and smoke your drugs like you want to, and you ain't got to be begging no guy or mess up your reputation.

So I was turning tricks again, this time to get money for crack. The reputation that I didn't have on Figueroa was that I would suck peter for crack. The reputation I *did* have was that I was a ho. For me, that made all the difference. Being a prostitute and making money meant I was in control. I bought my own shit and smoked where I wanted to. I wasn't going to give a blow job to a drug dealer for a hit off a pipe. It made dudes respect me. That's how I managed to keep some cool relationships. Dennis and I continued to be friends. The last time I saw him was after he made the song "Don't Look Any Further." He was working on that when I met him. After that, I think he got back with his girl, and he stopped messing with them drugs. Dennis had contracts, and he couldn't fulfill them because of the drugs. He almost didn't make it. A bass player I know was telling me all this. The dude was telling me, "I'm a studio musician and my money comes if Dennis completes this project. And I literally had to break the pipes for us to go to work one day."

Crack got the best of a lot of people, but Dennis pulled out just in time—and just as I was really getting deep into it.

I was in my second year in California. Drug dealers really liked me because I was so friendly. I was an entertainer. I would entertain the shit out of fools. They thought I was hilarious. And they were impressed with me because I was a hustler and I would be their girl— well, until I didn't want to be their girl. I could do all of that because I didn't have a pimp who claimed me. That was my California shit.

This is when I got the name Breezy. This girl named Joyce, she had kids, and she used to invite me over her place because I was the person who would get her high. So I would stay over there and hang out at her house. Sometimes Joyce would walk out with me. I mean, she wouldn't turn no tricks, but she would watch my back. People do that to make sure once you make that money you come back. So Joyce named me Breezy because I did shit so fast. She said never saw somebody come and go so quick. Most folks she dealt with said they were going out to get some drugs for her, would take her twenty, thirty dollars, and take a day and a half to come back.

"Yo ass is like the breeze. I be talking to you one minute, and the next minute you gone. That's what I'm gone call you, Breezy, cause you be fast."

I was over at Joyce's house when I met this drug dealer named Dean. He was chocolate, with curly hair, because he had a Jheri curl, a texturizer. Medium height. He always wore these dark sunglasses. Really good-looking. He had a bunch of drugs, bunch of money, and a couple of cars: a Mercedes and a Porsche. He was one of those dudes with a real tough-guy voice, real gravelly. I was over at Joyce's sleeping on her couch when Dean walked in the door.

He said to Joyce, "Hook me up with that."

Somehow, I was the hook-up girl. *Hook me up.* I was always hooked up with somebody. Dean had all the hos, everybody was his woman. He had all the girls who came by and bought drugs from him. That was the way he had it set up. And in return, he had this little house where we could come and sleep, take a nap, he would buy us clothes.

A drug dealer once told me, "Breezy, you be with everybody. The Bloods, the Crips, the Grape Streets, the Rolling Sixties."

I said, "Nigga, don't you know what my color is?"

"What is it, Breezy?"

"Green, nigga. Whoever got it, I'm gonna be with. I got no time to be flying no goddamned colors. How am I gone get money if I just date the Crips? Shit. Y'all ain't got enough money for that." He cracked up.

I would be in Crip territory, wearing a red dress, and then one of them gangbangers would say something to me. "Yo, girl, what you doing up over here in a red dress?"

"Nigga, every ho got a red dress! Why y'all keep mistaking me for a gangbanger? I'm a ho; hos have to have red dresses." And I could get away with it, too. Cause I'm a prostitute.

They start laughing and giggling up. But those were the same brothers who would come looking for me when they wanted to party. They would take me to these swanky, nice-ass hotels, and we would wreck the room. We had so much fun in there. Liquor, drugs, laughing, kicking it. I would turn on the music and do all kinds of little dances and shit. Dealers sat up there smoking blunts. It was like they were at the movies. Cause I was the bitch who was a party. That was me. They had a lotta money, and I had what they needed and I supplied it. Sometimes I would take another girl with me, but she was under my rule. She was in on my party.

So California was rolling. I was based in LA, but I roamed all over. I had the little gangbangers, all them chasing after me and liking me. I would trick with different guys who would take me into the mountains or take me up to Pomona, Pasadena, or Long Beach. I'd find myself in Compton. I'd hop in the car with a Low Rider, and he'd take me to San Diego and Oakland. And in between that I would go to jail because I got busted by vice, and then I would go spend sixty, ninety days in jail for prostitution. Once, it went all the way up to six months for prostitution. That was the most they ever gave me, a hundred and eighty days. In a way, I appreciated it. Those were rest times for me. Sometimes I would be so worn out. I thought about trying to get off drugs when I was in jail. I could give my body some time off, gain my weight back, and be pretty when I came back out. In the twelve years I lived in California, I was in and out of jail a lot. I got busted pretty frequently, but getting busted saved my life. Once, I had syphilis, and another time, I had pneumonia. If I hadn't of gone in, I would have just kept getting high and got sicker and sicker. I always kept my booty, but I would be so tiny, and that was unnatural for me.

I remember one time I had gotten out, and this girl walked over to me. "Come here, Breezy. Where you been, in jail?"

"Yeah."

"I'm so sad to say it, but I'm glad you went to jail. Cause girl, you was walking around here little as hell, looking like a stick with a bobble head." She had me laughing. I mean, it wasn't funny, but it was. That crack had tore my ass up. But once I got out of jail, my monkey would turn into a gorilla. It was crazy the way the obsessive-compulsive behavior hit me once I got out. My mouth would be dry.

And that hit they'd give me for free. Drug dealers wanted to be that guy who gave me the first hit and did me that favor so that I would only come back to them. I could be a very loyal customer. They would even ask for me. "Breezy out? Tell her come see me." I always had good intentions while I was in jail, but the minute they released me, I made a beeline to the drug dealer. "Here you go, Breezy." And once the drug dealer started me, I'd be off to the races. I would go and spend every dime I got on crack.

The only reason I continued to make money was because I would take care of my appearance. I was fresh and looking good right from jail. The other girls who looked stank couldn't get. I still thought I was all this because I kept a clean outfit on and carried myself a certain kind of way. But my thinking was all wrong. That was me: always trying to make something work for me and make it seem like it was better than it really was. If I would have taken a hard look at what was really happening, it probably would have destroyed me.

Chapter 15

Friends? How Many of Us Have Them?

What really saved my life, such as it was, was that I was rolling with the Do-Low Crew, off Sixty-Fifth and Denver. Pleasure, Jazzy, Lynn, Momma Jelly, Beverly, Stephanie. Those ladies were my friends and they had my back. We called ourselves the Do-Low Crew because we spent most of our time doing some low-down shit. We were a crew of female assassins. Just kidding. Well, we thought we were. We were a mess, but they would save me from shit and I would save them right back.

I met the first member when she was hanging in the neighborhood. Stephanie. She had never seen anyone like me. I was very advertisement-like. I was out on the level. I was funny and outrageous; I was a ho and a crackhead and none of that was a secret. You knew I was on something. It was like, "This bitch get her money."

I started seeing Stephanie around, and she'd peep me out and say, "Hey."

"Hey. There you are. How you doing?"

I thought I was running into her, but she was following me around. She was trying to find out who I was. Where did I come from? Where this bitch come from with all this flare? Popping a ponytail all over the street. In this leather-ass, tight-ass shit. But that's what I was doing to survive. It took a minute, but we hit it off. Stephanie was—and is—cool people. And she was just one of a bunch of ladies who kept me safe. I met Stephanie first. But once we all got together, we stayed together. We were ladies out there in the life, watching each other's back.

We used to get into fights with guys. Them dudes would be like, "Y'all think y'all tough."

And Stephanie told them, "Yeah, it's tough, nigga." *Pow, pow*, fists flying. She was a gangsta for real.

And then there was Jazzy. Jazzy was one of those girls that was like, "My crew might be laughing with you, but I ain't, bitch." She watched our back real good. Laid-back. She's still alive. I still see her now. I see Stephanie, too.

+ + +

The Do-Low Crew got into trouble, and then we got out of it. Sometimes. I picked up some real street smarts from those ladies. Like, it was Lynn who hipped us to the clothesline. Before we knew it, we were all doing it. We became the clothesline hos. So here's how it went. We would be out all night. In and out of cars. We were up and down the streets, and we'd be dirty. And when daylight came, we'd feel dirty. We wanted to wash up and put on some clothes, but we didn't have our clothes and we didn't really know where we left them. Sometimes I would find some guy and tell him, let me take a shower at his place. That was how I would do it. But one time, we were in this garage smoking when Lynn walked up in these clean clothes. "Bitch, where you get them clothes from?" We had just left from over at Buddy's. Stephanie, Momma Jelly, and me we were talking about going to the store and get something to wear.

"Clothesline. That's where I shop at."

"You lie."

"Yeah. You better gone get you some 'fore they wake up."

So when folks were in bed, we'd sneak in their backyard, trying on their clothes and seeing what fit. Crack is a hell of a thing. We would come right back in the neighborhood, right across the street where the people lived, and we would look at them crazy if they said anything. "What?" You know how crackheads can be: "What? What you looking at?" We looked at them full in the mouth and dared them to say something even though we were wearing their clothes.

Then Jazzy invented the pillowcase outfit. We would go to the hotel and take the pillowcase off the pillows, cut it open and roll it up so it could be a little skirt. And Jazzy would make a halter. We would have a pillowcase skirt and a halter top. Crackhead clothes! Do you understand me? We were having a ball and pulling it off. I was walking down the street with a pillowcase skirt and a pair of leather boots on. Like, I'm killing 'em.

When we weren't taking folks' laundry or getting high, we were running from the police. I remember the first time I went to jail in California. This cop got out of his car and I took off. He went running after me. He caught me. "Why you run off like that?"

"I thought y'all was robbers."

"Oh?"

"Yeah, I never been arrested before and I don't know how y'all do it around here."

So he gave me a little statement, and then he said, "You really was running."

"Thank you." I wasn't used to California. I didn't know that they really sent you to jail. I mean, you could get a bond, but you had to post the bond at that station at that time. So I did my thirty days, and then they let me go. A month inside hadn't changed anything. Crack was still hot. So many young drug dealers had money, and so much money was bouncing around, it was a goldmine. I was staying down there with John Hunt and the lady he was staying with in the back house, which was two blocks away from the stadium they were using for the Olympics. I would tell her I was going to the store, but I would always come back with money. The tourists were everywhere. And I didn't look like a prostitute. Kept it real low, but sexy. That went on for a couple years in that area.

Doing that kind of stuff made me think I was different from a lotta girls. And it made me think I was better. I wasn't any better. But that feeling was something I was trying to hold on to, and if I did, that would make everything okay. People keep asking me if the person I was back then helps me out with the ladies I work with now. But no. That's not it. It's about what Momma Jelly, Pleasure, Stephanie, Lynn taught me: they taught me about relationships. They taught me how to be a friend—and stay a friend. They taught me that I can build a relationship.

A while ago, when I was working at Dreamcatcher, the foundation I opened to help women caught in the life of prostitution, two old dope fiends came and worked outreach with me. They would play with me—shoot the shit with me, crack up with me. And they would ask me, "What you finna do?"

"Oh, I'm 'bout to get these other bitches and make them take a break from sucking all these dicks. Help them out, you know?"

"Go get them bitches, Brenda."

So when I get them girls, I remember when I was hurt and the friends who helped me through, and then it's not that hard to make a relationship.

First, I got to ask them, "What you want to do?" Cause we can't go nowhere unless I know what you want to do. I can't get to that point with you, unless you stabilized.

It's a waiting game with me. That's why when I'm out there now on the streets, the first thing they need to know is, "Alright, we still here." The waiting game is all about her making that first step to call me, and when she calls me, we get into the car, and after that I try to make sure that I can make what I'm doing as appealing as it can be to help her make a decision to separate herself from the life she's living right now. And I can't do that real fast; I got to do that step by step because we have to make sure that's working. If it is, we've got to wallow in it for a minute and get used to it. And then I'm like, what else I got to do to get to step three? I got to do this and I got to do that. I've been clean twenty-two years without drugs and prostitution. And I'm still growing. I'm still growing, because for thirty-nine years, my growth was stunted from the abuse in my life and all of that. I was not where I should have been mentally and spiritually. When I work with my young ladies, I can connect with them because I know how it feels to want to come back, to be whole again. I know how awful it is to feel lost, and sometimes it's your girlfriends who help you through.

Close as we were, they couldn't save me from everything. They couldn't save me from getting raped. They couldn't save me from getting robbed. But we tried to save each other, and I did the best I could for my friends. Like my girl Pleasure. I was getting Pleasure out of trouble a lot because at that time, when a ho had AIDS, everybody would spread your business. If you had the virus, and you were working in prostitution, the police would pick you up and put you in jail. That was Pleasure. She had AIDS and she was working, and it got around, and people knew she had the package. So she would have to hole up somewhere, but she also was owing some guy, and when they found her, they would bust her in her head. Every time it happened, she would tell them, "Go get Breezy. Go get Breezy."

They came get me, and I said, "What's going on? How much money she owe you, nigga? You that petty? I'll bring it back to you." They knew I would. I loved to have the money and just throw it in their faces like a little punk. "Here, take this money, bitch."

"Stop disrespecting me like that, Breezy."

"Hey, you acting a fool like this. Come on, Pleasure."

She was a sweetheart. I hated to see her die like that. Sweet little chocolate, and she got caught up. Some fool gave her AIDS on purpose. This brother she was messing with.

As I said, we in the Do-Low Crew tried to look out for each other, and lots of times, we managed. But when we failed, it meant somebody got killed. Like Lynn. Lynn got killed. She was married to a very volatile man. She ran away from him, but she would always tell us she was scared he would turn up. We would stand on the corner, and she would look scared. "Bitch, what's wrong with you?"

"Bitches, I got to look out for my husband."

"Bitch, your husband?"

"Yeah, bitch. My husband. That motherfucker looking for me." But we didn't believe her because she had been gone from him for some years. But she kept on saying that. What's the worst he could do? Try to take her back home? "Nah, that motherfucker gone try to kill me."

One day her husband caught her. He rolled right on up, sat her down in the car, and blew her head off. He blew her brains out.

That messed me up, even though I didn't see it. I was a block away from it. This man walked up to me and said, "Dude just shot your friend in the head."

"What?" I was at the hotel, and I came out and walked down the street. "Damn, he got her."

The ambulance came and took her. Her husband just killed her. He got into trouble, but he killed that bitch. She was a pretty girl, big booty, little waist, and just crazy. She had a girlfriend by then—this little young thing who used to follow Lynn around—and when she found out what the husband had done, it broke her heart. I feel bad about Lynn because I never thought it was that serious. And if it was, damn, she took a lot of chances. And then her chances ran out.

And just like I couldn't save Lynn, my ladies couldn't save me from everything. I got syphilis. At that point in my life, I was struggling on the streets. I had gone too long without rejuvenating my body. I had begun to look like a street bitch. Shaggy. The shaggy started to come in. One time I broke out in all spots. Up and down my body. That can happen with the second stage of syphilis. I started telling tricks I had an allergic reaction to something. One guy didn't care, so I'm pretty sure I infected his ass. Stuff as important as that became a gamble, and I was willing to gamble it. Not for the money, but for the drugs. I was able to turn down anything except for drugs.

So I'm getting high, and I'm up here, floating and rolling. This surge of energy had got me like *eeeeee*. Then that whole thing starts to crash down, or I smoked so much, I stopped feeling it after a while. You just smoking, you can't get no higher. And maybe my body is exhausted, but I couldn't stop smoking. There's no reason, but you did it. So when I came down and crashed, I got really paranoid. And then everything I wasn't aware of, I was aware of. My shoes were dirty; I got dirt on my dress. All kind of stuff like this. I looked like I been up all night.

You get fixated on trying to get out of that situation. I knew I didn't look proper. Sometimes I was able to say, forget it, and I was able to handle my business. And soon as I got me some money, I would go straight toward a store and do whatever I had to do to clean myself up.

But looking clean isn't the same as being clean.

The only time I was really clean was when I was in jail. Sometimes I feel like I spent half my time in California at Sybil Brand, the women's prison. When you first go into Sybil Brand, you get processed; the cops bring you in and they put you in a holding cell while they wait for your prints to go through. Your prints tell them everything about you. You may have a warrant on you. They find out you caught some shit they didn't know about. Cross your fingers. So you get through that process. Of course, with me, I always had a prostitution case. Now, I still haven't gone in front of the judge. They haven't even given me a bond yet, I've got to go in front of the judge before I get a bond. And while I'm waiting for the bond, I'm being put in jail.

I've got to go and get changed into jail clothes, and then they send me into this big receiving dorm. It's just a big, big room with rows of double bunk beds. It's about eight bathroom stalls, about the same number of showers. And in the front of the room, there are about four deputies standing behind this glass partition. On the side of the deputies, the way you came in, is a dayroom where you can watch TV. But it stayed locked most of the time. Because the women acted up all the time. When folks act up, that's the first thing they do, lock up the dayroom. No dayroom, ladies. Go sit on your bunks.

They had about a hundred and fifty women in there. Sometimes the receiving room is half-empty, sometimes it's filled to capacity and they have to pull in mats and women sleep on the floor. You never know. The women who come in there are straight off the street. You tired, you sleepy, you been smoking crack, you smell, you might be beat up. You might have just come from the hospital, the infirmary. When you get your sentence—and I had gotten a hundred and eighty days— you go to the receiving dorms. And the working dorms sleep seventy to eighty people. Upper and lower bunks. In jail, they have three working dorms, and three floors—the basement, one, and two. Three floors and about five or six tiers on each floor. And those are dormitory-like settings, and in the receiving dorm there are like a hundred and fifty women sleeping in the same room. It was a cesspool of germs. Some of the nastiest people were in there. They had outbreaks of lice. People shitting in the shower and dumbass shit like that. Everybody wanted to do their time and get out of there. Everybody wants to go to the working dorm—the laundry dorm, the kitchen dorm, the cleaning dorm, the sewing dorm, the dock dorm. Otherwise, you just sit around and talk shit, braid hair until it's time to go to sleep. If you sitting around in the dorm all day, you're going to get into a fight, into squabbling. And the way the officers ran it, if one person got into trouble—got caught doing drugs or having sex—everybody got punished. It's two, three o'clock in the morning, and they wake everybody up; make you stand up next to your bunk and tell you another inmate just woke you up in the middle of the night. Or they toss your box. See, they give you a little cardboard box where you can keep your little possessions; you accumulate a couple bars of soap and what have you, and as punishment they take your box and toss it in the garbage.

When you first go to jail, you have to go to the clinic. HIV wasn't real yet—later they started coming up with cases, but not then. Syphilis they tested you for. So I went to the infirmary, and they took my blood, and they called me in the middle of the day to come back to the infirmary, which was embarrassing. I found out I had syphilis. They had to keep me up there and injected me with antibiotics because I was in the second stage. I had Blackness in the palm of my hand. I didn't know what that shit was. So I got saved. And you know what? I was so glad I was treated. I had been in such bad shape. I had an abscess on the side of my leg that was so deep they had to dig a plug in my leg. Abscess was just a poison in your body and it didn't have nowhere to go. So it was coming out in weak spots and stuff. I was bald-headed, didn't have no hair on my head. I got some old mug shots. I looked a mess. I had to stay in the infirmary for almost two weeks before they let me go back into the dorm.

I put in a request to work in the kitchen, but you can't have syphilis and work in the kitchen. So I got a job at the docks. Now, a job at the docks was where they shipping all that stuff that came into the jail. The Sybil Brand Institute was a working jail. It was the county jail for women, but it also had programs, before people were even talking about programs. Sybil Brand was a rich millionaire woman, and she and a bunch of her friends built that institution up there to rehabilitate prisoners.

Every year, Ray Charles came in and did a free concert. We all would be standing in line, and Ray Charles would be popping. I worked on the docks, and there was this sheriff there, and she was really nice to me. She ran the laundry and I was in the laundry. I did the officer uniforms. So the officers would put five or ten dollars in their uniform shirts to tip me and make sure I handled their shit real good. So I got money and I would get my hair done. Cause nobody sent me money when I went to jail. Every time I went to jail, it was on me. Just Brenda.

Nobody had my back or sent me shit, unless I had a trick who I could tell, "Yo, bring me some shit." Sometimes I would get lucky and have him running me in things and shit. "Bring me some gym shoes. Some underwear." But most of the time I would just try to make do. I would sing for bitches. Crazy shit. They would ask, "Hey, Breezy, sing me that song."

"I got you, boo. Give me some chips." Cause, you know, I loved a snack. I had a connection in the kitchen and we would trade. They got me something and I would get them something because I worked on the docks. Or, when I went to do laundry, I would have a few dollars.

Up there at Sybil Brand, the Mexican girls had everything. If one Mexican come in, then another come in after her, that new Mexican is gone be alright. They would pass a pillowcase around, and everybody would throw something in that pillowcase for that new Mexican that came in there. Cause it was always like, "This is my cousin's sister's daughter's niece. You know what I'm saying, mi amiga? She's cool, she's cool."

They always took care of their people, but I could get shit off them, too, because people liked me. I didn't have too many problems because when I whooped somebody's ass, I whooped their ass. Nobody was messing with me because I wouldn't beef with nobody. I would be stupid and funny, but other than that, I maintained myself.

I spent a lot of my life in that damned place. It's not there anymore. They tore it down because they needed a bigger facility, because the population of women prisoners is increasing by 125 percent. That's how fast women are going to jail now. Almost as fast as men. But Sybil Brand was my second home in California. And it saved my life a couple of times.

It even saved my baby, because I was in jail for the middle of my third pregnancy. In fact, for most of my pregnancy.

I had had a pregnancy test in jail, and they had told me I wasn't pregnant. So they let me go to Mira Loma Detention Center. You couldn't go to Mira Loma if you were pregnant because it was an old army base. But everybody likes it because you get to walk outside there if you want to. You don't have to be stuck inside for six months. Sometimes, I'd step out on the dock, and I looked around, and I felt like I had just left a spaceship or something. Who are all these people outside, aliens? Shit was crazy.

Anyway, even though I took that pregnancy test and it came out negative, it was wrong. I was pregnant. I was in Mira Loma, pregnant. I didn't know who the daddy was. He was a trick, I guess. Anyway, they caught themselves. I went in to the medical office for a regular checkup, and the test came back and said I was pregnant. They said, "Okay, you got to go back, we can't keep you here and you pregnant. You got to go back to Sybil Brand."

"I won't go. I love this place and I'm going to stay here forever!" Pancake Day was the best day there! They just laughed at me and sent me back, and I got out of jail pregnant. I was four months pregnant. I didn't know what to think. But since I was pregnant, I was trying to find me a goofy who I could pin it on. I remember asking a couple of people in the community who knew me and I knew them, if they got my baby, would they keep it safe. I asked two people. I asked Stephanie's momma, Ms. Hatchett, and Ms. Lee. I knew Ms. Lee from the neighborhood. She and her husband were wonderful people. She had a couple of sons who I smoked cracked with. Ms. Lee said, "Let me think about it." But then she said, "But then you gone try to get your baby back, ain't you?"

"I don't know, Ms. Lee. I mean, if shit keeps happening like this, I might not make it."

She said, "You gone be alright."

I didn't think I was going to have a future. The streets were very rough on me and that was all I had. The night before I had her, tricks were coming back to back to date me. Tricks don't care about you being pregnant. Okay? In fact, they even have a myth that pregnant vagina's hot. So here I was, all these tricks, and I had almost four hundred dollars on me that night when I decided to stop turning tricks. I was on my way to get me some breakfast, and then I was going to get to Bubby Jackson. Bubby was this dope dealer. He had this deep, deep voice: "You know Bubby Jackson gone hook you up." Folks would be like, "Is that voice real?" Was his name real? Anyway, he had left town, but he told me I could lay low at his spot. There was nobody there but me.

The day I had my baby, I had the big-ass breakfast over at this place called Tom's. They would give you tons of food. You could get chili cheese fries in one of those closed-up boxes. Get pastrami with all the works on it. Oh my God. The best chili cheese fries in the world. I think they were still using government cheese. Can I just say how good government cheese was? It was so good it was ridiculous.

So when I got to the house eating my food, I had thought to do some cocaine, too. But I said, no, I ain't doing that shit right now. I had eaten real good and I was laying there, and *knock, knock, knock*. "Come in." Pleasure. Here come in Pleasure, and she had gotten in some mess, then got out of it, and she was telling me all about it. She had a little something to smoke and I was letting her smoke.

She said, "Here, take some."

I said, "I don't want any."

We talked a little bit more, and she insisted I take a little hit. She wasn't going to let it go.

"Take some."

But I said no, because I wanted to get to sleep.

"Take some with me." So I took a little hit. I hit that pipe, and as I inhaled, I could feel my water breaking. And as I looked at her, I made a decision. I gave her twenty dollars.

"Here, go get us some more." I knew if I gave her twenty dollars, she wasn't coming back. Twenty was enough to get you caught up. And she knew I wouldn't care because she was my buddy. When she left out the door, I saw that another guy had taken another room at Bubby's. I asked him to call the ambulance because my water had just broke.

He said, "For real?"

I said, "Yeah." I went back into my room, and I cleaned up and sat down. When the ambulance came, I started not to tell them that I had took the hit and I had been smoking. I wished I hadn't. But I did tell them. They started treating me like I was a crackhead. Not the paramedics, but when we got to the hospital. Those nurses. Bitches. They acted like I had killed their momma or something. They didn't know nothing at that time about drugs and crack. Bitches were treating me like I had killed the pope.

If I asked for water or ice chips, they might as well have said, "You don't need no goddamned chips." The tone of their voice was, "We don't like you, you smoking on this baby, bitch." That was what they wanted to say, but they couldn't, professionally. I was hollering; I was in so much pain I didn't know what to do. Eighteen hours of that shit going on.

Everything was so wrong. She had to go straight to the incubator because she was a preemie. And she was addicted. They had to do all that to that poor baby because she was a drug baby. She was shaking all over, cause that crack was in her system. I was wrong for that. And because of it, there wasn't an epidural in town for me. You ain't getting no epidural, I'm letting you know that right now. And I was like, damn, did I kill Christ? Although, I might as well have, because that was some horrible shit. I guess I deserved all that shit they threw at me. And they had probably seen some awful shit in that hospital. The kind of people who were coming in because of the crack. We were destroying babies one crack rock at a time.

At one time, I actually had enough in my heart to talk to other bitches like that: "Naw, I'm not giving you anything. You pregnant. Give the baby a chance."

But what right did I have to say that? That day in the hospital, I hit bottom. I hit it. That shit was messed up. That shit was so messy. And there was nothing I could do. The doctors were ready for me to go home. The baby was in the incubator, and I could come back and visit every day. But it was time for my crackhead ass to get up out of there. I did the paperwork, but they wouldn't let me take the baby home because there were drugs in her system. And now what I had to do was come back up there every day and come see my baby, and on top of that I had to deal with some social worker trying to figure out if I could keep my baby. That's what I should have done. And you know what? The worst part, when I left the hospital and went to the hood, people would ask me, "Where your baby at? Where's the baby?" But when I went back to see the baby, the nurses and the social workers were talking about locking me up. It scared me.

They gave me a court date for her. The day I was supposed to go to that court date, I went to an abandoned building and I got me some crack and got me a bottle of wine and I broke windows and I kicked in walls and I cried. There were twelve people in there with me. I didn't know why they were there. I was kicking in walls and breaking windows, and I couldn't stop crying and crying. "I'm sorry, I'm sorry, I'm sorry." Because the truth was, I didn't have anywhere to take her. "I'm so sorry." I didn't even own a blanket to wrap her in. "I'm sorry, I'm sorry." I started praying to God, let somebody come get her who's good. God, let me see her one day and she'll be with some rich-ass family. Let her have a good momma. "I'm sorry, little baby. I'm sorry, God. Amen."

Chapter 16

The Facts of Life

I was in California for four more years after that, but it wasn't any fun anymore. Trouble was all around me. It was time to go, but I was still hanging around. Todd Bridges, that guy from the TV show *Diff'rent Strokes*, had come into our community. And that says a lot. The crack epidemic didn't discriminate. It tested everybody. How did this kid, all the way from Beverly Hills, Hollywood, get himself to South Central? But there he was, getting high, smoking crack with the Do-Low Crew.

He was such a little bitch. I ain't having sex with Todd; me and Stephanie were just partying and getting high with him. But as soon as he got him a white girl, he would lose his mind. That was a part of his issue. He was a kid star who couldn't handle what was going on.

One time, we were at a friend of mine's house on Sixty-Fifth and Flower. Cisco had a really nice house. If he would have kept it up, the place could have turned heads. Todd's momma knew Cisco. Todd had his BMW parked right outside, and the doorman (and when we say *doorman*, we mean the dude who gets paid with drugs to answer the door at the spot) asked Todd if he could use the BMW to go and pick up his momma from the airport. He didn't bring that car back.

In the hood, you get called out if you don't retaliate. But Todd was such a baby that he didn't do anything. I mean, the dude took his car, and Todd just stuck his thumb in his mouth. I saw Todd Bridges on TV, talking a bunch of bullshit about this story, and he was telling a bunch of lies, making like he was handling guns and he was a gangster and all that. No, he wasn't! He was a punk. Todd wouldn't shoot nobody; that wasn't his MO.

When I saw Todd on TV, talking that bullshit, I thought, *I wish I was there, so I could bust his ass.* Because he was just lying. He should have told the truth. Crack was the great equalizer. Being a TV star didn't protect you. Being rich didn't keep you safe. Instead, Todd wanted to tell this lie about how he went from pampered movie star to OG gangster. That just didn't happen. The only time Todd acted up was when he was with white girls. If they came around, he didn't want to let you in.

"Okay, little bitch. Keep it up." So I stole his shit, and brothers would tell him, "Man, you don't know who you messing with here. You have no idea—this is *Breezy*." The truth was, if you let me, I could pull off some pretty outrageous shit. One time, me and Stephanie had a Cadillac, but the Cadillac belonged to this guy Lionel and he didn't like me. I didn't care. Him and Stephanie were together—they later got married—and he didn't want his woman out there sucking wang, which might happen if she was out there hanging with me. Okay. But when he met her, she was sucking wang. She sucked *his* wang. Anyway, he had this Cadillac, but the Cadillac didn't have no front window in it. We were driving down the street. That was some stupid shit. I looked at Stephanie and said, "Bitch, this stupid." The wind was kicking our ass because it was blowing right in our face; it's like riding a motorcycle in a car. Everything hitting you in the face and shit. We went through all of that to go and get some rocks. All of our missions were about getting rocks. Getting high and going back and forth from Sybil Brand was my life in California. That was my life.

One time, John Hunt's boys let me in his drug house, and when he came in, he said, "Oh hell naw. You let Breezy in here?" He said it like I was a disease. "Y'all got Breezy in here? Man, I'm violating you niggas."

"John, don't be talking about me like that. I ain't taking nothing from these niggas."

Without meaning to, I found myself wandering from one piece of drama to another. At first, I was with this pimp named Rick in Hollywood. I was making my little money, and all of a sudden it was evening time, and evening time was a great time for me. It was going into dusk, when people start relaxing and having their little drinks and picking girls up. All of a sudden, people started throwing beer bottles and shit on the street. And these were white folks. White folks throwing shit at me on the street. I was confused. I didn't know the verdict had come out from the Rodney King trial. I saw this Black dude and hopped in his car. "Nigga, take me back to South Central." I went to the hotel where Jazzy sold drugs but wasn't nobody there. I can't remember what happened next, but for some reason we parked and watched people loot. People were going in stores, pulling out safes, and rolling them down the street. Refrigerators and couches were on dudes' backs.

"This shit fucking up all my motherfucking money." I couldn't suck nobody's Johnson when shit was like that. How was I supposed to get paid?

I told my new homeboy to take me back around the Do-Low Crew area. And everybody was doing something different. Jazzy was selling drugs, and she had her man. Stephanie was I didn't know where. I was kind of on my own, and I knew this drug dealer around the corner who liked me. He was about two blocks down. They had put a curfew on the city. How you gone sell twat just till seven o'clock? This has to stop. How was I supposed to eat? So I put a catsuit on and my big hoop earrings. And I went out there to talk with the National Guard. The National Guard was sitting there, and I entertained them. "Who's first? Cause this is discount time. I won't charge you full price."

They got tired of my ass and made me leave. I still needed my money. I was still rolling, baby. I never had such a depressing time in my life. Bullshit. That was so depressing. It was just all messed up. I said, "Don't y'all do that shit no more."

I started hanging with a guy who liked me named Chug-a-Lug. Chug-a-Lug was hilarious. Really cute. He always had a great idea. Like how to get high and sell drugs. So I was hanging with Chug-a-Lug, we were up there, after we had gotten our drugs from the Freeway Boys. There was a documentary about the Freeway Boys—about how the FBI used them to put all this crack cocaine in the Black community. They would sell drugs to and buy guns from the Freeway Boys. There was a whole conspiracy that the FBI was behind. The Freeway Boys liked me. I used to knock on their door and ask them, "What y'all doing today?"

"What's up, Breeze? What you want?" And then I would open my coat up, and I would have on like little pasties and a G-string. Or I would have a little maid outfit on with no panties on. And they would crack up because they were just drug dealers, living life. They would let me in the drug house, and I would play with all the guys, and they would give me a lotta drugs and some money.

So I'm kicking it with Chug-a-Lug, and he was selling drugs out of this little apartment he had in Crips territory. This girl, Oriana, was in there with us. We didn't really have any beef. She was just a crackhead. I had already given her some drugs but didn't really want to let her in. But I did. She was so scandalous, subject to do things that made you hurt her. The guys would say, "She's too scandalous, so I had to hurt her."

But I said, "Nah, let her in. She's my friend." But she wasn't. I used to think she was okay, because crack had a way of turning women into anything. Women would do anything for it. I never got to the point where I would do anything for crack, but I also knew I was walking that road, so I felt sorry for her. For me, there was a cut-off, but all around me there were folks who had surrendered. I would be the person who said, "Okay, today the day it's just not for me to get. I can't go that far." But I had my share of bullshit I did. Some of it was embarrassing or degrading. But I never got to the point where guys could come up to me and ask me to do something so humiliating. They wanted to watch you have sex with a dog. I couldn't get with that raggedy shit.

Anyway, when Oriana left, she took Chug-a-Lug's gold chain with her. Like I said, she was scandalous. And I'm like, well, you know. But then I saw her downstairs. So I asked her, "Why you take that fucking chain?" And the Crips and shit were all around us and those were her folks. I was talking crazy to her. I mean, I saw that that bitch was gone bolt, so I knocked her down. She got up, and we started fighting, and I whooped her ass. But see, if I was going to whoop her ass, I should have whooped her ass and then got up out of there. Because all of her people were there. She's a Crip-a-lette. I was not. I'm from Chicago, still thinking I was with the Vice Lords. I needed to sit my ass down or get up out of there. I didn't do that. I headed back upstairs to Chug-a-Lug's. I heard the bottle when it broke. I heard somebody break a bottle. Then I heard footsteps. *Boom. Boom. Boom. Boom.* Like somebody was running. I got up there to Chug-a-Lug's to knock on the door, but before I could detect that anybody was running up behind me—because it was a dark stairway—she was all the way up on me, and she had that broken bottle in her hand. And I raised my arm to try to stop her, but the bottle cut my face. My nose was open. She opened up my face. Blood was shooting out my face like a fountain. Chug opened the door. I fell inside, bloody. I scared the shit out of him. The police came and the ambulance. I was so high. That was why I was losing so much blood; my adrenaline was high. The firemen were trying to calm me down. I was screaming like a pig, "Oh shit, oh shit, oh shit. I'mma die. I'mma die."

And this smartass fireman said, "Yeah, you is, if you don't shut up." Because they were looking at the situation: we were at a drug house, they knew I was high. They didn't treat us right. They didn't treat crackheads like human beings. I mean, they were like, "They're crackheads. Who cares?" They took me to Killer King Hospital. There are some hospitals in California where everybody says, don't go there. They'll kill you up in there. But you know what? Killer King saved my life. Twice.

I went there in the ambulance, and the ER doctor came in and looked at me, and he said, "You a pretty girl. Let me see if I can get somebody down here and see if they can fix your face, so that you won't be disfigured for the rest of your life."

"Okay, anything."

There was a plastic surgeon on staff at the hospital. He came down, and I remember him saying, "If we stitch your face, it will disfigure you." He was looking at the keloids on me already. "But if I butterfly it, and you take care of it, you'll have a chance." He butterflied my face, wrapped me up, and the hospital dropped me off at a shelter. They had an overflow of people there, but they couldn't turn me away. They made me a pallet in the broom closet. They took out the mops and stuff. There was a bathroom across the hall. I guess I needed the privacy. And that's where I laid down, because I had no place to go.

They forgot I was there. I laid in that broom closet for two days. I had a lotta painkillers and shit in me, and I was tired. I actually peed on myself because I was knocked out. I was so embarrassed. But I didn't know what my body was doing. But coming out that closet, and realizing that the people didn't even know I was there, it was like . . . some shit can get to you. I thought, this is what happens to you when you are in pain and you're disfigured. For a minute I thought, should I call my family? Should I let anybody know? But I made the decision not to, because why should I call them and upset them? I wasn't doing anything for them. I did an inventory of what I had been up to. All the mistakes I had made a long list. What were my options? Where was I going to go? Who cared about me anymore? None of it was good. Everything I did was dependent on my appearance. I couldn't figure out a way out of the situation I was in. When I came out of the closet and started walking around, the man at the counter asked me where I had come from. I told him, and he said, "Oh, shit. We forgot you were there." He looked embarrassed. I told him I was alright, but I wasn't. I began to feel as invisible and insignificant as it comes.

Meanwhile, word got out this bitch cut up my face. I had to go back into the neighborhood with that. And that means now folks would think they could just come and whoop my ass anytime they felt like it. All I could think about was vengeance. Because the worst-case scenario was worse than worst. Folks were looking at me like I was an alien or like I was about to drop dead. People would give me a dollar or two out of pity. I hated the pity more than anything. And it was kind of like that for a minute—until I got better, because I wasn't hanging with nobody until my face got better.

But there was some guys around who really liked me. I had done some things for those brothers. I had set some of them up. They had gotten money from me, and I had helped them when they were on their last leg. And those same dudes went and whooped her ass because she thought she could go anywhere and cut a bitch up.

One of the guys, he had just gotten out of the joint. He was buff. Fine and shit. I'm messing with him. I was always the kind who wanted to spoil somebody, give them my money and shit. That was me. Even though they weren't asking me, I was still in that mentality that I had to pay for my friends, my men, and my love. I always bought friends and bought love. But this guy was real cool. I had given him seven hundred dollars, and he was gone and go get his package. I thought we were together. Come to find out, he really needed that money to go and see his kids and he had no way of getting there. When I found out what he really did with the money, his woman was the one who told me. We were in the hotel getting high together and she told me, "He went to the kids and gave them that money. You is where he got that money from."

"Yeah, that was me." We were cool; we laughed about it.

That guy was the one who knocked Oriana out.

Then another dude who was really cool with me, and was a real gangster, came to me and said, "I'm gonna kill Oriana for you."

"Nah, don't kill her," I told him.

Now what I did do was put this dude Barry on her who had HIV. I told him to take her to the hotel and stick it to her.

Barry said, "I got you." That was low. But it was low times.

California was starting to catch up to me. My face had been cut open, Lynn had been killed, I couldn't sell much sex because I was in such awful shape. Even when I tried to do the right thing, it came back at me twice as bad. Like when I testified against this dude for killing this prostitute friend of mine.

Her momma came to me and said, "Breezy, don't just let this go. Say something." At the time I was with this guy named V-dub, and he had gone to jail, but before he left, he told the brothers in the hood, "Watch out for my girl." Everybody knew I had seen that guy who killed my friend, but the police hadn't caught him yet. I heard he was looking for my ass. So V-dub told the brothers in the neighborhood, "Don't let anything happen to my baby." So the dudes in the neighborhood found the guy before the police and they beat his ass down. Beat him with bricks and left him for dead, but he didn't die. He was in a nursing home. The police weren't really paying him any attention because he couldn't walk. But he got better real fast and started walking and left that nursing home and was back out on the streets looking for me. I was being careful, trying to dodge him. And some people were protecting me. But then the police got the bright idea to lock me up. For my own protection, they told me. They kill me with that shit. Why they got to lock me up? Why can't they lock up the man who was after me? So now I was locked up for my own protection—how does that sound? And this brother was out on the streets.

Finally, I did testify against him. Later on, I found out John Hunt was the killer's chief. I didn't know that. I would have never testified if I had known that. John asked me about it later, and he said, "You know that's one of my guys. I can't believe you did it. You testified." See, John didn't believe I testified because people knew me. They knew I'd stand up. I hadn't forgotten what Coolie taught me: never snitch.

I told him why I did it: my friend's momma had asked me to. John looked at me. "You know you can't come out on the streets no more."

"Yeah. I pretty much know that." I knew I was fair game, and he couldn't help me now. I needed to figure out my next step.

+ + +

I decided to try to stop taking drugs so I could be a better ho. First of all, it wasn't really safe for me to hang around with the drug dealers. I couldn't pop up to the drug houses like I used to. It got so bad, folks wouldn't sell me any dope. Me and my friend, Momma Jelly, our feet were hurting. The only steady trick I had was the stalker, Alrick. This dude was staying with his momma, and he wanted me to come stay with them. He wanted me to get clean and marry him. Man, please. It was too much. This boy was crazy. I'm like, man, I'm just a ho on the streets. But I didn't have a lot of choices. So we went to treatment, me and Momma Jelly.

Momma Jelly stayed, but I left early, and I went back on the ho stroll. I developed this infection in my finger; I still have a discoloration on it right now. You know, when you cut up that cocaine all the time with a razor, you can get an infection. I always used this finger to cut up cocaine and I had gotten all this bacteria in it.

One day, I was in so much pain, I couldn't believe it. I took some crack to help with the pain. Momma Jelly was telling me I was relapsing. But really, I didn't want to be clean in the first place. She was all in tears. She got me to go back into the little treatment stuff at the Salvation Army. And that bitch called my brothers. I go to this recovery home in South Central and I get a call the third day I am there.

"Telephone."

"Okay, who is it?" It was my brother. It was Todd.

"Hey, girl. Listen. I'm 'bout to go to the airport right now, get your ticket, and I'm going to call you back with everything. You come on home. You come on home now."

I was bawling like a baby. How many years? It was about four-teen years, because I left in 1980 and it was '94 now. I had been gone all that time. When I had last left Chicago, my brother gave me his money, and I was supposed to come back but I didn't. They kicked him out his place because I didn't show up with his money. I couldn't face him, so I decided to go to another town. But even with all that, he still sent for me.

I got on that plane. I just left. I didn't say goodbye to anybody. I didn't tell none of the girls left in the Do-Low Crew I was leaving. There was nothing for me to pack up or pick up. My name was trash on the streets, and John Hunt couldn't protect me. I needed to get out of California. My brothers, on the other end of the phone, told me to come on home.

+ + +

I will say one good thing about all that mess I did in California. No one brings up your past—because they did the dirt with you. I don't have too many people who are still able to call me. But if you don't die, if you make it to the other side, there is redemption, and it comes to you in phone calls, and clips on Facebook, and hellos at picnics. I'm still friends with my stalker. *Hey, Brenda Myers, this is your friend. How are you in Chicago? I was at the airport and I was thinking of you. I hope you and your family are doing well.* His family call me. Alrick's family adored me. Jamaican people. They call and say, "Girl, we so proud."

Spud, my little sweetie, called me one night. "Hey, baby, I seen you on TV. I'm telling my fiancée, you used to be my girlfriend."

"How you doing, Spud?" And he put his girlfriend on the phone. She laughed and told me hello.

People still hang with me, because I'm a lotta fun to be with. Brothers remember that shit: "Baby, you was a lotta fun." I don't have anybody who I'm not alright with. That's living. If you can make it, if you don't die, such kindness can come to you. It almost makes those awful times worth it. Almost.

Chapter 17

Madison Street

I came back to Chicago in 1994, stayed with my brother, went to Harold Washington College, and got my Certified Nursing Assistant degree. Graduated top of the class and started my internship at Cook County Hospital. I was working with these Jewish people out near Skokie. You know, those people take care of their old parents. I was making a lotta money. I was doing real good. I wasn't close with my girls, but when Prune came by to see her uncle Todd, she said hello to me. Peaches was almost out of college. They both knew I was trying to make it work.

Those old ladies I was working with were just as crazy as they could be, but they were sweet. They used to call me their girl. One lady, she had sundowns. All day we would kick it, but then at sundown she would start regressing. I would knock on the door and let myself in, and she would look at me and whisper, "Hey, there's a Negro in the house."

Her daughter looked her and said, "That's Brenda, Momma.

Don't call her a Negro." I told her I wasn't upset, she didn't know. That old lady was funny. She looked like that old lady on *The Golden Girls* because she used to carry around this little straw purse.

I worked with this old man who pinched on my titty while I gave him his Medicare baths. I looked at him like, *Mister*, but he just giggled and kept at it. Dirty old man. But I liked those old people. And I liked the money. I liked that my daughters were starting to thaw toward me.

But I liked dope even more. I missed my old life. I started getting high again.

You know, all that time I was clean and going to school, I don't think I was really doing that for myself. I was doing it for my family. I wanted them to be able to say, Brenda's doing good now. But I wasn't ready to stop. Didn't nobody pull me out there. I stepped out there. I set myself up. I got back out there, and I was news in the neighborhood again. I stopped going to my job because I wasn't ready to stop hoing. I was addicted to the lifestyle. I liked the fast guys, the fast money. I wasn't ready to be Brenda. I was still Breezy. Breezy was worldly and dangerous. Being a square, working a job, that was like wearing a costume. Life on the streets was my real life. Breezy was the real me. I needed to get back out there.

So much had changed since I last strolled Madison Street. I heard Coolie was selling drugs. When I went back home, I ran into him there. Coolie had gotten on heroin, but you couldn't see it. Then word was he had a stroke, and he never came back from it. Nobody told me because I wasn't connected with people in the game anymore, but I found out through the grapevine that he passed away. They told me that at the end he was down at the shelter. Even now, I still think about Coolie. There's something about him I can't shake. "I gotta walk away from love"—that's David Ruffin, and Coolie used to sing that to me. When I think of him, I remember how much music we had in our house. Coolie was a hand-holding man, and he loved it when I followed him around. I went to jail for Coolie. Gladly.

But it was more than just Coolie who had changed and passed

away. The last time I was in Chicago, I had hung out with my cousin Deborah. She had a pimp named Cold Jones. There weren't too many women I was allowed to go out with. Cold and Coolie controlled our lives. Anyway, we hung out and went out every Sunday to the North Side, the nice part of Chicago, and out to the nice restaurants. It was our Sunday out, and we could do what we wanted to do. We would sit at the bar and eat cheese, drink wine, and be toasty as hell, then go eat something. Maybe stop at a lounge on the way home. Sunday was ours.

I didn't hook back up with Deborah when I got back out there. I tried to look up Jackie, but I found out she died when I was off in California. Overdose. When I left Madison Street, it was my street. But coming back after California, I realized it didn't have as many stores as it used to have when I was a child. It still had a bustle and a swing. It was still the place where everybody shopped. But it wasn't the same. There was a tailor shop over Mr. Kim's wig store, and everybody would go and get their clothes tailored there. I was Miss Thang on Madison Street. I was known for my jazzy walk, tiny waist, big booty. Here I go: "*Hi!*" That was what Madison was to me before I left. I had a lotta fans on Madison. Maybe that was why I got back out there. I missed the excitement of my past.

+ + +

So I left what was supposed to be my good-news story and headed back to hoing. There I was, the frontline story.

I went to do this trick on Cicero. He was a little country guy. He was hilarious. I was coming down the street, and he was standing in the alley. And he was like, "Oh, girl." I was thick. Nice thick. "Where you going?"

"Nowhere," I said. "What you doing?"

"I live right there."

"Okay, that's nice."

"You gone come sit down for a minute?"

I had to go get my check from my job, but I was like, *Forget that check*. I said, "Yeah, I wanna come sit down." I mean, I wanted a check, but of course I wanted to sit down with him a minute even more. He didn't know it, but he was inviting me back to my old life. It was an invitation I couldn't say no to.

One thing led to another, and now I was staying with him. Everybody was teasing him because he had a ho living with him. But I didn't care what they felt because before I left, everybody in that apartment complex liked me. At first, his landlord kept on telling him, "She gotta go." But by the end, the landlord was like, "You okay, Breezy?"

I was still living on Cicero when I saw Sonny. I was out strolling for some money, and here he comes, looking swell. He had just gotten out of the penitentiary. I thought he was the finest thing. Pretty brown skin. He had finger waves in his head, he was cut. I was like, *Oh God*. I was like, *I need that man*.

He was giving out testers—and he handed me a bag of heroin. "I don't do those kinds of drugs," I told him, and I gave him the bag back.

He said, "Okay, you don't need that, then."

"What's your name?"

"My name's Sonny, baby. You?"

"You can call me Breezy." He left and the girl he was with stayed behind.

I turned to her. "Is he a pimp?" She told me who he was, and I said, "I like him. I'm gone get him. Let me go get me some money."

So I went and got me some money, and I looked for him for about a couple of weeks. I finally found him. I was up there near Augusta, and he was in this liquor store. I went in and I said, "Hey!"

"Hey, girl."

"I been looking for you."

"Well, here I am."

"Yes, you are. With your fine ass."

"I'm going to this clubhouse over here."

"Can I come back and see you?"

"Yeah."

So I went on inside the little clubhouse with Sonny, and now we were flirting with each other. I told him all about me, and Sonny was telling me how he gets down, what kind of brother he was. Stuff like that. He said to me, "Well, how you get down?"

"I get money. Do you?"

He started laughing. "Yeah. I got a little product to sell right now."

"You do? How much you got?"

"I got rocks."

"I said, how much you got?"

"How much you need?"

"How much you got, for real?"

"I don't know. Let me see." And he reached down into his pocket. "I got about three, four hundred dollars' worth."

"Give me all of that."

"Oh. You got it like that?" He leaned back and started laughing. I knew what he was thinking: this big-booty bitch just doing it. Showing out.

He gave me all of what he had, and I got a lump, and this brother saw me peel off money. I gave him five hundred. "Here. Make it light on yourself." Of course, I knew he wanted my ass.

"Okay. Okay. You ready to do something with a nigga?" he said.

"Shoot. You the only one sitting here."

"Let me get us a ride." He didn't have a car because he had just gotten out the joint. He got a dude's ride, and he took me to this hotel that was on Madison Street that was called the Grand. "So you and I gone do something?"

"You got something for me?"

"You know it." I reached down and gave him the lump, which was about twelve hundred dollars.

"I like a lady like you. Girl, you gone make me fall in love." I knew that was bullshit, but I also knew I had impressed this pimp. He left and was gone some hours. Then he came back, and he got in bed with me. We spent the night together. Usually, Sonny didn't just jump into bed with girls, but I had come on pretty strong. So the next night, we were getting ready to go out, and he introduced me to this other woman named Bridget. I got in the car with her because I knew I had to take control of this situation. I needed to let this bitch know who I was. What's going on was just a mind game between two women, and I'd played it so many times it was clockwork to me. I jumped in the car, looking at her. On a good day, she wasn't as sharp as I was. Her good day would be my worst day.

Sonny introduced us, and then she looked at me and said, "I ain't in on all that." I grabbed her by her face and stuck my tongue down her throat and kissed her.

I said, "Come here, baby. You my motherfucking bitch now."

Sonny cracked up. She was furious. "Don't be doing that! Don't be doing that!"

"You know you like that shit," I told her. "I know you a freak."

Sonny looked at us both and said, "Breezy's something else. She strong."

It was just a matter of mind games and letting a bitch know you. We went and got a hotel room and played around. Sonny had bought me some rock and didn't get her nothing. Cause she wasn't making the money I made. I was hitting this dude with money.

So I was sitting there putting my makeup on and my wig on, and this bitch put her cigarette out in my pop can. I reached over to get it and all I had was ashes in my mouth.

I turned around, "Bitch, you put your cigarette out in my pop can?" *Boom. Boom.* I start hitting that ho.

Sonny crossed the room. "Oh, I got to keep my tiger in a tank somewhere."

He was talking about me because he knew I wasn't playing with Bridget. I came in and claimed my turf. I took his ass from that bitch. Now, let me tell you something: he had known this bitch for years before I came. He still liked that bitch. But he could not turn down the type of money that I was bringing. He separated from her completely and was with me. Bridget was making good flat-back money—three hundred, four hundred—but I was coming up with fifteen hundred, two thousand, three thousand dollars on a lick. Every week. It was back-to-back, seven hundred, eight hundred. My money looked like that. She couldn't compete. She never could. And money, that's our power on the street. Like being the lioness with the lion. And we were together, until we weren't no more.

I mean, I had spent all that time in California without a pimp, so when I hooked up with Sonny, it was nice. I had company again. It's nice to have a pimp and have somebody in control. I had somebody I could go and share my shit with, instead of spreading it all over the street. I became prostitute legal then. And the thing about being on the streets, if you ain't got nobody, other pimps put their hands on you because they could. If you get a real pimp that other people know, nobody will mess with you. I mean, if you hoing without any representation, you could be sitting up and not bothering nobody and a pimp can come in and pop you in the mouth. "Bitches need to break they self." And I knew they were talking about me because I was the only bitch in there who didn't have a man. And these dudes weren't even pimps, they just acting up because they knew about me. I mean, men would take my money if they had a gun. That's how guys would do you.

The thing was, after California, I was a bitch who really liked to squabble. One time, I was hanging out with this young girl used to be out there, kind of like a goofy me. We were out there with her man and all of us decided it was time to cop some drugs. You know when you out there, you give your money to the guy who can point out the guy who has the drugs, but before we started any transaction, I used to tell them, "Listen, if he ain't got no drugs, I'mma come back and whoop your ass." I was about to give some random dude some money and the other guy who pointed him out to me had to guarantee that he was, in fact, a drug dealer. Sure enough, this time the drug dealer disappeared. I turned around to the guy who had pointed him out. "I told you."

He said, "I ain't got nothing to do with that. Maybe he'll be back in a minute." I looked at that man and didn't say nothing to him. I went over to a car with some light-skinned dude behind the wheel.

I said, "You got a piece in your car?"

"Naw, I got a bat. What you gone do?" But he popped the trunk and gave me the bat. I went over and got two good ones in before he went *vroom*.

I looked around. "Anybody that fuck with my motherfucking money, understand!"

A friend came and got me. "Come on, Breezy. Let's go get you some money, cause you gone wind up and whip the whole motherfucking block."

Everybody has a pressure point—even in the game, you have a pressure point. You either get your ass whipped out there, or you whip some ass. You either let folks know that ain't you, or it will be you. Sometimes you just take the bump that day. And that day, I didn't feel like it. There were days when I didn't feel like it. I would never tell a person that I was a total victim out there in the streets. Some days I was a victim and some days I was a victimizer. You cannot survive in the game and not be a predator, too. There were some days when I felt like everybody better watch out because I was out for mine by any means necessary. It can get dangerous for you with that mentality. It's such a negative energy. It's all over you. I have turned tricks and gotten into tricks' cars with such venom inside of me that I intimidated them so much they asked me to get out of their car, but it was too late because you let me in—and now I wanted all of your money. You weren't giving me a few fews and twos. White boys always had a real bad habit of reaching into their pocket and saying, "Here, take this and get out." Oh, yeah? I need *all* that. There is something that you start to be out there, that you don't want to be—but it pops up without your permission.

So I might have been a badass out there in the street or with Bridget, but that didn't mean I didn't get hurt out there.

The first time I got shot, I was next to Italian Beef's Restaurant, right there on the corner. Here's what happened. The potato chip man used to drop his deliveries off there, and I was always flirting with him. One day, I was standing by the end of the restaurant, where there was an alley, doing my thing, when I saw the potato chip man coming my way. He was doing his delivery, and I whispered to him, "Meet me in the alley." He drove down the alley, and I walked on in there, and I did my thing with the potato chip man. That was the first time he had ever hooked up with me, and I bet he wished he had never dated my ass, cause I took all his money. I stole the little white bag of money that was under his seat.

When I got out of his little truck, I was trying to get down the alley because I had stuffed the sack of money down between my legs. I had the date money in my hands—two twenties, forty dollars—and I was almost down to the end of the alley and here came another guy, and he pulled a gun on me. The potato chip man was gone. The dude took the money in my hands and said, "Gone in this garage."

I said, "I ain't going in this garage, nigga. No."

"You better get in that garage."

"I'm not going in no garage. What you gone do? Rob me and make me suck your dick? Give me my money back and I'll suck your dick."

"I ain't giving you shit back." He started laughing.

"Well, fuck you, then. The gun ain't real no way."

"Yes, it is."

"No, it ain't."

"Yes, it is."

"No, it ain't."

POW. I said, "Okay."

He shot me. In my pinkie toe. The bullet went in right there.

"Okay, where you want me to suck your dick, for real."

"Fuck you, you crazy."

"No, I ain't. I'm not crazy, nigga. You the one crazy."

"I'm getting away from you." See, I was kind of tipsy off that Wild Irish Rose. That shit makes you fight. Fight a telephone pole, if you want to. So now I was hopping down the alley, shot in my boot. I went to the corner by the restaurant, and I grabbed the pay phone and called 911 and the ambulance to come get me. Then I called my man Sonny. And that's the first time I got shot.

I was laid up for a minute after that. I remember, Sonny came back to the hotel room to check on me. "Guess what? I just saw Big Neecy." Big Neecy, Denice, was a friend of mine. "Guess what she did?"

"What?"

"That bitch just gave me three hundred dollars. She told me, 'Go take care of my friend.'"

I'll never forget that woman. She died in my arms. She had been in the joint, and she had gotten out of jail. She wasn't the most attractive girl, but she made a lotta money. Me and her used to sneak off when we wanted to get high. I was with Sonny and she was with this pimp name Steve Yo. When she used to take a hit off the cocaine, she would freak out. "Get it off me! Get it off me!" She'd start shaking all over.

I'd let her trip for a little bit, but then the people around us would say, "Stop her from doing that."

"Leave her alone. She okay." I would look at her and say, "Look at me. Look at me! Ain't nothing on you. Take a drink of this wine. Drink this wine." She'd drink the wine down. "Calm down, bitch. Calm down."

Then she would look around. "Bitch, where my shit at?"

"I got it, bitch. Sit down." People would take her shit when she was high like that. "You got to calm down off this one first."

Anyway, because getting shot meant I wasn't able to work, Sonny put Bridget to work and got a replacement for me. She was ugly. He came back to the hotel and told me, "You know what I just did? I just sat on the ho stroll for five straight hours and didn't nan bitch break luck. One too ugly and one too high." I started laughing because that wasn't my MO when I was out there. He couldn't damn near drive around the corner before I would be ready to go.

"I'm ready to go"—that's what he was used to. I could go to a guy's car, lean in, and talk to them, play with them. "Say, what you got down there?" I would be playing with his penis, but with my other hand I would steal his money. Once you have their wang in your hand, you got all their attention. Listen. I should write a book about Mr. Peter. I need to. Just like Steve Harvey wrote about relationships? I need to write a one-eyed monster book. And I can tell women how to handle that shit, how that shit goes, how you can be the queen. There are so many things you have to know how to do out there that relate to the weakness of men. And what they like. Listen: if a trick comes out on the street and leaves their house, tells their wife, "I'm going to go get a pack of cigarettes," and she says, "Take the baby with you, so that the baby can ride and go to sleep," and he's riding around with his baby in the car, his seed, his child, and he tells you to get in and suck his Johnson while his baby is in the back seat, who is in control? His wang. He has stepped outside the safety of his child, and that's what I knew. And I knew, when I stepped outside and was going to get somebody's money, I knew the one-eyed monster was in control out there. That's some cold shit to see. Me and some girls had gotten to a point where we said no to those tricks. We started hollering at them. We threw shit at their car. Sometimes we would tell the police, "He got a baby in that car." We wanted to shame them so they would get out of there.

Folks want to make us the most awful things on earth. When you say *prostitute*, people think "nasty bitches." But what about these nasty men who come to these nasty bitches? These men went through some changes to get to me. He came from the suburbs, he came down the highway, he had to do some shit. There were some things they had to do to pick me up. Some chances he had to take. And your wang said, "Fuck it. Let's go for it." People always trying to make it okay for these guys, but hos are the most awful people in the world. But that's just not true. Bitches just looking for love in all the wrong places. And we get caught up with these guys who take advantage of us. People think, oh, these girls decide to do this, this is their choice.

But what was her choice when she first started? Was it her choice then? Was she coerced? Was she kidnapped? Before this became her choice, she's four years old and she's gotten into this so early she doesn't know what a choice is. I know that for a fact, because I was forced into so many different types of relationships before I got clean. Lord knows, I had to go through so much trouble before I was able to get to the other side.

Even when I wasn't looking for trouble, for hurt, it found me. Like when I got shot the second time, three bullets in the arm. The Million Man March was going on and Sonny said he was going, but actually he was going to a bitch in St. Louis. But he wanted me to believe, like I was that dumb, that a pimp was going to the Million Man March. Said that to my face.

So I got this trick, and we were staying up at Sonny's sister Lois's house. The trick got me and Lois high. We made a run, but on the way back, we had a car accident. I didn't stay because there was a warrant out for me for prostitution. I ducked down the alleyway, and Lois and the trick stayed there for the police because the trick said he had insurance. After all that, they came back to the house and we continued to get high. When he was coming to the end of his money, I felt it was time for him to go. I didn't keep tricks around who didn't have money. We left, and then I went back on the stroll because when Sonny came home, I needed to have some money.

I left the trick parked right there at the corner, just before Cicero and Bloomingdale, and I cut through an alley where there was a vacant lot, just down the street. I caught a Mexican trick, and then I took his money. So now I was coming back down the alley, trying to get away from the Mexican, and just wanting to jump in the trick's car so we could get outta there. But when I got there, I saw more than one head in the car. I thought to myself, *Didn't I tell his ass don't let nobody in the car?*

Then a man stepped out the passenger side, and when he turned, I saw him come up with the pistol. I crouched down low and started running, and as I was running, I pumped my arms, and that was when my arm caught the bullet. I was running with my head down low, my arms swinging back and forth. Had I been standing up, I probably would have been shot in my back. I remember once being told, if somebody is trying to shoot you, run zigzag, don't run straight. Zigzag and get low. I didn't know why that came to me, but it did.

That was the kind of crazy nonsense I found myself caught up with. Crack was as bad in Chicago as it had been in California. All in all, I've been stabbed thirteen times and shot five times. When Sonny got back from his pretend Million Man March vacation, we got into it. Again. He and I went back and forth. He was another one of those brothers who was like, "You can't be with no one but me." And I was like, "Screw you." He wasn't as strong as Coolie. Maybe Sonny and I would have lasted, but he had gotten too regular with hitting on me. Maybe he would have gotten away with that kind of shit if I hadn't done all my traveling, if I hadn't gone through all that shit in California, if I hadn't learned all those hard lessons from Ma'Dea. But Ma'Dea prepared me for when she wasn't going to be around to protect me. In her own way, she prepped me to take a licking and keep on ticking. "She ain't gone be no pushover, when I get through with her ass." And I wasn't. Fighting was not a problem for me, cause it just seemed the right way to be. That's why I was always running and being an outlaw. I took some ass whippings from some men, but I fought some men, too.

That kind of shit went down between Sonny and me. He would catch me and see me on the street or something, jump out the car. "How much money you got, bitch?" I would lean back, because I knew he was going to go in my titties and get my money. But being with him was too confining. And he overworked a bitch. I was tired.

That day, I hadn't done anything but went and got money. I hadn't even finished working; I had more work to do. I had been out there when it was twenty, thirty degrees below zero. That's why I was taking a break. And he was talking about how he was gone beat my ass. Sometimes men would be feeling bad about something else but they want to come and jump on you about it. And I wasn't ready to get whooped that night. I ain't did nothing. It was funny: something in me said, *Are you really gone go in that house and have him beat your ass?* Cause I knew he was going to do it when we got inside. And I'm thinking, *For what? What did I do? I didn't do nothing. Got his money.* He told me what he was going to do when we got in the house. And when I got out the car, he talking about jumping me.

He grabbed me up. "Bitch, get in that house." And when he grabbed me, I coldcocked him. We got to fighting outside. I was tearing his ass up. Sonny couldn't believe it. I'm not saying like I'm a man, but I handled his ass that night. I was so angry; I was so mad about everything he had ever done to me.

There were three brothers across the street. And all of a sudden one of them came from across the street and said, "Alright, muffin man, back up off of her."

Another one reached down and said, "Back the fuck up off of her."

"That's my woman, man."

"Yeah, but back the fuck up off her, man. We not gone watch you out here." I was all over the place. Breathing heavy and crying and shit, but I really wanted to keep fighting. So them dudes looked at me and was like, "Come on here, baby," and walked me away down the block. Sonny vroomed off.

I was still crying. "That motherfucker . . ."

"Calm down, baby."

They calmed me down and I said thank you. But they were like, "Naw, baby, you had it. We watched you. We just gave you a chance to whip that nigga's ass. But you had it. We just came over there to stop it. You handled that." I'm all emotional. Then this light-skinned brother stepped out and said, "Breezy, you a *motherfucking G.*"

I thought to myself, yeah, I was the motherfucking hero.

Chapter 18

Chicago, Take Two

Sometimes I make this seem like an action movie and I was the hero, and in a lot of ways it was. I was out there dodging bullets, beating up pimps. I was a part of a lifestyle that had me going back and forth with street people. And let me tell you something: people go through shit in completely different ways. Sometimes you wild out, sometimes you hide. You get to this place that whatever jumps off, you feel like that's how life is supposed to be. One thing about street people is that they don't look at responsibilities the way they should. And you accept those weak spots from each other. Just like I made a whole lotta money, but my pimp was always broke. Sonny wasn't that bad because he didn't do no drugs. He might not have been broke; he might have been stashing his money. I don't know. I guess I'm saying we all learn to accept shit like that.

But just because you accept shit doesn't mean you like it. At some point, you think to yourself, screw all this. You know how me and Sonny just died? One night, Bridget, Sonny, and me were all in a room together. He was in one of his rages for no reason. He just came in and grabbed the broom and started swinging, and I blocked it. He hit me on my left arm, on the bone. It swole up. And then he took Bridget and me and dropped us off at the ho stroll.

Bridget looked at me with my broken arm and said, "If you stay on this stroll, you a fool. Because I'm gone. Fuck him."

I looked at her and said, "Do what you got to do." She and I weren't tight enough to be discussing him like that.

So I had caught a trick, and I went to the hotel with him, got his money, and I went to the spot out in the Grange where I met up with my friends Skip, Pete, and Reggie. They were all boosting. And they said, "Come go with us, Breezy. You don't have to go back to Sonny; you can come with us." They were sweet guys. And they were very funny. They weren't trying to have sex with me or anything like that. They were just trying to take care of a sister. And I needed that. I wasn't ready to go to the hospital yet. They knew my brothers, and they wanted to tell my brothers that this pimp done broke my arm. "Don't do that," I told them. My brothers were the kind who would deal with a situation, and I didn't want my brothers to go to jail for dealing with Sonny. More important than dealing with Sonny was doing something about my arm. I was in so much pain.

I took a hit of cocaine, but that wouldn't let the pain go. Skip's sister gave me some ibuprofen. I took two or three, and there was still pain. I had been out there for two days. My buddies said they were going back to the city. I said, "Hey, drop me off at the hospital. Where y'all gone be at and I'll meet you?" They put my arm in a cast at the county hospital, then I went back to Sonny because I didn't really know where else to go. I didn't want my brothers to see me like that.

When I went back to Sonny, he was acting sad and shit, like he wasn't the one who did it. He opened the door and said, "Baby, what happened?"

"You broke my arm."

"I didn't mean to do that. Come on in."

There was Bridget sitting up in there. I turned to Sonny. "You got this broke bitch up in here? I'm gone." I went to the door to go.

"Don't leave, don't leave." He went over to Bridget. "Get up. Get on and get out." But Sonny and I weren't right after that. I made a point of leaving and staying gone for a while.

Weeks later, she brought up the incident. "Do you remember that?" Bridget asked me.

"Yeah, I remember that."

"He knew that the real money was at the door and was 'bout to leave."

Do you see the relationship? What it is all about? Money. I knew he had a real liking for Bridget, but when it came to his money, Bridget could go and sit down somewhere because Sonny was going to follow the money.

I started hanging with this dude who was a Mad Black Soul, Randy Johnson. He was like a big brother to me, cause his woman was cool with me. On the night of the Players Ball, I turned to Randy and said, "Let's go to the Players Ball." I had gone to the Players Ball before. Once, I went to one in Chicago. I went to another in New York. This time I was super excited, but looking back, let me tell you the truth about the Players Ball: the Players Ball is the grimiest, most stupid bullshit that has ever gone on. But it's so exciting for the pimps because they love watching grimy shit. The only thing that saved it was that folks would put on the best outfits and show up in the best cars, even if they had to rent the car for the night. Even Sonny would go out and rent shit. I would look at him and think, *You so fake*. The whole thing represents so much garbage.

When you go into the Players Ball, dudes are grouped up with their stable. Then you have the men who come in there to cop a bitch. The drug dealers who came in there have women with them. And then you've got participants who came in there to praise the pimps and shit like that. You might have somebody like Ice-T in there. Or Snoop Dogg might come. But they don't stay for long, they just come through, cause they want to see how these clowns be acting out. It's just a big old party.

It's like walking into a club of ego-hungry dudes who have nothing better to do than stare at each other. It just makes you want to throw up. But for those who were involved in it, this is what they would tell you: the Players Ball is a glamourous exploitation of what we do 365 days a year. It represents the pimp's ability to hold on to his stable for 365 days. And the point is, they need to control the same number of girls that they had at the beginning of the year. And whichever pimp has the most flawless lifestyle, the most bitches and money, they become the pimp of the year. And they can prove that, because everybody knows everybody's business. Pimps are like hos; they like to sit around and brag. If a bitch breaks bad or runs off, everybody knows. I was considered one of the baddest bitches out there, but I always ran away. So Sonny never got any recognition. I used to think it was my fault, but you know what? Sonny never had any game.

All the pimps come together and vote on who was best at sustaining their stable for that year. And you get a trophy. A pimp trophy. It's like two feet high. Somebody just picked it up at the trophy store. How stupid is that? And then you get your name out there—you're King Burt or King Frank. You're all that and a bag of french fries. Hos want to pay you and choose you, cause you the coldest pimp out there. And I'm not gone lie—I liked it when I was involved in it.

So, like I said, when I wanted to go to the Players Ball with Randy, the only question was the money. Randy told me, "We ain't got no money."

I said, "Alright. I'll be back."

So I went up on Cicero, and I beat a white guy off—hundred dollars. Came back. Went to Walgreens, got some smell goods. Got my little outfit. Put my shit on. I got my cast on, but check this shit out: what I did was, I had some sequined pants, and I cut out the bottom of them. I put sequins over the cast; that was how I worked with the cast. I covered it up, and it looked cute.

I went to the Players Ball, and I was sharp. And I saw some pimps I had never seen before, and I was definitely an attraction. And guess who was there? Sonny. So I was with Sonny, but those Don Juans were taking a look or two. I was out there posing with my booty out and doing my thing. Next thing I knew, some pimp grabbed my arm, and Sonny grabbed my other arm, and he said, "Naw, bitch, this mine."

He put me in the car. Bridget was in the car, too, and he had picked up some other little ho in the place. She was licking on him, and he was licking on her. Bridget got mad. She was driving, but it was Sonny's car—a rental—and Bridget ran into another car.

Sonny said, "Did that bitch just hit this?"

And I said, "Yeah, she pretty much did."

She slammed our car into another car. I got out the car. And Red, who was Sonny's sidekick, who had come along with us, got out the car. Sonny grabbed Bridget, and he was kicking her on the ground like a dog. The other woman who was in the car just up and left. And the ambulance came, and then Sonny turned to me like he hadn't just finished stomping on Bridget like she was trash.

He said, "Baby, you alright?"

I knew right then he was a dirty dog. I looked at him and told him I didn't have time for police reports and shit like that. "I'll see you later." He was looking at me like, *Where that bitch going? She knows I need her.*

Red knew I had money, and I told him, "I'm going to hit a lick, I'll be back." I handed him a few twenties, and I said, "I'll be back. Don't be following me and messing up my action," because I was trying to help Sonny out, because now he got a tore-up car. Like I said, you can't be a victim out there all the time in the streets.

After I got my money from the stroll, I went to his sister's house and he was in the kitchen looking all pitiful and shit. I was singing Patti LaBelle, "He's the right kind of lover!" His sister was singing; she's a big old fool. And I was dancing around, and I got my money out. I swiped my money across his face. "That's what you get for fucking with broke-ass bitches."

"Don't talk to me like that. Bitch, I'll kill you."

His sister was calling after us, "I told him stop fucking around with those broke bitches."

"Shut up, motherfucker." I could treat him like that because I was giving him money. That was the kind of girl I was and that's why I was exciting to him.

I was with Sonny off and on for three years. I'd walk away when there was too much drama, then I'd come back when things settled down.

+ + +

I started drifting and staying with other people. I met up with this dude DayDay and his wife, Yolanda. Later on, she became my sponsor at Narcotics Anonymous. She's still my sponsor today. I met them both when I was on the streets. DayDay was hustling with me, and he was still getting high, but she was clean. DayDay was good-looking, and white women especially liked him, and he used to have me step up to them and get him his money. That kind of work wasn't really his forte. He used to tell me, "Go tell that ho to give you the money, Breezy." And I was like, "Man, you scared to take money from a ho?"

But he was also telling me about his woman. Yolanda was in recovery, and she had a real job and everything. Day used to talk about her so much, I felt I knew her. They were struggling. I would kick him like two, three hundred dollars, because he would be scared to go home without any money.

By the grace of God, Yolanda was very laid-back and unconditional. She let her husband go through all of that. Once, I was with DayDay, and he was supposed to watch my back. This young Black guy walked up and wanted to do business. I told him I don't date Black guys.

"Baby, I got money. My money just as good as any white guy."

"But I don't. I got to get my money and you're not going to pay me what I want."

He was a drug dealer. "I got what you want. How much you want?"

I said, "Give me a hundred dollars."

"Bet. Get in."

I said, "Why don't you come back?" But he didn't want to come back. He was parked in front of me and wouldn't leave. I was watching all these white guys go by, and this Black man was blowing my money. I got angry, so I said, "Come on, then. Goddamnit. But I told you not to mess with me." We went around the corner, and I didn't just take the hundred, I took all his money. Men don't pay attention when you having sex with them.

The next day he came back, and he saw me walking across the street. I was about to get in the car with DayDay. We were about to go, because I got the money for the day.

"You got my money?" the drug dealer said.

Day said, "Gone, man. She tried to tell you to gone 'bout your business. But you wouldn't. So you got what you got. She warned you not to fuck with her."

"Bitch better give me my money."

"You ain't gone do shit to her." DayDay looked at me. "Get in the car, Breezy." I got in. "You get in, too," Day said to the drug dealer.

"What you fin to do?"

"I'm gone take this nigga where he need to go." DayDay was Vice Lord. He drove his ass right over there where the Vice Lords were.

That dealer got up outta there, but he was yelling, "I'mma get y'all!"

Shenanigans. I was back and forth in the streets. I was hooked up with the chief of the Mad Black Souls. I was staying on Jackson with my homeboy Benny Lee and his girlfriend, YaYa. And no matter what, I was strolling up and down Madison. I was out there doing all my wild-ass shit to get a trick.

One day my brother caught me at it. Todd had been parked

there, just watching. When he pulled up on me and I went to the car, I thought he was a trick. "Oh!"

"Yeah. I been watching you for about thirty, forty minutes. You been up here having a time. Get in the car." I got in. He started driving. "You was over there having so much fun, I'm telling you."

I'm laughing at him. "Give me twenty dollars, nigga."

"I ain't giving you no money. You need to go home with me. You need a break. Look at you. You look wore out."

I couldn't argue. I needed a break. And that's how I woke up that morning in Todd's basement. My other brothers came out to check on me. Jerome did; Jethro would come by in his truck. They never stopped coming by, they never stopped coming by to check on their sister.

Chapter 19

Chicago, Take Two, For Real

pril Fool's Day, 1997. The day I was dragged by that trick. The day I made that little girl see me for the mess that I was and I took her innocence away. The day those dealers cursed me out and hustled me off the streets. April Fool's Day was the day I learned the streets can reset you even if you didn't want them to. I went straight from the hospital to Genesis House. If you came to Genesis House the way I did, they would let you stay three days, and then you would have to go to treatment and come back, because they had to stabilize you before they let you stay in the house, because you were a threat to the other girls because you fresh from out there, getting high. They want you stabilized off drugs. Which means that I had to be drug-free for a minute. It took thirty days for me to dry out, but it took another sixty days to get that gorilla off my back. I had to be put on routine: get up every morning, make my bed, eat real breakfast and lunch. I gained weight. Now I knew if I got the urge to get high, I should pray or think about something else. It was the same way with my prostitution. Sometimes I would sit in my room and I would hear car horns blowing outside. And I would think that the car horns were blowing for me. Friday and Saturday nights, the streets were active. I felt pulled toward the noise. I so wanted to go outside and hop in a car. But if I could hold tight, the urge would pass. Nobody had told me that before. That's what the other programs never did for me. They always just threw me in the program, and I wasn't even drug-free in the residential. They called in the ninety and ninety: I needed to be stabilized for ninety days before I started my treatment that lasted another ninety days. They didn't send me to treatment until I finished with all my doctor's appointments from the county hospital from my face being messed up.

I went to treatment with my face still all messed up. The doctors at the county hospital had given up on me. I was a sight; I looked like a mummy. Only one of my eyes was visible, and blood and pus leaked through the bandages. This girl walked up to me. She was tall, thin, and chocolate. And she was handsome, like a man. She said in a deep brass voice, "Bitch, you look like a monster." Finally! Someone was saying to my face—or what was left of it—what the others were saying behind my back. We both cracked up. That was how I met my Stephanie. That's how I met my ride or die, friend for life. Stephanie didn't know what had happened to me, but she could see I was in pain, and she wanted just to make me laugh. She looked at me like she wanted to say, "Where are those people who did that to you? Let's go beat them up." I could tell right away she was a good person, so good she could make me cry, because she was saying it out of love even though she didn't know me yet. I was mostly ostracized at the treatment center. But I could do a little hair, so the girls were always bringing their gel and stuff to me. "Could you do my hair?" I would give them the pineapple waves. I was good at that. Little finger waves. I could do that one real good.

One day, Stephanie walked up to me and said, "Quit doing these bitches' hair. They don't like you."

I looked at her and smiled. "I know."

"Fuck them. You my friend. I don't want you fucking with these hos." I just started laughing. It was so funny, because I was thinking, *They don't like you either.* We could be ostracized ladies together.

At the center, they had us two, three girls to a room. I only had one roommate. Every night, Stephanie would slide in my room. "Hey, what you doing?" She had never met a prostitute before, and she just peppered me with questions. "Girl, I keep thinking about this shit. Tell me another story." She liked to listen to me. I told her about my childhood and life for me out in the streets. It was painful, but I made it funny, too. Because out there, sometimes it was hilarious. I needed to talk about it, and Stephanie was a good listener. A lot of times, when I tell my story, people don't believe it because so much happened. Stephanie believed me. Believed in me, too.

I really took to treatment this time. I had some good mentors. I had this Muslim lady who was just awesome to me. She told me, "You are God's doorway to life." Ms. Jerry. "I want you to think about that and come back and tell me what that means." But I couldn't think of anything . . . God's doorway. Doorway to life. God's doorway to life. How does that feel? I couldn't figure it out.

Three days later, she says, "So how you doing with it?"

"I don't know." I couldn't figure how God's doorway to life had anything to do with me.

She said, "Through you, God creates life. You bring life into the world. God felt so special about you, Brenda, about women, that he gave us the gift of making life. That is more important than anything. Imagine if you bring in the next Martin Luther King or the next somebody who cures cancer." She made it sound like this grand event. Like I was a part of this spiritual thing between me and God. So I began to think of scenarios like, *Damn, suppose women didn't want to have no more babies and stop populating the world and they stop letting men get their poon. The world would be messed up. I'm God's doorway to life. If it wasn't for a woman like me, none of these men would be here.* I began to feel special to God, more than even a man. I came from a family of Christians where men were in control. Men were head of the house. Men were the head of the church. Women didn't have a place in the pulpit. She couldn't even lead a damn song. That's the way I was raised. My grandmother used to tell me that if I didn't learn how to cook and I didn't learn how to clean and I didn't learn how to make a husband happy, he was going to whoop my ass. She told me that, because that's all she knew. Men beating women's asses. I used to wonder why she would wish that for me. She beat on me, and then she wished when I got big somebody else would beat on me? I didn't get it.

When Ms. Jerry told me about being the doorway, a lotta stuff started poking me. If I was so damn special, why was I out on the street selling it for pennies? I was so much more valuable than that. And I started to make decisions about my body after that.

Then there was Ms. Ronnie. Ms. Ronnie had Spiritual Hour. During Spiritual Hour there was this song by Shirley Caesar called "He's Working It Out." When that record came on, I couldn't maintain myself, cause I was hoping that God could work it out for me. *The child who's on cocaine, through prayer he can change.* I used to hear that and say to myself, *I can change, I can change.*

I used to cry during Spiritual Hour. I cried because I hadn't really cried before. On the streets, when I was crying, I would take a hit of cocaine and stop, because I didn't want to feel that shit. I was holding in all this shit in my body from my childhood: molestation and Uncle LC, all the abuse, the beatings, the bullshit that people did to me . . . how unfair it felt that my mother was dead. I felt that life had really handed it to me.

I cried on that floor in that treatment center, cause all that shit was coming to me and I didn't understand why it was happening. I cried. And Ms. Ronnie gave me a place to cry. Stephanie was in the Spiritual Hour with me. It was a help to have her there. But still . . . I cried all the time, till finally Stephanie would say, "Stop crying, bitch." But she didn't know I had never really cried; that I was always fighting, always running, always going somewhere. She didn't know that I always had somebody's foot on my neck. There was never freedom. And I was always scared that I might do something and somebody won't like me. But here, I was here now and drug-free, so I was crying and crying and crying and I couldn't stop. I didn't know why I cried, I just knew it seemed right to cry. I wasn't in a place where I could tear up shit or get rid of this pain, I couldn't fight anymore, and Ms. Ronnie was giving me a venue to start getting rid of the pain.

So I did treatment, and Stephanie and I talked about being better girls, being better women. Being successful. We didn't want to get clean and not be successful. Both of us had great ideas and we were thinkers. We were intelligent people. We said to ourselves, "Okay, let's get clean. I'm not going to get on welfare and get a check."

At the Genesis House, I started getting my days together. I saw a psychiatrist. He diagnosed me as being bipolar, and I thought, well, let me listen to this short white-ass man; I didn't like him too much, but he might have a point. I was so unbalanced. They put me on antidepressants. I was on Paxil for a while. And then I said, "I don't like this. I don't like this medicine. I'm drug-free now, how this work?"

They told me, "You probably won't be able to get a check if you don't take this medicine."

"I don't want your check," I said. "I don't want to live limited." A check limited me. If I was getting a once-a-month check from the government, that's a limitation, cause the government doesn't want you to make any money. I didn't want to be under somebody's thumb like that. No more. Plus, I was a hustler. I had no fear my bills wouldn't get paid. I just didn't. I've seen in a lotta girls' eyes, *What am I going to do?* How were they gone make it when they stopped using drugs? I just knew I was going to be alright. I was willing to do whatever it took for me to make it. And it wasn't going to be prostitution because I wasn't going to sell my body *anymore*. I had made that decision when I was in the drug program. I never wanted to have sex again without loving it. For the first time in my life I was going to be in control of my body. Who got to touch it was going to be my decision alone. I was God's doorway to life. I was valuable. My body and my mind had worth. I had been lowballing myself. I couldn't sell my body now that I understood that. But I still needed money, and that meant I needed a job. And it wasn't going to be illegal. I just knew I was willing to work hard. I did not want that kind of check.

My first minimum-wage job was with an agency called Help at Home. I was cleaning up houses for people who had disabilities or for the elderly. After ninety days, they decided if they were going to keep you or not. After ninety days at that job, they made me supervisor. People started calling in, "We like her. Send her back." They would send me for a couple of weeks to somebody and then change up my schedule, try to send somebody else, and the people would call in and say, "Naw. We want Brenda back."

My supervisor, a jazzy old Black lady, was real down to earth. The first time I got a check, I told her, "This is wrong."

"What's wrong with it, Brenda?"

"Somebody named FICA took some stuff out of my check."

She said, "Baby, that's Uncle Sam. That's the federal government."

"Who the hell is Sam?"

Now, I had never worked "regular" jobs. I was trying to find out who these people were who were taking my money out of my check without my permission. I didn't sign my money over. Okay?

She laughed so hard. Every time she passed me, she would whisper, "*Sam*."

"Girl! Go on!" She was my mellow. She liked me a lot because I was good at my job. She had gotten so many frustrating calls from people who wanted me to come back because I would go in there and treat them like they were my momma. I would clean up their houses and sometimes I think they had me doing shit that didn't nobody else ever do, like go under the bed and clean up. There was so much shit up under those beds. I would put a plastic garbage bag over my hair, cover up my face, and put some gloves on, and I would say, "I'm going in, Ms. Jenkins!"

I made them laugh, and I took care of them. The way they were supposed to be taken care of. Remember, I was a CNA, I knew how to take care of people.

I had some Black guys who worked for the railroad and had some very good careers and lived on the Gold Coast; they probably got a little subsidy to live in those high-rises, but they were there. They used to sit back and tell me, "Girl, if you want to, you can just come and stay with me. Cause I can pay you."

"That's alright, Mr. Robinson." I always said no, because prostitution was still prevalent in my body. If I didn't look out, I would have sat up there and smoked the man's whole house. But I was good at work. Genesis House would take a third of my money for rent, and then they would take a portion and put it in my savings account. They were saving my money for me. And because all of my needs were met, I didn't have to worry about food or none of that. They would give me the rest of the money that was left over. That way, I could go and get my toiletries, go and buy a little outfit from Rainbow. Rainbow was my store. I was doing okay. I stayed at Genesis House for a year. I needed that structure. I needed to learn how to live by myself, live through a job, live without any outside contributions from men. I needed to stop using myself. And I learned how to do that.

If I would have left the treatment and got an apartment with Stephanie, which is what she wanted, I would have been getting high because I wasn't ready. I needed to be at the recovery home. Stephanie understood, but she would come knock on the door and come and see me. She came up real quick, with her little fast self. She would come switching her little ass in there to come and see me. She had all this nice jewelry on; she had a car. And I was like, "Damn, bitch. You came up fast."

"Bitch, come on. Come on and stay with me."

"I will. But you got to let me do what I got to do here first."

When I got ready to leave, my program wasn't too keen on the idea of me going to go stay with Stephanie. They knew she was still on drugs and doing some dangerous things to get it. They knew she was running with criminals, and if I hung around her, I was likely to fall back into trouble. They wanted me to do something else, but I had already decided, I was going to stay with her.

+ + +

Sometimes, I can be very blind when I care about people. I knew she still was getting high. When she was high, Stephanie used to go in the bathroom and become a dermatologist. She would have hair growing out of her chin and she felt like if she could get the follicle out, she could get to the root of it. So she would have needles and razors and she would cut on her face until you could see the white. She would tell people she had a Rollerblading accident. I told her, "Bitch, ain't nobody gone keep believing that Rollerblading shit." Everybody knew what she was doing.

One day I came home and she had sold my jewelry. I told her, "I'm gonna leave, cause I can't stay here, or else I'm gone whoop your ass." And I left.

She was so broken up. She was like, "I'm going to go to treatment tomorrow, so I can straighten my life up." I was still going to the meetings and sharing. My friends were telling me, "You got to leave, Brenda." I didn't really know what to do with the situation. I loved Stephanie so. On top of that, Stephanie needed me.

I used to have to get men up out of there. She would give me all her money and her jewelry when she was back there with them dudes. This one guy, he came into my room and said, "You know what? You need to go and give that girl her money and her shit." I was laying down, watching TV, getting ready to go to bed because I had work in the morning.

I said, "You right. You right." I got up. "I'm going to give her her shit. Don't go nowhere." I pulled a bat out—and he turned around and ran. *Boom, boom, boom.* Dude ran out the apartment.

Stephanie came out from her room. "What's going on?"

"Bitch, quit sending them niggas in my room. Cause I'm gonna hurt them. I'm not giving them nothing. Now, if you wanted it, you could have came and gotten it. But you sent that nigga in there, cause you knew I would bust his head."

She got raped in our apartment one day. I wasn't there. I mean, this was a pretty man. And he raped my baby up in there. She was so vulnerable. I didn't want to leave her.

She woke me up one morning. "Hey, come meet my friend Bob who I used to work with." He used to work for, like, Spring Spring, back in Sprang Sprang. Okay, what? I get in there, and this little old white man look like he was about a hundred years old. He's so frail, he's not sitting in the whole seat, he's sitting on the edge of the seat. Little frail guy. Stephanie's sitting up there, getting high with him.

I looked at her and I looked at him, and I said, "Bitch, you gone kill this man. He gone sit up here and die. And, bitch, you the one who is going to jail for killing this old white man. Not me."

She was talking about he used to work with her. Listen, this old man had retired by the time Stephanie was born. He ain't worked nowhere, sitting up there like one of those Catholic priests or something. There was a halo around his face, that's how close he was to Jesus. Shit. I told Stephanie, "Bitch, get this old-ass man out of here before we all go to jail."

Stephanie, she was hilarious. She was still funny when she was high. I love that bitch. We had great days. That wasn't one. But we had great days. I wished she didn't have a problem. She kept promising me she was going to go to treatment. And I just thought I needed to save my baby.

Nothing made me make a decision until Prune had a baby. She was twenty-six, unmarried, working downtown at a bank, and a little girl was on the way. I was almost forty years old, and I promised myself I was going to be a better grandmother than I was a mother. Prune's stomach was like she swallowed a pumpkin. She had this gray jogging suit that she used to wear all the time. When Peaches brought Prune by, with this pumpkin stomach, I thought, *Okay, you got to walk away from this life.* My girls kind of knew what was going on. And they said, "Momma, you know we can't bring the baby over here."

Nothing was going to stop me from being with my grandbaby. Nobody. Nothing. I loved Stephanie with all of my heart. But I had to go. Peaches lived on the North Side and was working as a therapist at a hospital. She was in a building that had a vacant apartment, and she talked to her landlord. I gave him my money, and I moved in.

Stephanie's sister moved in with her. Stephanie's sister always used her, even when Stephanie was high. It was easy to do because she always had a lot of money. Stephanie always had some kind of white-collar-rigmarole scam going on. She was that kind of girl. You could say Stephanie did prostitution by bringing strange men in the house, but her game was always having some side shit going on. She had unlimited unemployment payments because she knew how to play the unemployment system. That sort of thing.

✦ ✦ ✦

I was clean, and then Mimi was born! My little bundle! My grandbaby! But I still heard from Stephanie. She would call: "When you were here you broke a mirror and the mirror's worth three hundred dollars. You need to come over. I need my money for that mirror, bitch." She was calling me at work. I just went *click, click*. Stephanie thought I had abandoned her, but that wasn't true. I loved the shit out of that bitch.

But what was going on with my friend wasn't cute. She was almost dead. She called one morning about five o'clock. She said, "Listen. I need you to come get me and take me to treatment. Don't come now, because I know you have to go to work. Come when you get off work."

"That's true," I said. "I can't come get you." But I heard something in her voice, and I changed my mind. I knew I needed to go and get her right then, because if Stephanie took a nap and got her strength back, I knew she was going to buy more drugs, and she was going to die.

I got over there, and she couldn't hardly sit up. Her breathing was weak. She had smoked so much. But just like I thought, she had money. By the grace of God, no drug dealer had answered their phone for her, and she was too weak to walk up on Howard Street and get somebody. She was laying down, sweating. I looked at her in bed, and I told her, "I'm not going to work. You sounded like you needed me, and from the looks of you, you definitely do." Stephanie could hardly talk. I said, "Come on. Let me get you somewhere."

I put her in my car and drove her to this place called Ad Detox. I went in and told them Stephanie needed a bed. They told me they didn't have any beds.

I said, "Come here!"

"What?"

"Come here." I took the man out to my car. "Now, you look at my friend and tell her you ain't got any beds." He looked at the back seat and said, "Bring her back at twelve o'clock." So I took Stephanie to Genesis House, and they allowed her to lie on the couch until the bed was made available. Come to find out, she had pneumonia. Genesis House took her straight to the hospital.

+ + +

After that, our relationships, all of them, took a turn. Both of us had a habit of picking the wrong men. You know what I was always attracted to? Jail brothers. You just get out the penitentiary, looking buff and fresh, and I am going to make you a better person. I'm a better person, so I'm going to take you, because you're just out and looking good. You don't have to go back to a life of crime; you are going to be my man now. And I'm going to make you the best man in the world.

That was my mindset. I still was falling in love the way I fell in love when I was in the streets. Superficial. Flesh. Flash. I still had this thing about buying love, even when I didn't have to. I didn't know how to have relationships without paying a guy, taking care of him. He's a grown, full-ass man, but I'm Captain Save-a-Ho. So I would always attract the wrong guys. And the only time the relationship was good was when I was in the bed with them. It wasn't emotional, spiritual. Well, I would be emotional; they wouldn't be. These dudes didn't care about me. All my friends could see it. My sponsors, my mentors, my friends from Genesis House, they all knew that I was being used.

Two ladies I knew from Genesis House who had been there before me, Olivia and Louise, would knock on my door when I would be going through depression because some man had stolen my money. I'd be so embarrassed. My rent would be due, and I'd lost my assets to some random guy. I would isolate myself and not talk to anybody. Olivia and Louise would come over there. They would bring Louise's daughter, Paris, and tell her to knock on the door, because they knew I might not let them in, but I would let Paris inside. She'd knock on the door. "Please let us come in, Auntie Brenda. I love you."

While I was going through all that, I was still trying to build a relationship with my daughters. Prune wasn't there yet. Mimi could come over, but she couldn't spend the night. Both of my girls were worried; they didn't know if I was going to get high again. Peaches used to live right up over me—that was how I got to be with Mimi a lot. Mimi would always be over Peaches's house. It was a minute before Prune said, "Okay, Mommy, you can come and get my baby." When I went and picked my grandbaby up, Prune would tell me before I left, "Mommy, take care of my baby."

"With my life, Prune."

I used to hate that they felt they had to say that to me. But I understood.

Prune and Mimi came to live with me, and I loved it because I could spend all this time with Mimi. Prune was a great mom. In the morning, she would get up, get her baby ready, get herself ready to go downtown, because the place where she worked had a daycare in the building. She'd walk out the door with the diaper bag and her purse, baby wrapped up snug in the winter, walk to the train. I just thought: How can I help? And so sometimes, Prune would leave Mimi at home with me. And me and Mimi would go out to the pancake house. That's where I found out my little grandbaby was a diva.

I used to buy her these little outfits—little pleather suits, the little Mexican dresses and shit. Prune would be like, "Momma, don't buy that." My two daughters dress very conservatively. And I'm flamboyant. But Mimi liked the way I dressed and she liked to dress that way, too. Anyway, she was sitting up there in the pancake house with her little pleather suit on, and she looked at me and she said, "Nana?"

"What?"

"Did you get me this outfit from the big-girl store?"

"Yeah. I got it from the one across the street." You could see the Rainbow store from out the window. "In fact I did."

"Can we stop over there when we get through?"

"For what?"

"So I can get a blouse to match my suit. The one I have on doesn't really match my suit." I was stunned. I was like, okay, she's only three years old, but she's clearly been here before, and in her past life she was a fashion designer.

That kind of stuff just blows you. I was finally getting a chance to have what I missed with my kids. But then me and Prune got into it.

I had started dating this hunk named Pookie. The man had a body like a Mandingo warrior and dick in his shoe. Understand? It was like an addiction. I was addicted to that sex. He was so awful. I mean, nobody put they hands on me when I was clean because I wasn't allowing that. I knew I could fight, and I wasn't afraid to stand up for myself. But I didn't stand up for myself where it counted. Pookie could always talk me into shit. He was the kind of brother who would steal my money—then help me look for it. A lotta people have experienced that: steal your money then help you look for it, to throw off the scent. "You sure it was here? You sure?" I mean, what? Ain't nobody but two people here, me and you.

Prune wasn't supposed to be home, so I told Pookie he could spend the night. Well, Prune came home at like two o'clock in the morning and she wanted me to put Pookie out, but I couldn't bring myself to do that. So once again, I disappointed my daughter.

After that, Prune started talking jazzy to me, no matter what I did. And I just felt like she couldn't talk crazy to me. Once I got so mad, I chased her ass down the stairs. But now I can see her point. I was always putting men before my kids. I can see her point, and I feel awful about it.

Things had gotten really bad. I still had a job, but I had gotten an eviction notice; Pookie was robbing me blind. I couldn't keep up with shit from trying to keep up with him and his habit. This was not working. I remember sitting on the floor crying for about two hours and then I got up off the floor, thinking: *What are you crying for? You been shot, you been stabbed, all of this shit, and you have made it this far.* So I thought, okay. I'm not going to tell anybody what's going on with me, I'll just go to a shelter and keep my job. I'll regroup.

That was my plan.

Later on that day, here go Peaches at my door. "What's going on, Mother?"

"Nothing."

But she had already heard from the people in the building. They had informed her. She said, "You done packed up. Where you going?"

"I don't know. I haven't really made no decisions."

"Okay, Momma. Here." And she handed me an envelope. It had a check in it. "Momma, gone pay your rent." Peaches walked to the door, but then turned around. "But you need to think about why you need to pay your man."

I wanted to smash her in the neck. But it was so true, I couldn't. She had closed the door, and I was still sitting in the same place. I kept running through my mind, *Why do I do that? Why do I do that?* What Peaches said shook me.

I paid the rent. There was this white guy named Jeff who had this hole in his neck that he had to breathe through. Sometimes he would take the tube out and clean it right there in front of me. It was disgusting. Jeff was fat, and everybody used to abuse him; they called him "fatso." But you know what? He was the nicest man. I started to talk to Jeff about my situation. He said, "You know you need to get out of there, right? Because he's not going to leave."

"Well, I've got to find a place."

"I'll move you."

My cousin Gwen said there was an apartment over there in her building. She lived ten blocks away. I talked to the landlady, Delia; she was a Greek lady, and she told me she'd let me rent a place for seven hundred a month. She and her husband owned the place. I gave her money and she gave me a move-in date. And me and Jeff got ready to make the great escape. He gave me a framed piece of paper; the poem was titled "The Art of the Impossible." It became my mantra.

I prayed and talked to God. I told God, "I need this to be lifted from me. Help me."

It didn't come at first, because when I moved to my next apartment, I have to admit, I got back with Pookie one more time. But it was all wrong. And this time I wasn't blind. I saw him for what he was and who he was. One day, I came home from work and there was a bad feeling in the place. Pookie was sitting on the couch, high. He had just got out of jail, again, and he was talking shit to me to make me overlook how high he was. And I said to myself, *Why don't you get the hell out of here, sister?* Out loud I said, "I guess I don't do shit right."

"Oh, you want me to get out?"

"Yeah. Why don't you just go. Because this ain't working." I went in the bedroom.

He started putting his shit, and my shit, in his bag. Which was actually my bag. I had bought all his clothes, and his TV, too. It was one of those penitentiary TVs, made of clear plastic, so you could see right through it, so inmates couldn't put shit in them. It had the old-school back on it, not the flat screen. I don't know what they have now, but that's what he had.

He picked up that penitentiary TV and took it with him. I said to myself, *You petty asshole. I didn't want it, but you petty.* I don't even think it was a color TV. But he took his petty-ass TV and I watched him do it. I had a cat named Aretha Franklin. We were at the door as Pookie left out. And my cat was looking at me like, "Let him go. You'll be fine."

I closed both of my doors, locked them, and I went inside my bedroom. I look out my window, and I saw Pookie standing there. Whoever he called hadn't gotten there yet. But they showed up and came and got him.

Now how do I get through this period of me leaving Pookie?

I decided to become abstinent because clearly, I didn't know how to have a relationship. I needed to learn how to love myself before I could love anybody else. I had all of these great self-help books, and in the meantime, I was journaling. I started to date myself. I would go out to movies by myself. I would go out to dinner by myself. I would go shopping and go and people watch. I would sit up in the house and take long bubble baths. I would powder and lotion myself. I watched my weight. My hair was growing. And sometimes I would take it down and play with it. I would call my little cousins and tell them to take a picture of Auntie. They would laugh at me. I just decided to spend time with the kids and my grandbaby. It was my period of learning self-love.

I told God, "God, I don't know what You have in store for me, but if I don't get in a relationship, I think I'll be okay, because I'll have a relationship with me, finally." I believed that. I was just being with me. I was on this abstinence and I was dating me. Me and my cat, Aretha Franklin.

Chapter 20

Me, Living with Me

In the daytime, I was a bill collector. But when I got off work, I would go and volunteer at a shelter, help women who were in recovery. People asked me, "Why you go and do that when you get off work?" I was living by myself, and I had this extra time on my hands. And I wanted to follow the pattern of the women who had helped me in treatment. Ladies would come to Genesis House and volunteer. It made sense that I should volunteer. I wanted to give back the way those women gave back to me. I had been so happy when they stopped by. They felt good about it, and I wanted to live a life that I felt good about, too. It worked. I was at my best when I was giving back. There was a saying in the program, "You can't keep it unless you give it back." So when people would ask why, I told them, the job pays my bills, but the volunteering pays my spirit. Get it? It helped me live with me.

I had left Genesis House but still went over there to volunteer with Olivia and Louise. Coming back and talking to the girls—that was part of our required recovery. Everything was cool until they got a new director. She started telling the people who worked there we weren't allowed to come in and volunteer. That hurt. Later on we found out she was embezzling the money, but at the time all I knew was that it looked like she wanted to stop all the good work we had done. She didn't know anything about the women; she didn't know anything about the community. All she wanted to do was take over.

I still wanted to help the girls. So I used to meet them at the Narcotics Anonymous meetings. It wasn't the same, but it felt important to have some kind of relationship with my sisters. Louise, who was doing work at this place called Chicago Coalition for the Homeless, said to me, "Don't worry about it. You can do other things. I have this friend, his name is Samir Goswami, and he's doing this great work for the Chicago Coalition for the Homeless. He's starting this thing up for women in prostitution. You really need to be a part of that."

"Really?"

"Yeah. He's looking for somebody to do this speaking thing. You would be good at it. I'm not good for it because I don't like to do all of that. Talk to him. He'll take you out and buy you lunch and everything."

"They buy you lunch?" Back then, a free lunch sounded very good to me. I'm thinking to myself, regardless of what happens, I get a free lunch out of it. The fact was that I really wanted to go. When I wasn't at work or talking with the ladies at the NA meetings, I was sort of bored. This way I could go somewhere, meet some people. It would keep me positive. I went downtown to interview with this guy, Samir Goswami. We started having this conversation about everything prostitution. It was terrific. He asked where I came from. How did I feel about the women out there, the way I used to be? He told me that they were going to talk with the state senators because no one had ever spoken to them about prostitution. We talked about the challenges for a woman who was trying to get out of prostitution and away from the life. All of these things that I felt needed to be said, he was telling me, we should and could say to these powerful men. I had never heard anybody talk about helping women to such an extent. The fact is, women who had walked my road needed that level of help. We needed more than shelters or even treatment centers. We needed the law to change. We talked so much for so long that we ran out of time and I never got the lunch. If it wasn't for him, I don't know if I would have been put on the road to be doing it like I'm doing it. He became my mentor, he was my director, he was my friend. He was a gift to me.

Samir and I became like ninety-eight and two, like Jack and Jill. It was because of him that I started asking the big questions. And I started to feel women in prostitution don't have a voice. Who is speaking out for women? Speaking up for women?

Having a voice is a hell of a thing. A lot people don't, so other people have to speak for them. In the next week or two, I was speaking in front of state senators. I didn't receive any training. I had never done it before, but I wasn't nervous. I just thought, okay, here's my chance to say what needs to be said. Nobody was going to tell these folks the truth. *Let me say something to you some-of-a-bitches*—that was in my mind. And I felt that's what I was doing; I was speaking for girls who didn't have an opportunity to speak for themselves. I had to be careful about what I said, but I also needed to say what had to be said. I had to speak for the countless women who had died out there, who had been harmed, and who had never been able to speak.

The first time I ever spoke, I was talking about how the courts were giving out felonies to women who were prostituting. The felony upgrades were not helping the situation. They weren't fair. I told those senators to notice they weren't doing that to the johns. Nobody was going after the pimps. And they were only doing it in the areas that they were gentrifying, like Bucktown. I had worked Bucktown back in the day. They putting up million-dollar condos, and the residents had started showing up at court, calling their state senators and congressmen and all that to make sure the women didn't return to their neighborhood. But you know, even after the prostitutes had left the block, the tricks were still there. And the tricks were actually soliciting the women residents. Now somebody tell me what all that situation has to do with hos on the stroll? The hos weren't there anymore. It just goes to show that the problem were the johns. Throwing the book at the prostitutes wasn't going to stop the situation.

I had to become the voice and the face of prostitution, what they now call human trafficking. I had to take that role on, and if I was going to be that girl, I had to make sure that was okay with my loved ones. I talked to those senators first, and then I realized, oh, man, I've got to talk to my kids. My daughters and I had a long conversation about it. I asked them, "How you feel about that?"

"Momma, that's your story. You tell your story, especially if you are helping other people with it. Go tell your story."

You have to consider the people close to you when you put yourself out there, being known as "former prostitute Brenda Myers-Powell." I had permission from the people who really mattered. My daughters have supported me totally through this whole journey because they wanted me to heal. And if I wanted to help other people heal, then that's what my girls wanted me to do.

+ + +

The Chicago Coalition for the Homeless gave me a podium to speak from. The whole Chicago Coalition was like a family. It felt so good to be there. Everybody that was there felt so good to be there. They were organizers for the homeless. They were organizers for the rights of children to go to school if they were homeless. Everybody there had such big hearts. It was like you left your home and you walked into another home. Everybody was always bringing food in; everybody was working, but it was still family. It was a great place to be. I loved being there.

It became normal for me to go to Springfield and talk to senators. They called me the senator slayer because I used to walk around the offices when we were lobbying and have no problem talking to the senators. Some of them would call me in, and I would just rev up a conversation with them. Some of those senators could be kind of colorful if you let them. Some of them could be rude. They were something else, but so was I. I remember when we were trying to pass the Predator Accountability Act. One senator said, "Well, I don't want some poor guy to be railroaded by this bill you are trying to pass." And I told him, "Let's define 'poor guy.'" This bill would allow a young woman to civilly sue anyone who had coerced her to begin or started her in a life in prostitution. They didn't like that.

So let's define this "poor guy" when we talk about this "poor guy." Why and how was he involved with this woman? You're telling me he's this poor guy, so why is he in this circumstance anyway? How did he get from his wonderful home in Naperville to over here where this girl is? Let's talk about that one, sir. The bill covered both the tricks and the pimps. And winning a civil suit would cover the cost of her mental health treatment. People weren't ready for a criminal suit at that time because they were all about the poor guys. The women were the criminals. It was like folks wanted to tell me, "I mean, these girls were victims, but not really." Know what I mean? We were just coming into the concept of human trafficking, of women being survivors, but we weren't quite there yet.

+ + +

A couple of years later, I met Obama. I only met him once. Everybody was excited about him because even as a state senator we knew he was going places—he was the bomb. We were all at the Senate, and we're doing our thing, and here he comes, and we're talking and he's taking pictures with everybody. I get my chance to go up there with him, and I told him, "You know, we really need this bill passed, Senator Obama, because there's no way I can stand out there on the street corner. My knees don't work no more." And he starts to laugh, everybody was laughing. So when he starts to talk on the floor, he says, "We need to get this bill passed, and we need to get this bill passed today, because Brenda's knees don't work." When he said that everybody bust up laughing. And the bill passed. We came out all hugs. It was a good day.

During this time, I met a good man. Met him at a recovery meeting. His name was Keith. My brothers were telling him, "Ah, I wouldn't fuck with her. She's something else."

Keith said, "I ain't never asked any of you niggas for permission to fuck with her. Shit. I'm something else." And he really is. Keith is something else.

The first time I met him, he caught me looking at him, and I smiled. From his perspective, he thought I was smiling at him and I was. But I was smiling because his face was interesting to me. And his eyes . . . he had some old eyes. Like he had seen some things.

After the meeting, I asked some other members about him. I got different stories. He was with some woman. I remember I said to the girl who told me he had a woman, "I didn't ask you all that. I asked you about *him*." I didn't want to hear all that.

There was this skating-rink party, and we all went to the party. He was there with his kids, and I was there with my nieces. All the girls were in a circle, gossiping. I would turn my head to look at him, and I would see him looking at me. You know, we were doing the cute little shit people do when they are interested in each other. So he came over in his skates when I was in line to get some food at the snack bar.

"You got to quit stalking me," he said.

I looked around. "Boy, I ain't stalking you." I laughed and he laughed. We started talking, and I told him all the stuff I was going to do for my birthday with my girls. Blah, blah, blah. Later in the evening, he asked me could he take me out for my birthday, and I said sure. So we went on our first date. I had a car, but he didn't. So he picked me up at my house, and we left in my car.

"I'd like to buy you some flowers for your birthday."

I told him there was a florist right there on Clark. I parked my car across the street at this lot, and we went in to get the flowers. He bought me these beautiful peach roses; they were gorgeous. We get outside, and they had towed my car. And I was livid. I was cussing up a storm. "Calm down. Calm down. Promise me you won't let this change our date." So while I was sitting there stomping my feet and just about to go into a heart attack, Keith was looking upside the wall where they had a sign that told drivers where they tow cars to. "They tow them to right down the street. Let's hop the bus." We hop the bus and went to the towing company. Keith paid to get my car out.

"I'll pay you back."

"I didn't ask for you to pay me back. Let's just get back to our date."

He took me to this nice place to eat. We talked a lot. He told me he had a probation officer; I didn't know he was on probation. We went to a play after dinner. And then I dropped him off at his home. Now, as he was getting out the car, he told me he was living with this girl. I told him as long as he was living with her, he was her man. I was only interested in a 100 percent man, not a 50 percent man. I wanted a whole relationship. And I knew as long as he lived in this woman's house, that's the kind of stuff that would be going on. I'm not a fool. I know men and I know women. And in relationships, if you accept things in the door, it's going to continue. I wasn't bringing any more nonsense in my life. I was too old for all that.

But because I wasn't really thirsty for a man, I didn't fall back into all those bad habits I had had with other men. I wasn't going to give Keith all my money. I was going to let him take care of himself. I was feeling good about myself, and I liked being independent. My aunt Suzie was giving me advice on how to date guys. I mean, really date, like go out on dates with men to dinner and stuff like that. I didn't go out on another date with Keith until he had moved out of that girl's house.

Here is when I decided Keith was a keeper. I had gotten sick. I had this flu thing going on, and I had gotten a tooth pulled that day. He called me. I told him I didn't really feel like talking.

"Well, did you eat anything?" I said I didn't feel well enough to get up and cook anything for myself.

"Okay."

We got off the phone, and I laid down. About an hour later, I heard a knock at the door. That was surprising, because I didn't have people just showing up at my door. When I get to the door, it was Keith. He had a grocery bag in his hand. It was below zero outside. And he didn't have a car. So he must have caught the train and walked to the store, then walked to my house. He had brought me cold medicine and my version of comfort food: cream of chicken noodle soup and mashed potatoes.

He was in the kitchen stumbling around, asking me where did I keep the measuring cups. He made the soup and brought it to me. We sat up there on my bed and watched the news. I started to drift off. I heard him say he was going to leave. "I'll see you tomorrow, okay?" He locked the door behind him. Aretha hopped on my lap and I stared at the door. *You know what?* I thought to myself. *He might be a keeper.* He didn't have to do all that. And he hadn't pressed me for sex. Not once.

+ + +

So I was changing, but Stephanie wasn't coming along for the ride. We were still friends. I would still go up over there and run men out of her house. And she knew if she called me, I was coming. She would be sitting up over there, "I don't know what happened." I used to call her Erica Kane, you know, from *All My Children*. Every time something happened to Erica, she would say, "I don't know. Oh my God, Tom, Tom."

I told Stephanie, "You don't ever know what happened when I come over here." She was a fool.

Still, Stephanie was helping me out. I still didn't know how to manage money, and when I needed something, Stephanie always had it. She could write me out a check for a thousand dollars. "Come get it, bitch." Or she would slide the money under the door.

A lotta people say Stephanie is so overbearing, but so what? She's so my friend. With her overbearing ass. I know who she is. And you ain't got to hang with her, I'll be with her. Okay? That's my friend. You ain't got to claim her; you don't have to like her. I do. She never left me in the cold. She was there. And I was there for her.

When she lent me money, I never wanted to pay her back because I knew she would get high with it. Her son hadn't gone to jail yet, and he called me. "Go see Momma. She's killing herself." He was selling big drugs and she was stealing from him. She would just go in his room and get. The problem with Stephanie was, she had a pattern. She's educated: South Shore High School, top of the class, A-plus student; Illinois State, business and computer science; Chicago State University with a minor in computer science. She could go and get a job. And her pattern was: get clean, get a job, get some money, get some stuff, get an apartment, get a car, get a man. And then she's straight. Or at least she thought she was. She did that every time. The last time she did that, she married this man. Kevin. He was a womanizer, but according to Stephanie, he was such a good lover. And he provided. He liked coochie, but not just hers. Consequently, they had females coming over, females calling, bitches she had to show her marriage license to. I told her, "Why you going through all that shit?" But she loved him.

Now, in order to deal with all that, she had to get high. Kevin would try to hide his money in his pajama pocket when he slept. Stephanie's crazy ass was taking a razor blade and slicing his pocket open. She was getting that money. She sold his jewelry. She took his mink coat to trade to a drug dealer. She had gone down the back stairs where they lived. The only reason she didn't give it to the drug dealer was because she thought he was going to take it from her. My girl always had that keen sense of danger. She figured, "Here I am, a woman, on this shit, with this five-thousand-dollar mink coat, and that dealer would just take it from me." So she thought, she wasn't going to just take this coat and not have no rocks or nothing. She put the coat in the garbage and then looked up. Who's at the top of the stairs?

Kevin said, "I know that ain't my coat?" She didn't sell the coat.

They stayed in this dysfunctional-ass marriage. One day, when she hit the pipe, she started throwing up. He was in the bathroom at the sink. And you know what he did? He stepped over her. As if, *Bitch, die.* So now she was living in the house with this, but she couldn't leave. Cause he's paying the bills, he's good in bed; and it might be the cocaine that had her thinking this way. But he was a bastard. And everybody has a time; everybody has in them: no more.

So one day, Stephanie didn't go to work, but he did, and when he got back home, she was gone. She had gone to treatment. For the fifth time. But this time, something was different. She had learned some things in those other four treatment centers. In those other ones, instead of staying those thirty, forty-five, ninety days, she had left after two weeks, against the advice of everybody. "You not ready; you're going to use again."

But her ass had gotten kicked and torn off. And she was older, over forty. The streets were rough. Her little yank games she was playing, that wasn't working.

So Stephanie was in treatment. It was two weeks later, and she had a conversation with God. Ninety meetings and ninety days: "I'm going to do exactly what they say." She didn't know what's ahead of her, and she was petrified. But I know that kind of fear. The what's-next could be a step off a cliff. But you have to take it, cause you can't stay where you are. Maybe that's why Stephanie and I are so close. Maybe. But when I push on that thought, something pushes back.

There's no good reason why Stephanie and I are such good friends. Our closeness is divine—real but unexplainable. It's like God saw the two of us struggling and said, "Y'all should get together." I remember one time, I was at the treatment center, and Stephanie came over to see me. She wasn't stopping by to pick up any money from me; there was nothing I could have given her. She was just interested in me and how I was doing. I don't think I had had an adult relationship like that before. Every other person I had been with was "I'll give you this, if you give me that." But Stephanie loved me. She was becoming the sister I never had.

Chapter 21

A Funeral for Breezy

The funeral was my idea.

There was a woman at Genesis House named Carolyn Groves. She was this middle-class woman from Evanston. She taught theological studies at Loyola University, and she was a friend of my mentor, Edwina Gateley, a woman who had become a mother to me. Carolyn believed in journaling—that it was therapeutic to write letters to or journal about people in your life. She believed that this way you were able to look at your problems from another point of view. It's not like you are verbally talking about your problems, you're reading back your own thoughts and words. It is a way to see the things you want to free yourself from.

She told me to write about the people who had done things to me and tell them what they did. I wrote things about my pimp or people who harmed me. I wrote about Ma'Dea. At first it was all negative, and I remember Carolyn saying, "Okay. Okay. Now write about the good things that happened when you were with her. And the good things she did do." And I was able to write that. Ma'Dea used to say, "I'll eat shit with a splinter before I see you go hungry." I understand what she means now. She loved me. She loved Ernestine. I was her motherfucker. I didn't like it when she said that, but I get it now. I was her motherfucker. Good or bad. I was hers. I loved Ma'Dea. She was hilarious. Oh my God, she was funny. And she gave me the gift of how to tell stories. I listened to her for so many years, about being down South, how she grew up, how she got married and had kids. I listened to stories about what happened before I was born or when I was a little baby.

There was abuse, yes, but there was so much love in the middle of it. And there was so much pain. I made my peace with Ma'Dea when I understood that my life and my struggles were so close to hers. Nobody can deal with something that close in a healthy way. She was damaged by life.

With Carolyn encouraging me, I wrote about all this. But then it came to the place where I realized I needed to write Breezy. I didn't want to wear that name anymore. I wanted to be Brenda Jean. That's my name. I'm Brenda Jean, not Breezy. But what was I going to do with Breezy? Because she was alive. I realized I had to go ahead and let her go. She had to die for me to live. I didn't really like that. When I started to write about Breezy, all I could think of to say was that without Breezy, I probably wouldn't be here. She protected me, because Brenda Jean was not strong enough. I started to learn that even though I was ready to be Brenda Jean, Brenda Jean was still that little girl locked inside who was protected by the creation of Breezy. Breezy had done nothing wrong. All she had done was protect Brenda Jean. Things that happened: Breezy got shot. Breezy got stabbed. Breezy was being abused again. Brenda Jean probably couldn't have gone through all that. Breezy was this alter ego created to accept the beatings, the hits, the words, the curses, the challenges, the runaways, the moving around. To being independent, to being on the road like a hobo. Wherever I laid my head was my home. She was so wild and flamboyant, but she was always ready to come on with it. She definitely protected Brenda Jean. In those areas where I was vulnerable and soft, it was Breezy who popped out and said, "Fuck this shit!" Because Brenda Jean was about to get got. And so Brenda Jean had to step back, and I had to get Breezy. Probably in a lotta relationships, I did that. And when I came back with Breezy, it wasn't nice. She was very unpredictable.

So here's this Breezy girl who had been with me and to me wasn't a bad person at all. I didn't want to put her down. But the only hope of me becoming a strong, independent, positive woman that I needed to be was to get rid of Breezy. Breezy was too spontaneous. It was hard for me to say, "I don't need you anymore." Or maybe I wanted to say, "It's not that I don't need you, it's that you've done your job. You can sit down now. You can rest. Let me deal with this now." And that's how I wrote the letter about how she protected me, and how I had needed her, and how well she did protect me. And now, I thank you, but I need you to retire. I need to let go.

In accepting how it should be, I was able to be opened-minded and willing to change. Brenda Jean was going to grow. I realized I didn't know shit, and the shit I was going to be running into was going to be new shit. That was why I was so hungry to learn things, because I was like, Brenda Jean needs to catch up, she's still a little girl. I realized that some of the things I was experiencing, I came to wide-eyed.

One of the things that was therapeutic out of this exercise was that you write what you write, and you write as much as you need to write. And then you take that paper—it's almost like a ritual—and you burn it. And then you bury the ashes. It's like bringing closure to everything. Burying that. And that's what we did to what I had wrote about Breezy and how she needed to step back to allow Brenda Jean to take over. We buried her in the backyard of Genesis House. It was hard to do the whole thing. It was hard to burn the paper. Even if it was just a ritual, it felt very permanent to me.

Some of the girls who I was in the program with were there when I buried Breezy. Carolyn Groves was there, and some of the Genesis

House counselors were there, too. It was very emotional. Afterwards, without Breezy, I felt like a punk, because people would say things to me and make me angry and I wouldn't react. I knew if I reacted, my reaction wouldn't be healthy and it would get me in trouble. I had been going to anger management classes twice a week at Genesis House and I'm learning how not to react in anger. I'm learning how to take a deep breath and not say crazy shit. I'm learning how to walk away and come back calm. Where I was going, I couldn't take the anger with me. I had big plans for myself. Breezy didn't care about none of that. *Yeah, we in the police station, but you about to get your ass whooped right now.* That's Breezy. But Brenda would be: *We are going to make this police visit work.* Brenda needed to think her battles out and not just react to the battles that were happening. By doing that I realized how intelligent I could be. If you can just give me a second, I can think this through. I was able to figure out if the battle was even worth it. I started to smooth out and calm down.

I had the funeral in 1998. The ground was soft, the dirt was warm.

In some ways, Breezy is always going to be there for me. She's there when Brenda really can't handle it. But she's gone. Gone, gone. Keith has never seen her.

Even though I had held the funeral for Breezy and had written to everyone who had hurt me, I still had a way to go. I hadn't spoken to any of my family about Ma'Dea and me. The first time I said something, it was Thanksgiving. We were fixing the table, and I pointed to some old scar. I said something to the effect of "Ma'Dea gave that to me." Aunt Josie's look changed. And clearly, sometimes when you are trying to heal and you think maybe you can share things with some people, they may not be ready. This is what I do know. No matter what was going on with Ma'Dea, she was the glue of this family. And my aunts and uncles loved their momma. They loved Ma'Dea to death. And they remembered the best times with her.

Back in the day, on the weekends, Charlie and Dennis would come over or my aunt Suzie's kids, Renee and Gwen. Ma'Dea would get all the grandkids together, and we would go to the liquor store, and she would get her bottle and we would get our chips, or we would go to the restaurant and get our french fries, and she would bring all her grandbabies back to the house with her, and then we would go to the front room and we would get blankets and quilts, make pallets and tents and shit like that. Just mess up the living room and she would let us. We would have free-for-alls in the middle of the floor. She would be encouraging us, "Gone get her. Don't be crying. We don't like no crybabies." Because you had to be tough around her. Then we would all cool out and watch *Creature Features* on TV. Sometimes she would disappear, and then reappear in the window like she was an old monster: *"Ahhhh!"* We would start hollering. That would tickle her so. She would fall on the floor and just laugh at us. She would make me pee on myself, I was laughing so hard. She thought it was funny scaring the shit out the kids. And then the TV would go off, and she'd light a cigarette and she would tell us a story. And we would all sit around and listen to it because it would be so interesting. She had a way of telling stories.

So my family remembered the good times, but I felt like I was the only one who wanted to remember that Aunt Josie was the one who took me in because I had all those extension cord marks on my back. I'm thinking she would know better than anybody. I realized that was not something she wanted to talk about. You know how people want to talk about people in the past, "Yeah, Ma'Dea was this . . ."? Or talk about the wonderful things that they did, but never about things they have stuffed down?

Aunt Josie has two sons that are total assholes. And before I left, she put me in that category with them. She said, "You, Charles, and Dennis have to learn to stop living in the past and not to be bitter. Y'all got to stop that." I was surprised she put me in that category with them, because I didn't think that I was anywhere close to them. I've never said a cross or a disrespectful word to my aunt. I've never said a disrespectful word about my grandmother either. And we laughed about the stuff she did—how she had all these different ways and didn't take no shit. But I also experienced other stuff. I remember my cousin Dennis, we were all there and we were talking about that, and he said, "She never put her hands on me." Ma'Dea loved her boys. But they weren't there all the time; I was there. I was there to get on her nerves; I was there to do the little shit that Jeremy does to me now. And I get it, but I didn't get it before. Even Dennis once said, "Yeah, well, she used to beat the brakes up off you. She never beat us like that." So when Aunt Josie told me to stop living in the past, it hurt me so bad.

On my way back from her place, I said something about Ma'Dea that Peaches didn't agree with, because Ma'Dea was different with her. I think the same is true with Aunt Josie. Sometimes I feel like Aunt Josie is closer to my girls than she is to me. When I got home, I stayed in the bed for three days. I was so messed up. Crying. And for a while I didn't talk to my aunt Josie because it was clear I could not really talk to her.

Talking about my past abuse was hard to do with my family, but making sure I didn't turn into my grandmother as I raised my son was harder. Jeremy was a handful, and I was dealing with issues with that boy. My brother Jethro and his girlfriend, Melanie, were doing drugs together, and they had already had three kids. Jeremy was the fourth and the youngest. The other children were already in custody with my stepmom. But she couldn't take any more kids. She had custody of her daughter's kids and now she had Jethro's kids. There were a lot of kids.

When Melanie was pregnant with Jeremy, I talked her into going into treatment. I used to tease her, "If it's a girl, name her after me, and if it's a boy, name him after me." She had the baby clean, so they gave her the baby. I used to go by, to encourage her to stay in treatment, get her hair done, and all that. Jeremy was so adorable, the little stinker. I loved him. I would go and get him, bring him out to the house, and then I would bring him back to her. But then I started getting calls—she was using again. Some days nobody knew where she and Jeremy were. Melanie was on the streets. Once, I saw her. She saw me, too. She walked up to me and asked if I would give her two dollars, so she could get a can of ravioli so she could feed the baby.

"Where *is* the baby?"

"Oh, he over there in the car." She had put Jeremy, who was a couple months old, in an abandoned car. "He hasn't eaten today."

"The baby hasn't eaten all day? Give me the damn baby, Melanie." So I took him back home with me. I bought him clothes and food. I put everything in a box and take it all back with him to Melanie's. Back and forth, back and forth.

Months later family services called. "We have baby Jeremy and we hear you love him enough to come and get him. That's what the mother says." I asked them, if I didn't come and get him, what would happen? And they told me they would put him in the system somewhere.

"Somewhere?"

I talked to my husband, and we agreed we had to go and get him and keep him. Jeremy was sixteen months old. We had to do different stuff to become foster parents. I had to get letters of recommendation because I had a background. When we got him, we realized he was delayed in a lot of ways. He didn't talk, he was malnourished. I had to get help from Easterseals. In the beginning, Jeremy had real separation issues. I couldn't get out the car and walk around to take him out of the car seat without him thinking I was leaving him if I did that. He would start crying. I had to stay in his vision so he would know that I was just walking around to get him out of the car, too. "I'm right here, Jeremy."

He didn't know how to say he was hungry, so finally I went and got him a little cartoon plate—the *Toy Story* movie—and when he wanted to eat, he would put the plate on my lap. Finally, he picked up weight and was running around and laughing like a little baby. He was my little stinker. He was five years old when we adopted him. We waited that long because I thought Melanie would get her act together. But she never did. After we took him, Melanie never visited. Never. Even on special birthdays and stuff like that, I couldn't get her. She was busy in the streets. I would go and find her because Jeremy wanted to see his mother. It wasn't easy. Sometimes he would holler out her name in the middle of the night. And as he got older, he got more complicated and harder to deal with. I would struggle with that. One time Keith said to me, "I never knew your grandmother, but I do know her."

"How do you know her?"

"I watch you. Sometimes I see you be her. Cracking on Jeremy for no good reason. And you don't have to be."

I didn't know how to take that. I had to work through that. I had to work through realizing you don't always make the best choices or do the right thing all the time with children because you can become so caught up in a situation. I saw mistakes I made that Ma'Dea could have made. Being angry. Being mad. And then she would start hitting on me because she was a fighter. With me, I would tell Jeremy, "I don't fuck around like that, little boy. Let me let you know that." So I started seeing being in her position. And I said, *Please forgive me*. More than once she said to me, "Brenda Jean, what goes around comes around. And one day you are going to have to reap what you sow." Now, as a young kid, I got none of that. Reap what you sow? Go around, come around? You are going to have to answer for the things that you do?

Since I have been raising my son, I realize Ma'Dea has not lied to me yet.

I know of the things that Jeremy has done to me, and I can remember the times when I was like that with her. Lying. Disobedient and not even knowing why. I know mine came from anger and hurt and pain. But it also had a lot to do with my environment.

Now how's Jeremy's environment making him act the way he does? I needed to check myself and check the surroundings. I started to do that. And I started to feel that not only did Jeremy need some help, I needed some help, too. I was in a better place than Ma'Dea. I had Stephanie in my life. And Keith. And mentors. And sponsors. Ma'Dea just had Ma'Dea. And her bottle, when things got too rough. And things were too rough a lot.

I finally learned she did the best she could do with me with what she had. She wasn't the reason for my abuse, she wasn't at fault for my sexual abuse, my molestation. She was verbally abusive, but she didn't know how to be anybody else. She didn't know how else to handle herself without being raw. She just knew how to say what she had to say, and sometimes that was soul-shaking. It would just shake your core. She would say stuff to me like, "I'm too old of a cat to be fucked by a kitten." That's some hard-core shit to tell a youngster, because it sounds dirty. But what she was saying to me was that I had to get older in order to understand that the shit I was doing, she'd already done. I couldn't just tell her anything and fool her. She been through it already, little kitten. Now I'm looking at life, and things are coming at me like that, and I'm looking at my little kid Jeremy, and, "Boy, I see you coming."

I started healing when I saw how bad Jeremy would hurt me through his behavior. I was amazed at how hurt I was from it and how personal I took it. And he was only a kid. Same thing with Ma'Dea. I was only a kid, but that shit was so shattering.

I think she would be so proud of me now. Of what I'm doing. I think, at the end of the road, she would have said job well done. There's some tough-titty shit that happened with me, and I think that before my grandmother passed away, she had an idea that she wasn't going to be here to help me through it. *How do I prepare Brenda for what's coming?* Because she knew about the rain. She knew about the storm. *How do I prepare this kid for this shit, because I'm not going to be here to fight for her? And if I'm here, I'll be too old to do anything about it.* I feel sometimes that what I went through stressed Ma'Dea out. And the only way I can forgive myself for that is that, as I was going through all this, I didn't know how to tell Ma'Dea about it. If I had known better, I would have done better. I wish I had been a better child. I wish I could have saved her through being a better child. Maybe growing up and being better, I would have been able to take her out of those ghetto-ass apartments. I could have taken care of her, the way she took care of me all my life. I do wish that. I wish I could have taken care of my grandmomma.

In 2007, we started the Dreamcatcher Foundation. Stephanie had been thinking about a nonprofit that we could do together for a while. Ten years. Stephanie thought up the name. She wanted a name that inspired and said reach for the stars. Google was her friend, and she thought about dreams: carrying the dreams, reach for your dreams, and then she saw "dream catcher" and looked it up and said, "That's it." And that's how we came up with the tagline at the time: "Do you have any dreams you want to catch?" But it didn't tell people what we did. So then we came up with the tagline: "Specializing in human trafficking." Because people kept saying, "Dreamcatcher— what is that? What y'all do?" Stephanie didn't know about the story of the Native American dream catcher until I told her about it. How they put it over the bed, and it catches your nightmares.

Meanwhile, I had been working, and Stephanie was walking her journey. She met Michael Wilson. I remember when I first met him. Stephanie told me he was wonderful. She had told me about wonderful men before. But when I left her house, I felt that he was a wonderful man, too. I didn't know how wonderful, but I knew for some reason, she got somebody to take care of her heart. That's how he made me feel. Stephanie had a real man to take care of her now. I was so glad. I sat there in my car for a minute before I pulled off, thinking about that.

Stephanie had been in a meeting, and this man, who looked like a god, very handsome, was standing there. Cool. Very well dressed. And he said, "I'm Michael and I'm an addict."

She was sitting with a woman named Daphne, and Stephanie turned to her and said, "Bitch, who is that?"

She said to Stephanie, "Bitch, that's Mike. You know him."

"Bitch, I don't know him. Who is he?" And he went on to say how he had fourteen years, and he was in the program. And *woo, woo, woo.* Now, the rules of the program were that you were not supposed to mess with a newcomer. Okay? Stephanie, with her low self-esteem and insecurity, said, "I can forget it. I ain't got no clean time and I heard what that man just said. He's sober, he's in the program."

She put her head down and walked away. But you never know. Pam, Stephanie's sponsor, was good friends with Michael. She had made the introductions. He had gotten out of a marriage six years ago. He was a bachelor. Stephanie was doing her giggling thing. He knew she had no clean time, but he liked her. They went out to eat a couple of times, spent the weekend over his house. And that was it. They met in February, moved in in April. He proposed in June, and they got married in October. And that lasted sixteen years until he left the world. Liver cancer.

Throughout all that, Stephanie was going to get her master's degree in social work. She was working for a social service agency called ACCESS Community Health Network and knew other people who had social service agencies. Predominately with the AIDS thing. Stephanie just knew that together we could provide something important for the community. That in a real way, we weren't living up to our full potential. That's when she told me, "I will not sit here for the rest of my life in this going-nowhere job, and the only way I see my way out of this is for me and my friend to start our own shit." Stephanie was married to Michael when I met Keith. I was working as a bill collector. And in the process of that happening, I was getting stressed out with the bill-collector job. I'm volunteering at the Chicago Coalition for the Homeless and then hassling people to pay up from nine to five. I was living two different lives.

While I'm at Coalition, people started doing articles on me. The *Chicago Tribune* did a piece on me. And then the Coalition got a call from the *Washington Post*. They wanted to know who I was and how was I doing all this. How is this prostitute doing all this stuff and putting herself out there like that and speaking to these politicians? And what they were saying—"she speaks so well, so articulate"—oh, I know what that's code for. I was on the front page of the *Washington Post*. It was crazy. Everything got really big, really fast. This producer from the *Judge Hatchett* show called his friend at the *Washington Post*, and they were talking and my name came up. They wanted to do a show with me. They've got twin boys from California who want to be pimps. These little white girls were giving them their lunch money and started to think they're hos. They wanted me to come on the *Judge Hatchett* show and talk to these boys. I ended up taking Homer, a former pimp friend of mine, because I think these boys needed to hear from a real pimp. I listened to them and thought, *Womp, womp.* Then I told them about the West Side of Chicago and how this shit really goes. They can't believe it. I introduced them to a real pimp, and then they get really scared.

Kids. Girls. I did two more *Judge Hatchett* shows. But then one day a producer from the *Judge Hatchett* show kicks it with a producer from the *Maury* show. So I do the *Maury* show and met D. West, who was like a regular on the program. He would go on the show and scare everybody. I would go on the show and think to myself, *He needs to stop hollering at these girls. There's another way to do this.* But I never got a chance to do it the ways it should be done, because what they want is the hollering and carrying-on. It was one of the reasons why I backed out and didn't want to do any more shows. They wanted a dog and pony show. They only person who wasn't an idiot onstage is Maury. Everyone else is paid to act the fool. But you know what? I started getting letters from the girls who had been on the show: *Dear Miz Brenda, I saw myself and I didn't like what I saw. Thank you for talking to me.*

The thing is, I would talk to those girls after the show and ask them to make sure they watched themselves on TV when the show aired. "Tell me if you like what you see. And then think to yourself, all your friends are gone see you, too." So that's how that went. And meanwhile, I'm still holding down the bill-collector job. I was driving myself crazy. Driving Keith crazy, too. Till finally, Keith said, let them fire you and you can draw your unemployment. "I'll take care of you." I was off for about six months or so, and Stephanie said, "Come on down here and work where I'm at."

She got me a job where she was working, ACCESS Community Health Network. It was a medical center that dealt with a lot of inner-city issues. Mainly African American women who had HIV and AIDS were their clients. Stephanie was a case manager who dealt with infectious diseases. She helped get people's lives in line, get their medication in line. She was their counselor. She wasn't too far from her master's when she got that job. She and Michael were living their dream, and I started working there. It was a good job for me. I liked it. They gave me a lot of education. They were always sending their employees on trainings and just prepping you to deal with this transient population. That's where I learned about counseling, mentoring, and dealing with young girls.

But the entire time, Stephanie and I were still talking about starting our own thing. Both of us were thinking, *What kind of population are we going to serve?* Stephanie thought pregnancy prevention or some type of services for teens to prevent them having babies and help teens who already have babies. She told me about it, but I thought we should do something in prostitution prevention. The term *human trafficking* hadn't been invented yet. Now that's the term—*human trafficking*—to be politically correct, but back then it was just prostitution prevention.

It's all so polite now, so that's what everybody says. Nobody can say *dick* anymore; they want to say *penile connection to the body*. Girl, please. Anyway, I thought about serving prostitutes. Something like Genesis House. Like Christian Community Help Center. Those were places that helped women who were on the stroll, who had formed an addiction, who had developed an addiction to the lifestyle. We wanted to work with all of those women. Stephanie ran off and did more research. There were a lot of services being done for prostitutes, but there were not any services for the youth. No one was really servicing the twelve-to-twenty-four-year-old population, and there weren't any services being delivered by survivors.

One day Stephanie said, "Friend. We can do this shit. You are the expert. And everywhere I look, your name pops up attached to some TV show or organization."

That's where it all started. After that, we started evolving. We understood that we had an eclectic approach. It was both practical and clinical. We understood we had a lot of information that social clinicians didn't have, and that was the practical application in this arena. I knew this world, inside and out. I was doing my thing, but I was ready to take the next step. I knew I could help girls who were caught out there the way I was.

+ + +

We were unique. We were survivors, and we made an organization. We would be run by survivors. Everything would be done by survivors. And we started to get our shit together. Stephanie was still working her job. She would come in, do her clients in half a day, and then the rest of the day she'd do Dreamcatcher. And I would go over there, and we would work together. All those people in the office would get uncomfortably quiet when we were working. But Stephanie didn't care. She had four desks in her little area, and she used them all. Once, this guy took me to a woman who was a millionaire, for me to cosign his project. But when he got up and went to the bathroom—he was gone for about fifteen minutes—when he came back, I had the bag for Dreamcatcher. And when the millionaire met Stephanie, guess what she said? "If nothing else, Brenda is persistent." We came about this shit so funny, we didn't have a plan, but we had an idea. We would get in Stephanie's car and just ride around and laugh and talk to young girls.

"You alright?"

"You know how it is, Miz Brenda." And I did. It just came to be okay. I'm a character. And I love being a character. I love people. I think people are one of the best gifts God put on the earth. And because of that, we need to treat each other better. I like to treat people better. Girls gravitated toward me because I was the lady on the Maury Povich show. Girls would say, "Oh, we seen you on the *Maury* show." And I would say, yeah, that's me. And those girls wanted to tell me their stories. How people don't listen to them and their momma didn't listen to them. They needed a place for somebody to hear what they were talking about. "That happened to me, but I couldn't tell nobody about it."

And that's how that happened.

+ + +

Life doesn't stop happening just because you've got your act together. Life just keeps coming at you. During Stephanie's clean time being with her man, her mother left first. And then her dad left. Then she had to watch her husband make that transition in that same house. Michael was like that Prince song, "If I was your girlfriend, would you let me help pick out your clothes?" He would do that. He was a lovely man.

I'm grateful that God allowed her that time to be with him. And let her know what real love is. They had unconditional love. They weren't perfect, but they were perfect for each other. She misses him. But she's not going to destroy herself because he's not here. He would hate that.

I was afraid of losing her, but she would always reassure me. "Bitch, I might do a lot of things, but I'm not fucking with that cocaine." She would always tell me that. And I believed her. This has been a woman who has never been uncomfortable enough to not tell me the truth. Because now we are married as people. As two girl-friends, do or die. We like Thelma and Louise. And we went off the edge together. So when she was hurting, I was hurting. Am I going to lose my friend? Are we going to lose everything we worked for?

Sometimes Stephanie was mean. One time she ate me up during a cab ride. "Motherfucker, kiss my ass." And she said some more shit to me, and I was upset. Later on, she told me she was sorry, but I told her, "You already said that before, bitch. I forgive you. You said you were sorry that night. I got it."

I think about the women Stephanie and I are now. We are these ladies who married men who loved us; we speak for the voiceless; we get to have grandbabies sitting on our knees. Such joy. It took almost a lifetime, but I've learned I have to teach people how to treat me. I used to allow people to treat me any kind of way. I don't do that anymore. Sometimes I don't hang with folks no more, but sometimes I feel like, you don't know any better, so let me tell you how it is and how it's going to go. And then, if you don't like it, we don't have to hang out with each other. If I am telling you how to treat me and you are treating me in another way, we can't be friends no more. The only people who get away with that is my son and my husband.

+ + +

But more than anything, I am now in a place where I get to live my life and have my own opinions. My life is full of choices. Some choices are hard to make, others are easy, but I can't get over, this late in the game, how good it feels to choose something and live with it. Every day, I make a choice. Sometimes I can't make myself happy and my husband happy. I can't make Jeremy happy and me happy. Or Stephanie. Or even my daughters. I can't make people happy and me happy. But every day, I choose me.

I Make Plans, God Laughs

My life is now what I never expected it to be. I am surrounded by my family and loved by my daughters. I'm in love and married to a good man. My best friend and I help girls stay off the terrible road I walked, and for the women on the stroll, abused and drugged, we give them counseling and steer them to treatment when they are ready. I have a full life. And when I met Kim Longinotto, the director who wanted to capture a portion of my life on film, she thought so, too. The film, *Dreamcatcher*, followed me and the girls I help. I meet these young ladies in high school and some in junior high. Some of them are as young as twelve years old. They are already professionals. I'm not surprised. I started that young. Each of them is just about to start down the dark road I walked on. It's hard to speak to a child who is going through adult stuff. They've got complicated families and bad boyfriends. They're trying to juggle staying in school and having babies. You can still make a good life, I tell them. The work is rewarding, and I guess when other folks took a look at how Stephanie and I spend our days, they agreed.

The film won a Sundance Film Festival award in 2015 and was nominated for a NAACP Image Award. I was walking down red carpets and flaunting it. For a minute, I thought life couldn't get more exciting. Boy, was I wrong.

I remember at the time, I felt unbalanced. The producer on the film, Lisa Stevens, she had a new idea. She wanted to do another documentary with me, this one about me looking for the daughter I abandoned twenty-seven years ago in Los Angeles. She approached Stephanie with the idea, and I guess Stephanie told her she thought that was a great plan and that I should be a producer on it, too.

Well, Lisa called me and told me all about it. Oh, I was so mad at Stephanie. I went over to where she lived, stormed up to her door, and proceeded to cuss her out. "You can't have no conversation with nobody about my daughter. You need to stop advertising about my daughter."

If my daughter was out there, this was not the way I wanted to meet her—on live television. I felt like my punishment was not to know if she were living or dead. It was hard to even talk about her or think about her. I got so belligerent that Stephanie had to put my ass out.

She looked at me astonished. "Really, bitch? You think I would do something like that to you? Get the fuck up out my house."

"I ain't going nowhere."

"Get on out of here. Like I would do something to you." I left, but I was still fussing with her out the door. I was at such an emotional low with this. All you had to do was say something about it and I would have started a fight. It was unresolved and it was hurting me on the inside. Of course, Stephanie got that. Well, we made up. Cause we fall out, we make up all the time.

Later on, we had a brunch on Sunday, and there were some Hispanic people around and I started feeling emotional, and I told Stephanie, "That's what my baby probably looks like. She had coal-black hair. And she looked like a Hispanic. The only thing I could give her was my name, so I named her Brenda."

At the same time, my daughters were researching some things in their own lives. They wanted to find out the history about their dads. Peaches wanted to find out about her roots. About her dad. I didn't have anybody's last name. What my boyfriends told me, what their friends called them—that's the name I had. All I had was Spoon, so that was all Peaches had to work with. She was trying to find out through her DNA could she find him. Through Ancestry.com. She was searching and telling me all her background. She was part English and Indian and of course African, and she had some other things in her. She was telling me about that, and I was telling her, "Oh, that's so interesting."

✦ ✦ ✦

A couple of weeks later, my daughters and Stephanie told me that they were going to have a "Love Day." We do little stuff like that. We all get together and have wine and some snacks. Sometimes we call it Wind Down, but we wine down. Okay? Wind Down Wednesday. We do little stuff like that to rejuvenate ourselves. They said, we are having a Love Day.

That day at my house I was cleaning up and fussing around. You know how you try to get everything tidied up before you walk out the door? That was what I was doing. But everybody was needy that day. My husband, Jeremy. I wanted to lock them out the door. Finally, I realized, shoot, I had to get out of there if I was going to be on time. I just grabbed my clothes and left because I thought I could change over at Peaches's house. Peaches had already commented, "You be on time." I went over my daughter's house looking a sight for sore eyes. I had just gotten through cleaning, so I had my cleaning clothes on. When I got there, they met me at the door. Peaches and Prune shuffled me in. "Come upstairs." And they took me up the stairs real fast. I put my clothes on. "Hurry up, Momma." So now I was wondering what they had up their sleeves because they were rushing me so. I knew they were planning something, but I didn't know what it was. We do nice things for each other. Maybe they had somebody who was going to read some poetry, or maybe they had somebody who was going to sing. That's what was in my mind. For my birthday, they had had somebody come and sing to me. It's Love Day, so I'm thinking about a lot of things, but mainly I was thinking about my lost daughter.

This girl. I had come to a peace about her. I thought, she's my daughter, no matter who she's with, and one day I'll be able to see her and that will probably be in heaven. I had gone to a clairvoyant, and she told me my daughter was doing well. She was doing very well. In fact, the clairvoyant told me, she's looking for you. But I didn't really believe all that. Plus, what everyone wanted to do with the story, I wasn't ready to deal with all of that. I wasn't going to let anyone make a mockery of it. It was one of the hardest things I ever had to deal with. So my daughters were hurrying me to come downstairs, and then they shuffle me into my daughter's living room. First of all, we never hang out in that room. We usually do stuff in the dining room, right by the kitchen. We're women, we are always right by the kitchen. I'm thinking, *Why we going in here?* We were going into the good room. They sat me down in the chair. Stephanie's there sitting on the couch. Mimi's there. And my other granddaughter, Avery, she was there, too. They were all in the living room.

Now here came Peaches with this speech. "On this Love Day, we love the people of the world and the United States of America . . ." No, I'm just kidding. But she gave a little speech. Peaches kept saying stuff like, "Momma. We want to tell you that we share you, we see you, and we feel you." And I was like, oh, that's beautiful. She had put emphasis on "we hear you." They heard my pain. They had heard my heart.

Then Prune gave her speech. Hers was like, "Momma. You deserve to come full circle. Your life deserves to come full circle. And that means everything in your circle needs to come together." And I was thinking, yeah, that's right. "Momma. Someone wants to meet you." And then this girl walks in the room. I looked at her, and it was just two seconds, but I knew who she was. She was my daughter. I fell on the floor and I started to cry. I just couldn't hold it together.

"Are you—? Is that—?" I almost had a heart attack. I thought we were going to have to have the paramedics there.

I looked at Stephanie. "You knew all the time!"

"What can I tell you?"

+ + +

I turned to this beautiful girl and told her, "I prayed. I prayed for God to take care of you." She was holding on to me; I was holding on to her.

She looked at me and said, "I was very well loved and taken care of."

I wept. "You were?"

"I was." She was hugging me, and I started to smell her. Do you know how when you have a baby, you smell them? It was like I got her all over again that day in that hospital. I needed to smell her. She said, "Oh my gosh, you smelling me." I needed to inhale her.

That was a beautiful day. Her name was Brenda, but everybody called her Bree. That she had kept the name I had given her at the hospital felt like a miracle. They had kept my baby's name. It was the only thing I could give her. The woman who adopted her was named Brenda. How could God get so close? She's wearing the name of both her mothers. Bree had a sister, who she had brought along. Jenna. They are total sisters. Jenna was so great. So supportive. I was just admiring Bree the whole time. Looking at her face. I was looking at the smallest things. And I saw things that felt like her inheritance. The similarities. And I thought, *That's my baby*. You could just see it. It was nice.

Bree told me she found her father, too. He was a Mexican guy. My daughter approached him and said, "Hey, I think you're my daddy." And he said, "I probably am. I got about thirteen, fourteen kids." My daughter told me he was a tall Mexican. She told me some other things about her birth, and even though she didn't know it, she was explaining where I was in my head all those years ago, things I never knew until my daughter came back. You know, I do inventory on my life when someone comes from my past. I try to understand myself, then put it in a box. She said that I named her Brenda Market. My name is Brenda Myers. Her first name is mine, but I named her last name after Coolie. I'm in California, a hundred years later, and I was still . . . still . . .

That's some crazy shit about where I was and where my thinking was. Today in my life, I have dreams of Coolie, I have dreams of Sonny. I have dreams of some of the guys I been with. And sometimes I wake up and they're all interconnected, and I feel in a melancholy way about it. And that's why I have to put it in place, to where it really is and really was: these men used me. They used me to the point where I thought it was okay as to how they used me. And it's hard to separate the love I had for them with the part where they abused me. It's hard. That's why this shit is hard. That's why this lifestyle is hard for a girl. It's not a night where you don't lay down and wake up with feelings unless he's just really dogging up out. Tommy Knox? I could take him or leave him any day. Tra-la-la. But there are some relationships that I had with these pimps, players, that were intimate in their own way. No matter what over-the-top shit happened. There was some real intimacy, conversations, connections.

Sometimes I touched some pimp in his heart, sometimes he touched me in my mine. But neither one of us never loved each other more than we loved the game. Addicted to the lifestyle, and if the drugs don't kill you, the lifestyle will. The lifestyle comes with a deeper addiction and package, more than the drugs and all the other shit. It's an irresponsible lifestyle, and when it's good, it's real good, but the pleasure, the success is bad for you. You know how you're addicted to sugar and chocolate and shit like that makes you feel happy, makes you feel good? Those are the times in your brain, these things that you are doing in your lifestyle that tick off that area in your brain. The lifestyle is like a super-exciting rush. You get what you want when you want it. You do what you want to do when you want to do it. You start to accept the fact that I need to go to jail. You say shit like, "Shit, they can hold me but they can't keep me forever." You accept that you get robbed, you accept that bad things happen in the game. If you are a good hustler, you can recuperate from that shit. That's just a temporary day, I'll be back on my feet in no time. Cause that's a part of the game you have to accept. All you got to do is live through it. So I can't sit here and tell folks that I didn't love it. All that shit that was going on, it was like feeding a part of me. And it was always, but always, a distraction from the pain that was going on inside of me.

I had to grow away from that. I had to walk away from all that. I didn't get me through, God got me through. If He hadn't, I would never had held my lost baby in my arms.

+ + +

Of course, I wanted to know how they found Bree, or who found who. Between Stephanie and Peaches, I got the whole story. See, Peaches had kept on Ancestry and they came back with a hit that said we did not find your dad but we found a sister or a first cousin. It was Brenda. Before Peaches called little Brenda, she called Stephanie. Stephanie was about to go out dancing. Peaches said, "Stephanie, I think I found Momma's daughter. And I need you to be on the phone, because I want you to hear things. Maybe I'm too excited. I want you to hear what I hear."

They all got on the phone. They were all talking to Bree, and she's saying all the things I had told Stephanie over the years.

"My name is Brenda. I'm half Hispanic." All she knew was that she was born in Los Angeles, and she was left in the hospital by her mother. And she had been looking for her.

Peaches said, "I want Momma and Bree to meet."

"Okay, how do you want to do it?" Stephanie said. Well, Mother's

Day was coming up. It was two months away. Stephanie never spilled the beans, even when I had come over her house and cussed her out. Stephanie told me she was tempted to whip out a picture of Bree she had in her phone. A new picture. But she didn't, because she didn't want to ruin the surprise and it was already in motion for Bree to come.

Stephanie and Peaches had set up a date for Bree to fly to Chicago, and they invited her sister, Jenna, to come as well. They didn't want Bree to feel uncomfortable. She had been looking for me for a while. When I met her, she said she had sent me a letter on Ancestry: *Hi, I might be your daughter.* But I had never seen it. I'm not a big messenger person. Someone told me it might not have gone through, because you have to accept somebody on the messenger thing. You have to friend them and everything. I told her when we finally met, "I assure you, if I had gotten that message, I would have been there on a rail, on a jet." The only thing I had left to do on this earth was to find my daughter. And at that moment, the first thing that come into my mind was that God showed me who He really was. It's like He looked down on me and laughed and then said, "Huh, I told you I was God, didn't I?" This is God; look at Him do this whole thing. I mean, she never did a day in the system; I had asked God for that. The lady had adopted her right out the hospital. And the woman's name was Brenda, too. Maybe that's why she didn't change Bree's name. And some of our mannerisms are the same. The wigs, the big laugh. It's crazy. Little Brenda was loved well.

Three months later, Bree's birthday was coming up, so I went to California to celebrate it with her. And I met the woman who gave her what I could not. I absolutely adored her. I went to Things Remembered, the jewelry store, and we had stuff engraved. I had a jewelry box made for her, and on it I had engraved: *Thank you for doing what I could not.* That's what I gave her as a gift. I just wanted to let her know that she was the best part of Bree.

+ + +

So we are now trying to all make a go of it. We decided to make Peaches's birthday this girls' night celebration. We are ladies who know how to party. We raise our arms and lift a glass. My daughters, my friends, celebrating how we got through. Here we are, Lord. Together. I have everybody in my life who is in my front row and on my top shelf. Everybody was there, even my grandbaby Mimi. It was like something most women just dream of having. Coming from where I came from and to have that type of celebration with my daughters and my granddaughters, I can't describe it. I have been very, very lucky in regards to my family. Cause now I've got everybody.

The party was amazing. We went to Bolingbrook. It's this nice part of Chicago that has all of these restaurants. That night, we all went to this restaurant. They went and dropped me off, so I didn't have to walk so far. Then they went and parked the car. I'm the old one. I'm standing there, waiting for them to come. I saw Bree walking down the street, in between the cars, and she sang something. And she did a little dance. I thought to myself, she is crazy as heck; I do that kind of stuff all the time. Sometimes I have a song in my mind, and when it hits me, I've got to sing and do a little dance. And there she was doing the same thing. Anyway, we did dinner; there was a lot of laughing. We tried to tell her as much about ourselves as we could. She and Jenna told us about them. Bree still hasn't figured out what to call me. And I'm alright with that. It was a beautiful time.

After she left, I had to keep telling myself it was real. I couldn't believe God loved me that much. But He does.

Acknowledgments

First, God is first. And I say that because for a good part of my life I approached Him as if He were third or fourth. Without God I would not be here.

Stephanie Daniels-Wilson is second. She is my best friend who heard this book inside me before anyone else did. She pushed, supported, and encouraged me to write my story. You always saw the genius in me, friend.

And then, when I want to acknowledge and give praise, I get all the numbers mixed up. Who comes first, who's second? How can I enumerate all the loves of my life? My daughters Ernestine, Ruth, and Bree endured this journey with me and still love me for who I am. Yes! You are my first, best and treasured. To my aunt Josie: this story would read quite differently if you hadn't raised my daughters up to be the outstanding ladies they are today. I have granddaughters now, Amir and Avery Grace, who are my reasons for the season. Amir, when you were born, I asked God to allow me the chance to be a better grandmother than I was a mother. And He answered me: okay, Brenda Jean, I hear you. I'd like to give a special acknowledgement to my husband for giving me the love I thought I'd never find and for loving me for who I am today, not what I used to be.

God is first because He wasn't through being good to me. I have three other amazing kids, LaShonda, Lil Keith, and Debron, who I adore. Three more grandkids, Jason, Kaden, and Kamren, who are more reasons for the season. And He wasn't done blessing my life. God gave me my bonus child, Jeremy Powell, who keeps me going with all his energy and in the process lets me live my second mommy-hood.

My journey may have started lonely, but God made sure I didn't walk my roads all by myself. I'd like to give a special acknowledgement to those that helped me along my new journey. To Edwina Gateley, who I call Mother because she embraced me. I stand on the shoulders of the great woman she is. Yolanda Daniels Rocket for being a wonderful sponsor, friend, and mentor—one of the strongest women I know. May she rest in peace. Carolyn Groves, you helped nurture me into becoming a woman; Samir Goswami introduced me to the human trafficking movement and recognized my leadership ability. You helped me soar. I found my voice with you, friend. Thank you, Christine and Mike Evans, for thinking I'm special. Special shout-out to the Sophia's Circle ladies, Chicago Alliance Against Sexual Exploitation, Cook County Sheriff's Office, Chicago Coalition for the Homeless, and Rex Alexander, who gave me guidance through difficult and happy times in my life.

I want to acknowledge people who believed in me: Rachel Durshlag, Marian Brooks, Ann Sweeny, Dawn Trice, Lisa Cunningham, Olivia Howard, Tina Fundt, Anne Ream, Jerry Riles, Bill Leen, Eric V. Harwell, and all the officers from Division 17.

When I decided to tell my story, when I decided to be brave and tell the truth, I had so many to catch me with open arms. A special acknowledgement to Lisa Stevens. You are a beast. The *Dreamcatcher* film couldn't have been done without you. You, Geralyn White

Dreyfous, Regina Scully, Barbara Duncan, and women making films tell our truths with open eyes and open hearts.

To everyone on the Holt team: thank you for all that you did for this book.

To Pat Eisemann, my fabulous publicist: thank you for getting this book out into the world and into the hands of readers. Nicolette Seeback: thank you for this gorgeous cover.

Of course, I have to give a big thank-you to Rosemarie Robotham, a talented writer in her own right, for introducing me to my writing crew.

Steven Ivy: thank you for your great counsel.

And to seal these acknowledgments I'd like to thank my super women: April Reynolds, who wrote this book from my heart—you are the BOMB; my amazing protective agent, Jennifer Lyons, and my die-hard editor, Sarah Crichton. You made this all happen and believed in me not only once but twice.

Now I want to acknowledge why I wrote this book—for every little girl who has had her choice to be innocent taken away from her. WE DO RECOVER, and then it gets real.

While writing this book we found my daughter Bree, and my final acknowledgement is to Ms. Brenda Butler, the amazing woman who adopted and raised my daughter when I could not. I am forever grateful to you.

About the Author

Brenda Myers-Powell has been advocating for victims of sex trafficking since 1997. She considers herself fortunate to have survived many challenges in her life and to be able to use those experiences to assist others in their personal journeys of empowerment and recovery. She co-founded and leads the Dreamcatcher Foundation as its executive director. She's also served on the board of several other organizations including Sophia's Circle, CAASE, and PART. In her role as a community organizer, Brenda rallies and trains victims to speak with legislators to bring change for their communities. A seasoned public speaker herself, Brenda regularly gives talks on poverty, violence against women, and criminal justice reform. She has worked on every level to bring greater support and awareness for women who have been abused, even leading several research projects related to violence and the exploitation of women as the key researcher. She has been recognized with several honors including the Chicago Coalition for the Homeless Recognition Award, the Illinois Coalition for Victims of Sexual Assault award for community activism, and the 2010 Chicago Foundation for Women Impact Award. In 2020, she was selected to serve on the United States Advisory Council on Human Trafficking. Brenda's work with Dreamcatcher and victims was the focus of the Sundance award–winning documentary *Dreamcatcher*.

+ + +

April Reynolds has taught at New York University and the 92nd Street Y and is currently teaching creative writing at Sarah Lawrence College. Her short stories have appeared in several anthologies. She has gone on assignment for the US State Department to lecture on creative writing and her own works. Published by Metropolitan Books/Henry Holt in 2003, her first novel, *Knee-Deep in Wonder*, won the Zora Neale Hurston/Richard Wright Foundation Award and the PEN American Center: Beyond Margins Award. Her second book, *The Shape of Dreams*, is forthcoming.